THE DIVINE DRAMATIST:
GEORGE WHITEFIELD AND THE
RISE OF MODERN EVANGELICALISM

LIBRARY OF RELIGIOUS BIOGRAPHY

available

Billy Sunday and the Redemption of Urban America
by Lyle W. Dorsett

Liberty of Conscience: Roger Williams in America
by Edwin S. Gaustad

The Divine Dramatist: George Whitefield and the
Rise of Modern Evangelicalism
by Harry S. Stout

forthcoming

William Gladstone
by David Bebbington

The Divine Dramatist

George Whitefield and the Rise of Modern Evangelicalism

Harry S. Stout

WILLIAM B. EERDMANS PUBLISHING COMPANY
GRAND RAPIDS, MICHIGAN

09 08 07 06 05 04   11 10 9 8 7 6 5

Library of Congress Cataloging-in-Publication Data

Stout, Harry S.
    The divine dramatist: George Whitefield and the rise of modern
Evangelism / Harry S. Stout.
        p.   cm.
    Includes bibliographical references and index.
    ISBN 0-8028-0154-4 (pbk.)
    1. Whitefield, George, 1714-1770. 2. Calvinistic Methodists—England—
Biography. 3. Evangelists—England—Biography. 4. Evangelists—United
States—Biography. 5. Evangelicalism—England—History—18th century.
6. Evangelicalism—United States—History—18th century. I. Title.
BX9225.W4S74 1991
269'.2'092—dc20   91-13549
                                                            CIP

For Mark A. Noll

Contents

Foreword

Historians commonly suggest that religious revivals, as we know them, were invented in Great Britain and the American colonies in the eighteenth century. They also single out George Whitefield, "the Grand Itinerant," as the most powerful and arresting revivalist of an age that includes John Wesley and Jonathan Edwards. Yet Whitefield has remained an elusive figure, far less understood than the founder of the Methodist movement or the theologian from Northhamption, Massachusetts, who wrote so profoundly about religious experience.

Stout's creative study brings Whitefield to life, capturing the essence of his meteoric rise and the arresting power of his preaching. *The Divine Dramatist* is superb biography in three respects. First, it is a vivid character study of a complex individual who was devoted both to sacrificial service and to fame and achievement. Whitefield was a man so passionate about his calling as preacher that he would allow no rival for his affections. He proposed to his wife without a confession of love and tolerated a marriage largely absent of warmth and passion. Spending as many as forty or fifty hours a week preaching, Whitefield was a man who lived almost exclusively for public performance. His private failures, frustrations, and ill health found their best cure in his proclamation of the gospel before an audience.

As history, this study also is brimming with original insights. It explains the power and significance of Whitefield's innovation: extemporaneous, open-air preaching to mass audiences. Whitefield became Anglo-America's first religious celebrity because he competed for public attention outside the arena of the churches — in the marketplace. Like his friend Benjamin Franklin, Whitefield also became a skilled promoter through the popular press. Stout's chapter on the remarkable relationship between the creed-denying Franklin and the deist-denying Whitefield sparkles with illuminating insight.

Stout suggests that the key to understanding Whitefield is the stage; drawing on his early affinity for acting, Whitefield transformed preaching from a bookish lecture to a powerful dramatic performance. He fused acting and preaching in such a way that audiences were held spellbound. Stout's dovetailing of the histories of preaching and of the stage greatly enriches our understanding of the power and significance of the Great Awakening.

The book's third strength is that it sheds light on the entire course of American religious history. Just as Whitefield broke the links that bound preaching to the church, so he envisioned revivals that would bring together persons apart from their ecclesiastical affiliations. He promoted the creation of a religious culture that subordinated churches to a larger reality — the individual experience of the New Birth. In this framework, personal experience replaced denominational creeds, sacraments, and communal covenants as the ultimate arbiter of authentic religious faith. In emphasizing the New Birth over against church and creed, Whitefield became the herald of the revival-centered voluntary movements that have been so characteristic of American religion.

Nathan O. Hatch

Acknowledgments

I gratefully acknowledge fellowship support for this book from the John Simon Guggenheim Memorial Foundation, the National Endowment for the Humanities Summer Travel to Collections, and to a Yale University Senior Faculty Fellowship. The Huntington Library and Art Gallery, in particular Martin L. Ridge, and the American Antiquarian Society, in particular John B. Hench, graciously provided grants for travel and residency, as well as a collegial setting unexcelled for scholarly support and stimulating conversation. The research staffs of New College Library, University of Edinburgh, in particular Dr. Murray Simpson, the British Library, and Yale University's Sterling and Beinecke Libraries gave unstintingly of their time and enthusiasm in tracking down Whitefield materials.

I am especially grateful to my graduate assistants at the University of Connecticut and at Yale University for tracking down fugitive Whitefield sources and offering timely criticisms of earlier drafts. In particular I wish to acknowledge Louise

Breen of the University of Connecticut and, at Yale, Christopher Grasso, Catherine Brekus, and Henry Blodget.

To friends and colleagues I owe more than I can say for their encouragement and criticism. At an early stage, my interest in George Whitefield was fueled by William H. Kenney. In a small way I hope this volume discharges a debt long in the making. Most recently, I have benefited immensely from the friendly counsel and criticism of my Early American colleagues at Yale. In particular, I wish to thank Jon Butler, Nancy Cott, John P. Demos, Kenneth Minkema, and Edmund S. Morgan for reading substantial portions of the manuscript and revising my thinking at several key points. I also wish to thank Jon Butler, Nathan O. Hatch, and T. H. Breen for supplying books and materials from their own research that bore on this enterprise.

My immediate family has offered infinite goodwill and assistance throughout this project. My daughter, Deborah J. Stout, devoted two summers to the rather thankless task of word processing, while my wife, Susan J. Stout, applied her skilled touch in ways too numerous to list. My son, James, offered timely encouragement, together with frequent voicings of every scholar's favorite question: "When will it be done?"

My greatest debt, evidenced elsewhere, is to Mark A. Noll, who read the manuscript in its entirety. His friendship and encouragement got me through the rough times, and his critical discernment is responsible for whatever final clarity of language the book may possess.

Introduction

To most historians George Whitefield is known as Anglo-America's most popular eighteenth-century preacher and its first truly mass revivalist. And he was. But in the course of writing this biography, it became clear to me that he was far more than a great preacher. Such was the scope of his fame and popularity that he rightly can be labeled Anglo-America's first modern celebrity, a preacher capable of commanding mass audiences (and offerings) across two continents, without any institutional support, through the sheer power of his personality. Where other influential preachers and churchmen wrote learned treatises and preached in meetinghouses and cathedrals to audiences totaling in the thousands or tens of thousands, Whitefield wrote best-selling journals and drew audiences that must be totaled in the millions. White and black, male and female, friends and enemies — all flocked in unprecedented numbers to hear the "Grand Itinerant." Wherever he visited, people could do anything, it seemed, but stay away. For comparison one must look to an electronic age and comedians, movie stars, athletes, or evangelists like Billy Sunday, Aimee Semple McPherson, Oral Roberts, Billy Graham, and Jimmy Swaggart. In the eighteenth century there was only Whitefield.

Considered as a religious celebrity, Whitefield must be understood in social and cultural as well as religious terms. In a career spanning three decades, during which he preached over 18,000 times, his impact as religious revivalist was uniformly powerful in England, Scotland, and North America. In all of these places he showed how religion could be made popular. But in colonial America his significance had an added dimension. There he became not only the prototype for future mass evangelists but the prototypical culture hero as well. In Whitefield, colonial Americans discovered their first intercolonial hero, the first in a long line of public figures whose claims to influence would rest on celebrity and popularity rather than birth, breeding, or institutional fiat.

True, most of the American self-made heroes have been political leaders whose names are identified with the creation of the American republic. But this should not blind us to the fact that America's first hero originated outside of the political arena. Pre-Revolutionary America was very much a religious culture the primary common symbols and rituals of which were substantially sacred in nature. So it is not surprising that its first hero emerged in that religious setting. Unlike England or Scotland, moreover, America had no single established church. Thus it was uniquely receptive to an interdenominational appeal that could fuse an intercolonial sense of religious loyalty and common identity. Whitefield's American legacy was doubly significant. He not only saved souls and swelled church memberships but rallied as well an entire group of disparate and previously unrelated peoples into a common movement for revival, a group that looked to him as its spokesman. Out of his revivals there emerged a pan-American — indeed, an Anglo-American — common cultural identity.

Whitefield's stunning successes as the evangelical "marvel of the age" call for explanation. And here the biographer encounters a significant problem. Virtually all of the Whitefield primary sources, such as private papers and diaries, have been lost or destroyed. While a significant corpus of Whitefield's sermons survive, most of them were composed in the first five years of his ministry. To reconstruct Whitefield's character and times, it is necessary to turn to other sources. In place of private notes and journals the historian must rely on external sources including Whitefield's own published writings and letters, contemporary diaries, letters, magazines, and, most important, newspapers.

When all of the fugitive sources are consulted, together with general histories of the eighteenth century, a fascinating story emerges that reveals a surprising amount of information about Whitefield's personality as seen from the outside in and about the times in which he lived. If an autobiographical account of Whitefield's charisma remains inaccessible, we can nevertheless ask how it became manifest. How was his charisma discovered and expressed? How did he manage to transform charisma into an international reputation as the "Grand Itinerant"? How do we understand the man behind the achievement, and how do we interpret the significance of his achievements for both religious history and popular culture? These are the central questions addressed in this biography.

The more I studied Whitefield's career, the more apparent it became that the very lack of information on his inner and private life supplied important clues to the man. In fact, I became convinced that Whitefield lived his life almost exclusively for public performance. On many of his tours, he was occupied for as many as forty to fifty hours a week *in the pulpit*. This contrasts with totals a tenth of that for most other ministers and does not include the hours spent traveling between stops, setting up outdoor preaching locations, or exhorting in private groups. In reconstructing his public career as evangelist I was, at the same time, revealing his innermost biography.

Always at the forefront of this inquiry is Whitefield the

preacher. This I take to be his most distinctive contribution to his times. In the course of his extemporaneous, open-air preaching to mass audiences, he transformed the traditional sermon into something different: a dramatic event capable of competing for public attention outside the arena of the churches — in fact, in the marketplace. Whitefield showed that preaching could be both edifying and entertaining. Others had preached out-of-doors before him, to be sure, but none had ranged so far in ever-expanding itinerant circuits, nor had any enjoyed Whitefield's personal, transatlantic appeal. It was left to Whitefield to become Anglo-America's first religious celebrity, the symbol for a dawning modern age.

Studies of Whitefield have too often abstracted him from the age in which he lived. To his contemporary admirers and later filiopietistic biographers, he is a timeless man, located on a continuum of faith and revival stretching from Abraham and Moses through Paul and Luther to the present. While such hagiography serves important religious functions in the community of faith, it deprives the general historical community of another — I do not say better — story in which Whitefield emerges as a man who belonged very much to his times. As such, his significance is bound up and connected with the age of his contemporaries and acquaintances, such as the great British actor David Garrick and colonial America's "representative man," Benjamin Franklin. These too were symbols for their age who recognized the new popular forces erupting in their societies and exploited them fully. And what Franklin achieved in journalism and politics, and Garrick on the stage, Whitefield achieved in religion, for many of the same reasons.

Like his entrepreneurial contemporaries in politics and theater, Whitefield confronted a society in crisis. New social, political, and economic forces were rapidly reshaping traditional institutions and, in the process, redefining the rules by which "society" existed and held together. Increasingly the logic and structure of the marketplace came to stand as a shaping metaphor for society in general. In place of a local, face-to-face world premised on trust and personal familiarity, people were everywhere being thrust into larger webs of association premised on contract, mobility, and impersonal interest in common products, services, and markets. As the public sphere grew more impersonal and abstract, the private self gained proportionate importance as the repository of spiritual experience.

Inevitably these vast cultural transformations spilled over into religion. The religious crisis of the eighteenth century was not so much a crisis of thought as of mood and spirit. The sixteenth-century English Reformation and the seventeenth-century Puritan movement had successfully produced written constellations of ideas that would outlive their framers. The *Thirty-nine Articles* and the *Westminster Confession of Faith* would be their enduring monuments. The problem for the eighteenth century was how to make these inherited ideas come alive in ways that would speak compellingly to the rapidly changing landscape of eighteenth-century Anglo-America. The critical issue was less one of definition than of presentation: how to take the old verities and present them through new voices that would speak to the changing circumstances of eighteenth-century society. How, in a word, were they to make religion *popular*, able to compete in a morally neutral and voluntaristic marketplace environment alongside all the goods and services of this world?

In turning to the social and cultural history of the age in which Whitefield preached, we find that Americans and Britons alike were caught up in a "consumer revolution" stimulated by vast increases in manufacturing, capital, and leisure time. This trend would not become general until the nineteenth century, but already by 1750 the seeds were sown, first in London and then outward. Inevitably this revolution created what the historian T. H. Breen has called a "shared language of consumption," which increasingly characterized society in the impersonal, market-driven terms of producer and consumer, buyer and seller. This shared language threatened to overtake social discourse. But at first it did not include religion. Public religion was confined to the tradition of the old churches and meetinghouses. The public square was naked; there was no sacred vocabulary or ritual to fill its ever-expanding stalls of goods and services.

George Whitefield's greatness lay in integrating religious discourse into this emerging language of consumption. Before him there had been only established "churches" and tolerated "sects." Aspiring religious leaders and reformers could think of nothing grander than reviving their own denominations and convincing those in other denominations of the errors of their ways. Only Whitefield thought to transcend denominational lines entirely and, in effect, ply a religious trade in the open air of the marketplace. His "product" he offered to all who would voluntarily enter under its canopy and participate.

Given Whitefield's unprecedented success in marketing religion to the eighteenth century, we have to wonder what techniques he employed. My search for an answer took me to a most unexpected and ironic source: the eighteenth-century English stage. For centuries the stage and church had stood in mortal combat for the souls of their nations. The intensity of their rivalry derived from the similar — and competing — nature of their appeal. Both encouraged a suspension of belief in the experience of the everyday to introduce their viewers to different worlds. Theater, in its capacity to combine the pageantry of art, the intensity of poetry, the enchantment of fiction, and the movement of dance, represented a religious-like amalgam of art and energy that, as one contemporary put it, had the power to "get Possession of the heart." Not surprisingly, many clerics accorded the contemporary stage the status of a church: the church of Satan.

At an early age — as remarkable in his own right as the musical prodigy Mozart, the runaway journalist Franklin, or the boy genius Edwards — Whitefield managed to fuse a public amalgam of preaching and acting that held audiences spellbound. His early affinity for the stage is well known and recounted in virtually every biography. But these passing concessions to childhood experience do not go far enough. At heart, Whitefield became an actor-preacher, as opposed to a scholar-preacher.

Surely the irony of identifying Whitefield with the stage would not have been lost on him. From his early infatuation with the stage he later turned with all the fury of a spurned lover. But beneath the rejection lay a born actor whose intrinsic need and special gift for dramatic self-expression never disappeared, even as its focus shifted from stage to pulpit. He applied the methods and ethos of acting to preaching with revolutionary results. While damning contemporary theater as the "devil's workshop" on the one hand, he co-opted its secrets and techniques on the other. The fusion of these two arts produced a new philosophy of preaching that emerged first in practice and later in theory.

Before Whitefield, everybody knew the difference between preaching and acting. With Whitefield's preaching it was no longer clear what was church and what was theater. More than any of his peers or predecessors, he turned his back on the academy and traditional homiletical manuals and adopted the assumptions of the actor. Passion would be the key to his preaching, and his body would be enlisted in raising passions in his audience to embrace traditional Protestant truths.

Contained in this theater-driven preaching was an implicit model of human psychology and homiletics that saw humankind less as rational and intellectual than as emotive and impassioned. In eighteenth-century actors' manuals, the individual psyche was divided into a triad of feelings, intellect, and will in which feelings reigned supreme. An unfeeling human is a nonperson, a mere machine with highly sophisticated mental functions. It is the passions that harmonize and coordinate intellect and will. In fact, they control and direct all the faculties.

Whitefield himself was a performer rather than a theoretician. Instead of theoretical treatises on preaching, he provided pulpit performances so powerful and compelling in their emotional intensity that none — including his greatest enemies in the church and theater — could stay away. Like no preacher before, and perhaps since, he demonstrated that the passions *could* be as effective an anchor of evangelical preaching as the intellect. Beyond that, a passion-based ministry was able to compete with the growing range of goods and services in the public square. Indeed, so effective was Whitefield's competition with the theater that the two became implacable foes. This biography traces this rivalry and discovers in it important clues to Whitefield's success.

A new homiletics invariably produces a new sense of the preacher's art and a new sense of the Scriptures from which that art is sculpted. Whitefield's dramatic appeal to the passions encouraged pious souls to become actors themselves and to transform the world from a profane stage to a sacred stage on which believers could enact roles of godliness modeled on biblical characters. In the course of moving from mind to passion, he restored narrative to the center of preaching. No longer was Scripture primarily a set of doctrines; now it became a dramatic script with a cast of characters whose lives and roles served as models for later generations to "impersonate." Whitefield's great ambition was to characterize and impersonate the world of the biblical saint, as preserved in Scripture narratives, with such compelling pathos and urgency that it would draw consumers away from the false gospel of the theater and the "world" and bring people into the Christian church.

In preaching to mass audiences of disconnected individuals, strangers, Whitefield helped to introduce a new concept of religious experience that grew throughout the nineteenth century into a recognizably "evangelical" movement. In the new religious experience, piety was no longer something inextricably bound up with local community and corporate spirituality. The emphasis shifted to a more individualistic and subjective sense of piety that found its quintessential expression in the internal, highly personal experience of the "New Birth."

Indeed, the individual experience of regeneration, detached from a particular place and time and existing within the self came to be *the* badge of religiosity and true piety in Whitefield's revivals. We will see how the very meaning of "revival" shifted from a mysterious, local, communal event to one that was predictable and highly subjective.

As the theater supplies clues to Whitefield's stunning outdoor successes, studies of the actor supply important clues to Whitefield's personality and character. Few great people achieve fame without aspiring to it, and Whitefield was no exception. But the fame he sought was not that of the metaphysical theologian or the denomination-builder. Rather he strove to achieve the actor's command performance on center stage. From his youth, Whitefield wanted to be a star, and the particular egotistical self-promotion he displayed in his career was very much in the manner of the great actor.

Every actor is necessarily a detached individual in the sense that he or she builds an imaginary world around self. The best actors become so contained in their self-centered dramatic worlds that the dividing line between the stage and "real life" begins to blur. For many, life becomes most "real" when lived on the stage, in the moments of public performance. As celebrities, moreover, actors instinctively reveal themselves — and their egos — to the public. Their lives become an open book.

In his classic twentieth-century treatise *To the Actor,* Michael Chekhov echoes the conventional wisdom when he distinguishes two different attitudes actors have toward the stage:

> To some [actors] it is nothing but an empty space which from time to time is filled with actors, stagehands, settings and properties; to them, all that appears on the stage is only the visible and the audible. To the others, the small space of the stage is an entire world permeated with an *atmosphere* so strong, so magnetic that they can hardly bear to part with it after the performance is over.

Whitefield clearly fit the second category. His whole life was directed by the personalities from Scripture that he characterized and embodied in the pulpit. He lived his life for the public so exclusively and single-mindedly that his private life shrank into a small and relatively insignificant interlude between the big performances. Where many dissenters from John Bunyan onward tried to infuse their private lives with spiritual "drama," Whitefield sacrificed a private life to live wholly for his public.

In pursuing information on Whitefield's private life, one is struck by the paucity of information regarding his most intimate dealings with family and friends. This too provides important clues to his character that will be pursued in separate chapters on early methodist women of the revival and on Whitefield's own courtships and marriage. For the most part, he confined his energies and attentions to allies, male and female, in the methodist cause of revival. But in the case of Benjamin Franklin we find a fascinating exception that, like Whitefield's relationship with the theater and with women, has not been fully appreciated. Through that friendship we discover clues to both personalities that cannot be clearly seen in any other of their relationships.

As drama supplies the context for Whitefield's new brand of revivalism in this biography, "mass marketing" constitutes the means whereby he attracted — and directed — his mass religious following. Besides being a consummate performer, he was a self-promoter with sure business instincts. Earlier than his clerical peers he learned to exploit the emerging world of print journalism to promote his tours. He cared little whether he elicited adoring praise or vicious criticism: both served his purposes well. Through his own literary and journalistic innovations he succeeded in creating an image and presence that was larger than life. His *Journal* (itself an innovation in its printed form), together with newspapers and a letter-writing network of friends and secretaries, supplied the marketing apparatus for creating a truly transatlantic revival.

Finally, some caveats. The Whitefield who emerges in this biography is very much a "modern" or protomodern figure. In exploiting the new media and the emerging marketplace mentality, he anticipates modern evangelists, particularly those in the "electronic church." Yet there is a danger here of anachronism. Much in modern evangelicalism Whitefield would neither have recognized nor sanctioned. From first to last he was a Calvinist who believed that God chose him for salvation and not the reverse. His piety was molded by a conversion experience that, he passionately believed, was unmerited and of divine initiative. This same Calvinism informed his self-concept and placed even his most shameless self-promotions within a larger understanding of self and society molded by the premodern Calvinist tenets of total depravity, original sin, and unconditional election. If I have placed less emphasis on theology in this biography it is because it was of less importance to his *significance*, not because it was of less importance to *him*.

Whitefield's theatricality likewise requires specification. I have used theater as a window into Whitefield's career and personality, but, like all insights, it can be taken too far. In particular, analogies to the theater that apply to Whitefield do not accurately characterize the audiences at his revivals. Whitefield's intent in preaching was to activate his hearers to seek their salvation earnestly. In the best dramas, playgoers have a cathartic experience but they remain spectators, separated by the stage's fourth wall and usually addressed only indirectly. In contrast, Whitefield intimately bound himself to his audiences — or congregations: he preached to himself as he preached to them, and both were urged to action. Whitefield's audiences were told in no uncertain terms that they not only watched, but were being watched; the spotlight turned on their chairs, and they, with Christ, became lead actors in the divine drama. To the believers in the audiences, Whitefield's revivals were more participatory than theater.

If theater, newspapers, and the actor's psyche provide

keys to the interpretation of Whitefield's greatness in this biography, they are not meant to supplant or subvert traditional accounts of his piety. Beyond living a life for the public, Whitefield embodied the spiritual roles he played. Unlike many charismatic performers who followed in his footsteps, he remained undistracted by the allure of sex or wealth. If he was not a good family man, neither was he a hypocrite or one who merely "played" at spiritual roles for ulterior reasons. His personal character matched the biblical saints he portrayed, and his vast charitable efforts left him perennially near bankruptcy. It was his integrity that won the admiration of skeptics like Benjamin Franklin, who in time became his staunchest American supporter. In this sense, Whitefield was his own finest convert to the Christian lifestyle he proclaimed.

A NOTE ON USAGE

Throughout the biography, I have distinguished Methodism as a denomination, with the use of a capital *M*, from methodism as a reform movement within pre-existent Anglican or "Calvinist" denominations. When Whitefield spoke of his "beloved methodists" he did not have in mind an incipient denomination so much as a lifestyle and code of spirituality that, he believed, should be present in all denominations. This is quite different from the more institutionally grounded Methodism that came to be identified with John and Charles Wesley and that moved in Arminian and perfectionist traditions, which Whitefield rejected.

1 The Young Rake

I was born in Gloucester, in the month of December, 1714. My father and Mother kept the Bell Inn. The former died when I was two years old; the latter is now alive, and has often told me how she endured fourteen weeks' sickness after she brought me into the world but was used to say, even when I was an infant, that she expected more comfort from me than any other of her children. This, with the circumstance of my being born in an inn, has been often of service to me in exciting my endeavors to make good my mother's expectation, and so follow the example of my dear Saviour, who was born in a manger belonging to an inn.

So begins George Whitefield's gospel-sounding account of his nativity. The passage was written at age 26, by which time he had already established himself as the most sensational and controversial preacher in the great London metropolis. For one who had risen so far so fast, the analogy to Jesus in the manger was both terribly egocentric and, at the same time, perfectly natural. It expressed exactly the conflicting impulses that raged

1

in the young evangelist, pitting a deep-set piety against a determined ambition to be "somebody" in the cause of Christ.

Besides offering an unequaled window into the psyche of the young evangelist, Whitefield's *Journal* remains the only source of information we have about his youth. When the didactic and self-promoting aims are stripped away from the text, several critical facts emerge that help to locate the formative influences of Whitefield's youth. Taken together, they provide indispensable clues to the character and qualities of the future evangelist.

First is family. Whitefield was born December 16, 1714, in the Bell Inn on Southgate Street, Bristol, the youngest of seven children. If his circumstances were not as bleak as the analogy to Bethlehem suggests, neither were they the usual stuff of which an Oxford gentleman was made. In the sharply stratified and hierarchical society of eighteenth-century England, Whitefield's family circumstances could best be summarized as one of declining status. His great-grandfather Samuel Whitefield was an Oxford graduate and rector of Rockhampton in Gloucestershire, and his grandfather Andrew succeeded Samuel at the family estate as a "private gentleman of means." But there the upward climb seems to have stopped. George's father, Thomas, began his career as an apprentice wine merchant in Bristol and eventually took over the ownership of the Bell Inn. Although a respectable establishment, the inn was not especially lucrative or prestigious. From the edge of gentility, the family had declined at a time when many other mercantile families were moving in the opposite direction.

The slide grew even sharper when George's father died suddenly at age 35, leaving a widow, Elizabeth, and seven children. In 1724 Elizabeth sought to recoup some losses by marrying an ironmonger named Capel Longden. The marriage proved disastrous. After failing to wrest control of the inn from Elizabeth, Longden took what he could, deserted the family, and eventually filed for divorce. Of the marriage itself, Whitefield says practically nothing except that Longden's departure

2

was a godsend to his "troubled Mother." It was undoubtedly a relief to young George as well. As a result, however, Whitefield would grow up without a strong father figure in his life.

George's older brothers helped to run the inn and eventually owned it. But it was George's mother who exercised the major influence on his childhood. From earliest memory he recalled her singling him out as the son who would make something of himself and the family. As long as she ran the inn she refused to let him work there. Both mother and elder siblings protected George from the world and held out high hopes for him. Inasmuch as earlier generations had made their mark in the Church of England, Elizabeth pointed George in that direction too. A clerical career would recapture the family's lost distinction and reestablish it on the fringes of English polite society.

Though Whitefield linked himself to Bethlehem, his mother was no Mary, nor — her name notwithstanding — was she a New Testament Elizabeth. Her vision for George was probably more social than spiritual. There was certainly no deep spiritual concern or biblical instruction in Elizabeth comparable to that of a Susannah Wesley or an Esther Edwards. Nor did it ever occur to her to depart from the established church or to plumb the depths of religious experience for herself. In fact, Whitefield wrote to his mother in later life urging her to move beyond her nominal faith and examine her heart for evidence of the "New Birth."

The religious career that Elizabeth Whitefield encouraged was powerful, but more in terms of a lost status than any of the internal calling or character formation for ministry found in many dissenters' homes. In contrast to Baptist, Congregational, and Presbyterian dissenters, George grew up with no alienation from the established church, without even a nonconformist's sense that some "truer" or more "faithful" recovery lay outside the state church. Recovering lost status was as significant as kindling spirituality as far as the family and young George were concerned.

The psychological effect of declining status engendered a deep sense of inferiority in Whitefield. This sense, moreover, was not simply subjective; in the context of eighteenth-century society, it was a social *fact*. In the finely gradated society of eighteenth-century England, the only distinction that really mattered was that between "gentleman" and commoner. In George, this reality kindled a mounting ambition. He could not *claim* gentility, but he could *reclaim* it and win back the respect due his family and himself. Yet even while he continued to covet respectability and status, he nonetheless dismissed the trappings of the world, including the church. This love/hate relationship with the world, status, and achievement was evident throughout his life.

In part through his mother's influence, and in part through his own fertile imagination, Whitefield resolved this inferiority-based tension through an all-compelling sense of personal destiny. Unlike the destiny that many eighteenth-century gentlemen sought — personal fame and virtue, achieved through their own superior will, efforts, and abilities — Whitefield's sense of destiny was invariably tied up with a supernatural deliverer who would pick him up out of his lowly situation and catapult him to apostle-like status. Whitefield lived in an imaginary world of destiny derived from the humble saints of old who did not choose but were chosen from above to be luminaries of the faith. Such a destiny did not require class and social rank. The beauty of a divine sense of destiny was its social inversion. God often took the humble to instruct the great.

Along with his dreams of sacred destiny, Whitefield instinctively took on the words and language of the apostles — particularly Paul — for his own speech. While his mother's ambitions pointed to an administrative niche in the church, his personal ambitions transcended institutions in more personal, charismatic ways. As the church would be his arena, so Christ would be his deliverer.

Perhaps because he knew early on his mother's expecta-

tions of something great for him in the church, Whitefield
seems to have attended Anglican and Presbyterian services
regularly. Long before spiritual crises welled up within his
conscience and transformed his life, he practiced the moves and
mannerisms of the preachers he observed. While still a child,
he repeated before his family sermons he had heard, and on
occasion he recited some that he had composed himself. The
interest seems to have been dramatic and imitative rather than
spiritual.

Invariably the young boy's knack for mimicry and memory for dialogue surprised those attending his imitations. So
effective were his abilities that they came to the attention of the
pastor of Southgate Independent Church, Thomas Cole, who
found that the young lad was repeating his pulpit stories almost exactly as he had told them. Later in life Cole attended
one of Whitefield's sermons and was heard to remark, "I find
young Whitefield can tell stories as well as old Cole!"

Whitefield's talent for mimicry soon found other, more
dramatic outlets as well. In fact, theater and play-reading soon
became an irresistible outlet and preoccupation of his youth,
comparable in importance to home and family. By the time he
wrote his autobiography, he had become a mortal enemy of
the stage and so did not dwell on such moments as when he
read or acted his first play or what plays he found most enjoy-
able. But the very vehemence with which he renounced his
play-reading youth as devil-inspired "folly" suggests that this
pastime bordered on an obsession. Clearly he was born with
dramatic urges and instincts that demanded expression.
Indeed, they soon proved more powerful than schooling and
nearly undid his college ambition.

To a boy bound for ministry, schooling always figured
prominently. In pursuit of the family dream, a twelve-year-old
George began grammar school training at the nearby parish
school, St. Mary de Crypt on Southgate Street, near the inn.
Any hope the young lad had for a university education depended on his mastering Latin and reading the classics of

Greece and Rome. Yet he found this labor extremely difficult. His later confession that he was "so brutish as to hate instruction" was probably not an exaggeration. Throughout his life he remained indifferent or hostile to classical learning and sustained study. His late-life companion and chronicler Cornelius Winter recalled that Whitefield's sermon production involved great passion and practically no study: "He was never more in retirement on a Saturday than on another day. . . . I never met with any thing like the form of a skeleton of a sermon among his papers, with which I was permitted to be very familiar, nor did he ever give me any idea of the importance of being habituated to the planning of a sermon. It is not injustice to his great character to say, I believe he knew nothing about such a kind of exercise."

But if Whitefield was slow to pick up Latin grammar and rhetoric or to develop the habit of study, he quickly demonstrated a predictable genius for elocution and declamation. His memory for dialogue and gift for expression exceeded that of all his classmates and elicited the wonder of his tutors. In no time he was speaking before his classes and tutors, and by year's end he addressed the visiting members of the corporation.

As he developed his talents with speech and declamation, Whitefield discovered that he was a born actor. The young lad had undoubtedly encountered strolling actors at the inn and had accumulated a full range of characters there to observe and mimic. By the time he got to school, he was immediately given lead roles. So impressive were his performances that his tutor, Daniel Bond, composed dramas especially for him. In one uncomfortably memorable performance Bond cast him in the part of a girl — a role he had "often done" before, and which he played to perfection.

In eighteenth-century England, it was still common for males to play female parts; indeed, it was considered a supreme test of the actor's ability to take on the part of woman. Whitefield was no exception.

My master seeing how mine and my schoolfellows' vein ran, composed something of this kind for us himself, and caused me to dress myself in girls' clothes, which I had often done [in stage roles], to act a part before the corporation. The remembrance of this has often covered me with confusion of face, and I hope will do so, even to the end of my life.

In and of itself, there was nothing objectionable about acting women's parts. Yet in recollecting it, Whitefield registered extreme embarrassment and discomfort. Here we get the first intimation of a person uneasy with his own masculinity as it was defined in the eighteenth-century codes of virility and Spartan muscularity. Always protected by mother and elder siblings, Whitefield never possessed the physical courage and fearlessness so highly favored by the George Washingtons or British generals of his age. He made many male friends, but his dealings with them were always affectionate and cordial, never intimidating. Descriptions of young Whitefield's slight build, "comely" appearance, and "fair countenance" suggest one who adapted easily — perhaps too easily — to female parts. Later in life, he openly admitted his fears of physical confrontation, and, in moments of danger such as ship crossings or mob persecution, he confessed that his wife was braver than he. Only on the childhood stage or in the pulpit could he be fearless. There he could take on the bravest roles and the most courageous saints and play them to perfection.

The immediate result of Whitefield's early successes on the stage was his immersion in theater. Years later, when composing his autobiography, he would recall with regret how "during the time of my being at school, I was very fond of reading plays, and have kept from school for days together to prepare myself for acting in them." Here was an outlet that fit his personality and inborn talents as perfectly as the sermons he mimicked at home. Acting helped him to overcome his fears by "impersonating" greatness. But because acting and the stage existed in a nether world of questionable morality and inferior social class, George's mother could never recommend the stage for her child. On the other hand, she didn't have the dissenter's hatred for all theater as the "devil's workshop." So, receiving neither encouragement nor resistance from his mother, the young actor pursued the stage as his consuming avocation.

Whitefield's awakening interest in drama coincided with a great revival in English play writing that redefined the craft and won entirely new audiences among the middle and working classes. The young Whitefield undoubtedly encountered a broad spectrum of drama, from Shakespeare to contemporary comedy, historical tragedy, and biting political satire. He may have thrilled to the classical tragedy of Joseph Addison's *Cato* or such more contemporary tragedies as Ambrose Philips's *The Distrest Mother*, Nicholas Rowe's *Tamerlane*, and Aaron Hill's *The Fatal Vision*. Romances and ribald comedies — which Whitefield later confessed were his "heart's delight" — included such favorites as Anthony Aston's *Love in a Hurry*, Colley Cibber's *Love Makes a Man*, George Farquhar's international hit *The Recruiting Officer*, and Richard Steele's *The Funeral*. And it is likely that Whitefield sampled the biting wit of Henry Fielding's burlesque *Tom Thumb*, seeing in it the power of satire and ridicule in confronting established institutions.

In addition to reading plays, Whitefield also studied acting. In the eighteenth century as in the twentieth, this involved analysis of the passions. While other aspiring clerics in the eighteenth century were reading their Bibles and studying doctrine, young Whitefield was working on the passions. Dramatic plots could be strained and implausible, but that didn't really matter. It was the passions evoked in the actor and audience that counted most. Aspiring actors were less interested in the arts of logic or rhetoric than in the fine arts of painting and sculpture that focused on the human face and body. They asked how the face and body registered emotion in times of great distress, happiness, or repose.

We cannot know for certain whether Whitefield actually read actors' manuals, though they were cheap and readily available. Considered as homiletical texts, they reveal a concentration and emphasis almost exactly opposed to the intellectually centered manuals of the Puritan stalwarts William Perkins and Cotton Mather. In Aaron Hill's classic eighteenth-century manual *The Art of Acting*, actors learned that "the passions men are actuated by, must be the Objects they are most familiar with, and yet we find no Difficulty greater, than to represent 'em, in their due Distinctions." Beginning with the head, actors explored the full range of facial expressions and body language that would be matched with particular emotions in a spectrum of emotions ranging from sorrow and grief to fear or hatred, and ultimately to love.

Whether by theory or actual performance, aspiring actors learned to exercise their imaginations to recover passions. Their first mission, Hill insisted, was "to fix itself upon the clear Idea" of a passion and then "transmit" it to the face. To explain this "transmission," actors employed a science and epistemology every bit as comprehensive as that found in rhetoric and the liberal arts. Any idea or sentiment, Hill explained, acts "immediately behind the optic Nerves" and "stamps instantaneously upon the Eye and Eyebrow, a struck Image of [the] conceiv'd idea." The actor's face was the tableau on which he learned to sketch the passions of his part. In eighteenth-century theory, it was impossible to look one way and feel another: the face and body were a window into the passions of the soul. Actors began with the eyebrows, mastering a full range of expressions that in "progressive impulse" expanded outward to direct the face, neck, chest, and legs. In any performance the actor appeared to be assuming all the expressions simultaneously, though in practice he learned to break the passion down into all its body parts and master all the poses and inflections appropriate to that particular emotion.

Hill identified ten dramatic passions to which appropriate actions and facial expressions were attached: joy, grief, fear, anger, pity, scorn, hatred, jealousy, wonder, and love. With these ten tools the actor could play any part, for they encompassed the sum and substance of the human condition. Of Whitefield's great contemporary David Garrick it was said that he could entertain guests by "throwing his features into the representations of Love, Hatred, Terror, Pity, Jealousy, Desire, and Joy in so rapid and striking a manner [as to] astound the whole country." On stage, it was "no longer Garrick whom we heard: the change once effected, the actor disappeared and the hero was revealed, and the actor did not become his natural self until his task was done."

In place of thinking man the manuals substituted impassioned man and from there articulated a theory of self-presentation in public settings that was every bit as comprehensive and self-contained as a preacher's manual or rhetorician's text. In time, Whitefield would desert the theater, leaving forever open the question of whether he would have been Garrick's equal. But the lessons he learned concerning passion, body, and character were never forgotten and were to find dramatic expression in the pulpit.

In the end, it was practical necessity that ended Whitefield's schoolboy career on the stage. Convinced by his bad marks and his family's declining fortunes that a clerical career was out of the question, he announced to his mother that he had withdrawn from his course of study in the classics and was learning "to write only" in preparation for the trades. Until then his mother had always shielded him resolutely "from intermeddling in the least with the public business" of the inn. But in 1729 that prohibition temporarily ceased. For a year and a half he assisted his mother in the inn, washing sheets, mopping floors, and serving food, all the while observing a procession of guests representing all walks of life.

As an eighteenth-century innkeeper, Whitefield must have encountered all sorts of characters, including drunks, politicians, prostitutes, "gamesters," pickpockets, and a tippling cleric or two. All of these were far removed from the pious household of faith common to a Jonathan Edwards or John Wesley, but they furnished him with a rich store of characters that he later brought to life in the pulpit. Where an Edwards or Wesley spent time in the company of respectful parishioners and polite supplicants, Whitefield inhabited the robust and vulgar world of everyday England.

In Whitefield's new world the passions reigned. All of his playgoing friends fell into the roles of the characters they saw, and soon Whitefield followed suit: "I began to reason as they did, and to ask why God had given me passions, and not permitted me to gratify them." With no one or no thing to provide an alternative answer, Whitefield's passions dictated a role that he would play around the inn: "I soon made great proficiency in the school of the devil. I affected to look rakish, and was in a fair way of being as infamous as the worst of them." Throughout his life, Whitefield sculpted roles out of his passions. In the beginning, the "rake" won out.

Besides playing a role in life as though it were an extension of the stage, Whitefield used his experience in the inn to master the art of ingratiation. Social class, drama, and the inn experience together taught him how to get along with all sorts of people. Without ever forgetting his place, he could relate to people of all classes. He became a raconteur of the first rank and a conversationalist as engaging in the parlor as in the pulpit. Far sooner than he imagined, he was to put to use the skills with people he learned in the inn.

The lesson Whitefield learned most clearly from his experience in the inn was that the trades were not for him. The job of "putting on the blue apron" appealed to neither his social ambition nor his sense of destiny. It was merely a way station on a journey barely begun. After his brother Richard took over management of the inn, George had an unhappy falling out with Richard's wife, and so he left. His mother had moved into a small cottage when she gave up control of the inn, and so for a time George went to live with his oldest brother in Bristol.

The Bristol experience was short-lived but immensely important in forming Whitefield's spiritual character. He arrived there out of work and out of sorts with his hoped-for destiny.

11

For the first time he experienced a spiritual crisis that confronted him with the being of God and the reality of sin. He felt compelled to "look into my heart" and think about religion less in terms of calling and profession than in terms of experience and conscience. He began attending services regularly at St. Johns Church and, through the "blessed sacrament" of the eucharist, began to think of salvation and damnation. Although throughout his ministry he was to transform the religious experience of others through the sermon, his own spiritual initiation came through the sacraments. At its deepest level, religious experience remained tied to ritual and symbol. In those Whitefield found the greatest religious meaning. The pomp, ceremony, and ritual of the Church of England never constituted an obstacle to his faith. As his religious interests assumed ever-deeper personal dimensions, his sense of the church, worship, prayer, and piety were fixed by Anglican dramaturgy.

Filled with an unsettled and unsettling religious conscience, and still without work, Whitefield returned to Gloucester and waited on his destiny. He soon fell back into the old activities: "Much of my time I spent in reading plays, and in sauntering from place to place." But these activities didn't satisfy. Like many urban youths of his day, Whitefield marked time, waiting for his moment to come and knowing full well that for many people such moments never materialized.

The answer Whitefield awaited appeared predictably in the form of an epiphany. He recorded the moment briefly in his *Journal*: "One morning, as I was reading a play to my sister, said I, 'Sister, God intends something for me which we know not of. . . . I think God will provide for me some way or other that we cannot apprehend.' How I came to say these words I know not. God afterward showed me they came from Him."

Though the entry is brief, the moment was certainly pivotal in Whitefield's youth. The interrelationship of epiphany and play-reading is here obvious and testifies to the power drama exerted in his youth, beyond what he could have appreciated in describing the moment ten years later. In ways Whitefield never fully realized or acknowledged, drama informed his sense of destiny. In recording this moment for pious readers, Whitefield no doubt intended the juxtaposition of epiphany and play-reading as ironic: of God taking an immoral act (play-reading) and transforming it into a glorious alternative (mission). Yet at the time it occurred there was undoubtedly no sense of irony. His repudiation of the theater was still in the future; at this point, stage and pulpit naturally coincided in his mind. In the same way that he became a "rake" and sculpted a shape for his life from the romances he read, he also defined a destiny that would take him out of Gloucester and into a bigger, more significant world.

What made this epiphany so memorable was not its uniqueness but the fact that soon thereafter a life-shaping, seemingly providential, opportunity appeared. In talking with a Gloucester friend, Whitefield's mother learned how poor students could attend Oxford as "servitors" — servants to the wealthy gentlemen who left their private estates to study culture and the art of leadership in the colleges. Immediately Elizabeth determined that George would have such a place. She importuned Whitefield's grammar school master to intercede on the boy-actor's behalf and in that way won a servitor's place for him at Oxford's venerable Pembroke College. The news of his admission rang out like a bell from heaven. In recording the moment in his *Journal*, Whitefield instinctively resorted to a dramatic dialogue: "Upon that my Mother immediately cried out, 'This will do for my son.' Then turning to me, she said, 'Will you go to Oxford, George?' I replied, 'With all my heart.'"

With destiny in sight, Whitefield returned with renewed ambition to the painful study of Latin and the classics. Although still not stellar, his academic performance was acceptable. He continued also "seeing plays," but doubts began creeping in around the edges of his conscience, and he "began to have some scruples about it."

Now that a career in the church was becoming a reality

with the Oxford acceptance, he turned to the life of the soul with a single-mindedness that bordered on the obsessive. The lengths he traveled to bring his soul into conformity with his awakened conscience and clerical destiny are reminiscent of the struggles of the young Luther. A great destiny required great trials and preparations.

At age seventeen, a more focused Whitefield embarked on the first in a long series of bodily mortifications and ensuing illness that accompanied him through his Oxford years and beyond. Simple piety was not enough. Following a particularly meaningful Christmas celebration of the eucharist, he recorded that "I began now to be more and more watchful over my thoughts, words, and actions." During the following season of Lent he engaged in a thirty-six-hour fast and filled his evenings with devotional readings to his mother and sister. Rare was the day he missed matins and evensong. And with increased devotion came steady improvement in school: "I learned much faster than I did before."

Throughout this formative period, the determinative influence of Whitefield's mother comes constantly to the fore. She played a central role as both the instigator of his ambition and his admiring audience. The combination was all-powerful in shaping Whitefield's youth. At some level this imposed destiny undoubtedly raised resentments in the young lad and drove the two apart in later years. But it also fed a powerful ambition and gave it scope when he was most impressionable.

During Whitefield's periods of fasting and mortification he experienced new epiphanies in the form of dreams that appeared stage-like in their direction. An older Whitefield regretted mentioning these dreams in his *Journals* because his critics used them to document his "antinomianism," but they are indispensable windows into his late-adolescent experience. For one deeply sensitized by his mother to his destiny, dramatic by nature, and caught in a spiritual crisis, revelatory dreams seemed entirely natural. In one particularly graphic vision he saw God on Mount Sinai speaking to him. Upon conveying this dream to a pious "gentlewoman," he learned the dream was a "call" from God to pursue college and the ministry. Throughout that year as he readied for Oxford, he continued to have dreams and "impressions" during his waking hours that foretold stellar spiritual performances on his part. Invariably his dreams were cast in the general context of personal destiny and charismatic ministry. The dreams never featured others, nor were they in any generalized sense calls to mere morality. They were calls to a great destiny that Whitefield was certain belonged to him.

Fortified by revelation, he threw himself into an organized "round of duties" including monthly sacraments, public worship, and private prayers twice daily, and "fasting frequently." Scholarly preparation was necessary but not especially useful to his designs. He wanted to finish schooling as expeditiously as possible, for his calling was to "preach quickly."

With schooling complete, the most unlikely of pulpit giants embarked for his sojourn at mighty Pembroke College, Oxford. He fit no clear stereotype in Christian hagiography: he was religious but theatrical, Anglican but dissenter in spirit, poor but destined for greatness. His life was a series of tensions: he could not read enough plays and he could not get enough religion, he felt inferior and he felt famous, he lived by passions and he renounced passions. All of these conflicting strains would stay with him throughout his life. They would propel him to Oxford and, beyond that, to a career that had no precedent or parallel in the annals of English preaching.

2 Oxford Odd Fellow

In 1732 a determined but uncertain Whitefield arrived at Oxford to pursue his destiny. The experience would be both more and less than he anticipated. If Oxford was a ladder of success for aspiring gentlemen and clerics, it was also a microcosm of the larger society. This meant that not every student would begin on the same rung nor could every student aspire to the same heights. One's rung in the college hierarchy reflected one's rung in the social hierarchy of eighteenth-century England. For the socially insecure and inferior Whitefield, this did not bode well, for his rung was very low.

As one of the oldest and most respected Oxford colleges, Pembroke evidenced a deep respect for the prerogatives of wealth and social rank. Each rank afforded its own privileges and responsibilities, reflecting social realities beyond the college walls. At the top of Pembroke society were the "gentleman commoners" — the wealthiest, best connected students, who could count on the deference of their inferiors among both faculty and students. Many of these students endowed their

16

college while still students and built it up through the remainder of their lives.

For gentlemen students like Whitefield's contemporary Sir Erasmus Phillips, life at Pembroke college was a social feast. Phillips kept a diary of everyday life at Pembroke during the period when Whitefield entered the college. His entries reveal a constant round of dinners with local and visiting dignitaries, evening balls and parties, weekend trips to London, gambling at the race track, fox hunting, and island fishing. Young Phillips also held political office at his home estate at Haverfordwest and conferred frequently on matters of local governance. The academic side of school receded into this rich social background, though ample time was reserved for meetings with tutors, readings in the classics, and practice in the art of declamation. Like others of his class, Phillips remembered Oxford for its social associations and as the place where he acquired the classical culture and vocabulary of national leadership. At the end of his college experience, a gracious Phillips displayed the magnanimity of his position by hosting parties and receptions and "treat[ing] Pembroke College in the Common Room."

Below the gentlemen commoners, but still self-supporting, were the commoners. The most brilliant Pembroke commoner in Whitefield's era was the famed essayist and literary wit Samuel Johnson. Though students like Johnson paid their way, they always felt (and were treated) poor in contrast to the gentlemen commoners. For them, the academic side of college necessarily played a more central role — and it raised its share of resentments. Failure to attend lectures or meet with tutors was punishable by fines, leading an angry and impetuous Johnson to complain to his undistinguished tutor, "Sir, you have sconced [fined] me twopence for a lecture not worth a penny."

As the gentleman commoner's life was grand and the commoner's life was common, the servitor's life was servile. From without all Oxford may have looked the same, but once inside Whitefield learned otherwise. Each year a limited num-

17

ber of servitors were admitted tuition free, less to reward working-class diligence than to provide necessary services for the gentlemen students and the college masters.

The servitor's work was hard and often demeaning. When not acting as errand boys for gentlemen, they were often required to perform such degrading tasks as cleaning clothes and rooms and serving at parties. They also worked for the college master and assumed the unenviable task of checking rooms at night and reporting students who were not in their quarters. This understandably did not win friends among the gentlemen students, who would retaliate by going "hunting." Late at night the servitors would be chased through the college halls by angry gentlemen clanging pots and candlesticks in imitation of a fox hunt. Such experiences bred a spirit of resentment, anger, and inferiority. Even a commoner like Samuel Johnson felt the sting of elitism and hierarchy and vowed to fight back. Of his Pembroke years he later recalled, "I was miserably poor, and I thought to fight my way [to respectability] by my literature and my wit."

While Johnson got angry, Whitefield sought to please. In part, this was the distinction between a commoner's and a servitor's response to social pretension. But in deeper measure it reflects two contrasting personalities. One reads the *Journal* in vain for references to rage or anger at the abusive disdain a servitor suffered. When intimidated, Whitefield's first response was ingratiation and, failing that, complete withdrawal.

Whitefield's early years in the inn prepared him well for his role as servant. At first he adapted easily to his situation and picked up quickly on the art of the servitor. He well understood the rules of rank and deference and played his part to the full. Unlike the gentlemen who enjoyed their private quarters, Whitefield shared his room with several other servitors and found he was preferred above all: "I ingratiated myself into the gentlemen's favour so far, that many, who had it in their power, chose me to be their servitor."

But if Whitefield was frequently in demand, he was never

included in the social rounds of his superiors, nor, in contrast to Johnson, did he attract the attention of his tutors for superior scholarship. He was thus doubly bereft. He was out of his old world and peripheral in his new. Despite the favors of the gentlemen, he was a very lonely young man. Later in life he recalled with poignancy how he came to Oxford "without a friend. . . . I had not a servant, I had not any one to introduce me." Left alone in an unfriendly place, Whitefield turned to religion and the "holy life" as his only solace. The male life of card playing, drinking, hunting, and fishing passed him by and he it. He was at Oxford to become a cleric, after all. So he withdrew into a life of study, regular prayer, and devotional reading. Once more he sculpted a role for himself, but one no longer even close to the romantic gentleman-to-be. He turned in anger on his supposed "benefactors." Because anger does not accord well with a life of devotion, he never recorded it in the *Journal*. But the young student's frustrated rage is unmistakably evident in the fact that he abandoned the role of ingratiation and set out anew to be the antithesis of a secular Oxford gentleman. Instead of the youthful "rake," he now became a self-defined "odd fellow."

Now more alone than ever, Whitefield covered his loneliness in a series of self-imposed religious duties that occupied all his thoughts. The more alone he felt, the more he turned to spiritual exercises: "I now began to pray and sing psalms thrice every day, besides morning and evening [services], and to fast every Friday, and to receive the sacrament at a parish church near our college, and at the castle, where the despised Methodists used to receive [the sacrament] once a month."

The reference to "Methodists" is the first to appear in Whitefield's journal, but hardly the last. In fact, the young and miserable Whitefield was not alone at Oxford. In the midst of his loneliness he encountered another Oxonian, Charles Wesley, who persuaded Whitefield to join him in religious meetings with his brother John and several other pious students known derisively as the "Holy Club," the "Bible Moths," or, most generally, "Method-ists." Not all methodists were servitors like Whitefield. The Wesleys, for example, were commoners — impoverished and constantly in debt, but not servants. On the other hand, none were gentlemen. Indeed, insofar as gentlemen defined the essence of the institution, they came to represent the image methodists would subvert. In place of envy there would be unqualified — and unappreciated — disdain.

All methodist students were dissatisfied with the laxity and worldliness of Oxford, and they spurned rowdy comradeship with other students. Instead, they met daily for prayers and self-examination. They sought to govern every waking hour of their lives according to sacred rule or method — in its own way, another powerful "script." Many methodists kept diaries of their activities, noting spiritual exercises by the hour of the day. In stark — and no doubt deliberate — contrast to the journal of an Erasmus Phillips, their diaries contained no references to leisure activities. In their inverted campus ethic, the methodists sought to fill every waking moment with spiritual contemplation and good deeds. Like the young Ben Franklin pursuing his "Art of Virtue" and recording every activity in the day, the methodists felt that all of life had to be "useful." Social pastimes disappeared, and so to a considerable extent did academics. Like the seventeenth-century Puritan movement, the methodists originated as a purifying element within a compromised Church of England. But unlike the Puritans, they evidenced little interest in the arts curriculum or in *technologia* — the organization of all knowledge as divine emanation. In the dawning age of Enlightenment, they gave learning up to the universities and pursued their own anti-intellectual faith.

On a personal level, methodism offered these alienated students an element of control and meaning in a rapidly changing world. Their strict discipline spoke to the enduring Protestant need to discover meaning in the transaction between God and the self, and to impose that discipline on a chaotic world. If the world ignored or reviled them, they would ignore the world and appeal to a higher destiny. In Whitefield, the powerful inclination toward spiritual fame coincided with a rebellious methodist impetus against the world and its mores. As the eighteenth-century theater poked fun at elite morality and manners on the English stage, so methodism assaulted polite pastimes and preoccupations from the pulpit. Each in its own way was a powerful counterculture, standing apart from traditional order and proud of its defiance.

Whitefield immediately gravitated to his new "spiritual friends" and threw himself into their structured discipline. Fueled with a contradictory combination of humble piety and mounting ambition, he soon tried to out-methodize the methodists. At first he found the rule of morning and evening devotion and daily acts of charity to the poor and imprisoned almost insurmountably "difficult." But eventually he mastered their pious exercises and surpassed them in strenuousness and devotion. With the leader John Wesley, he "determined to be all devoted to God, to give Him all my soul, my body, and my substance." To attain this new Oxford identity, he drove himself so hard that he experienced "fits of illness" that plagued him throughout his Oxford career.

Whitefield's commitment to methodism became so all-embracing that it utterly supplanted not only academics but his old rakishness as well. Even thoughts of marriage and family were postponed indefinitely when supernatural "impressions" convinced him of the duty of celibacy: "our Lord, by His spirit, soon convinced me that I must know no one after the flesh; and I soon found that promise literally fulfilled." Whitefield did not elaborate any further on the nature of this "literal fulfillment," though he was clearly referring to a foiled love affair.

At the same time that he renounced the world, Whitefield made sure the world knew he renounced it. In a pattern he would follow throughout his early preaching career, he publicized his difference, incurred reproach, and then used that reproach as divine confirmation. Countercultures require public demonstrations, else they become merely a private piety or devotion, known only to the self and to God. Instead of avoiding the derision and persecution of other students, he actively sought it out, discovering in persecution a confirmation of calling: "These, though little, were useful trials. They inured me to contempt, lessened self-love, and taught me to die daily."

Of greatest moment for Whitefield in this period of wholesale repudiation and withdrawal was his renunciation of the stage. At an unspecified time in the first year of heightened spirituality, a single-minded Whitefield read his last play. His account is tantalizingly brief: "All this while I was not fully satisfied of the sin of playing at cards and reading plays, till God upon a fast-day was pleased to convince me." Soon thereafter, while reading a portion of a play to a friend, "God struck my heart with such power that I was obliged to lay it down again; and, blessed be His Name, I have not read any such book since."

For Whitefield, there could be no stronger symbolic statement of his movement away from the established church to the methodist counterculture than to renounce the stage. Behind his decision was a well-articulated and long-established body of dissenting thought that repudiated modern theater in its entirety, such as William Law's *Christian Perfection* and William Prynne's *Histriomastix, the Players Scourge* (1633). The same process of revelation and inward prompting that drove him to celibacy, mortification, and methodist rule now targeted his former love. Unable to reconcile the theater with his religious passion and sense of destiny, he resolved not simply to abandon the theater but to declare war on it. In repudiating the stage utterly, Whitefield took his place among nonconformist religious purists who had throughout the centuries denounced theater as sin. Unlike eighteenth-century Anglican critics of the theater who opposed the bawdiness and "tastelessness" of the contemporary stage while accepting its redemptive possibilities, the nonconformists rejected it in toto as intrinsically evil and incapable of redemptive applications. Theater was not a separate institution and pastime but a *competing church*. From Law's treatise, Whitefield learned that "though the Devil be not professedly worshipp'd by Hymns directed to him, yet most that is there sung is to his Service; he is there obey'd and pleas'd in as certain a manner, as God is worshipped and honoured in the Church."

As a church of Satan, the theater did its greatest evil in promoting immorality. As audiences observed sinful practices in the passionate atmosphere of the theater, they were encouraged to participate themselves. By the sheer fact of representing immorality and showcasing it in all its alluring essence, the theater in effect legitimated it and encouraged it. As the Puritan William Prynne pointed out, if "the casual sight of Bathsheba was sufficient to provoke even regenerate David to an adulterous act . . . will not then the premeditated voluntary delightful beholding of an unchast adulterous Play, much more contaminate a voluptuous, carnall, gracelesse Play-haunter, who lies rotting in the sinke of his most beastly lusts?" Prynne's objections were echoed in countless other tracts and treatises that in their sheer fury and intensity revealed a deep-seated fear of the theater as competitor.

As well as encouraging immorality, play-going was held to be an inducement to idle "amusements" that would draw attention away from the true object of passionate loyalty: unceasing Christian service. Play-going headed the list of a whole set of worldly distractions, among which Prynne and other purists included "effeminate mixt Dancing, Dicing, lascivious Pictures, wanton Fashions, Face-Painting, Health-drinking, Long haire, Love-lockes, Periwigs, women's [hair] curling," and even "excessive laughter." Most of these offensive pastimes were associated with sex and the passions.

Time and again nonconformist critiques of theater railed against the "effeminacy" of the theater. Men in dresses, men in women's roles, men with high voices — all of these came under attack and derision. Behind Puritan and Methodist attacks on the theater was the fear of a loss of self-control — the very badge of their manly, and godly, identity. Theatrical effeminacy threatened to impose directionless and chaotic "feeling" over "intellect" and "understanding." While feelings were acceptable and unavoidable, they had to be governed by intellect. Where godly passions were subordinated to the dictates of law and doctrine, profane passions governed the self and destroyed all control. At heart, methodist repudiations of the world were repudiations of feelings and a competing, passion-driven existence. A passion-driven self was an uncontrolled and uncontrollable self. Selves governed by worldly passions were like a raging sea overflowing its banks and disrupting all order. Or, in another metaphor of the time, they were like a woman.

To Whitefield these charges must have been especially intimidating. His very manner and personality exhibited precisely these qualities of passion and timidity. Clearly if he was to be a methodist and, by extension, a godly man, he must renounce all traces of the effeminate and passion-driven self within or at least rechannel them in appropriate outlets. By blaming the theater for his past excesses and renouncing it entirely, he could play the man for the methodist movement and transfer theatrical passions into the pulpit.

Most methodists had nothing to lose in giving up the theater. Many came from dissenting backgrounds where it was never a factor anyway. Whitefield, on the other hand, had a good deal to lose. And in the end, he couldn't rid himself of it. His antitheatrical theology and manly methodized living obscured but never managed to annihilate an inner personality that was impassioned, effeminate, and dramatic. In the end, theater won the contest for Whitefield's personality, even as methodism won the contest for his soul.

With rejection and otherworldly ascetic renunciation came increased illness. Throughout his career Whitefield was plagued by a series of physical and nervous ailments that led him to question his strength, and again, his masculinity. Perhaps they also expressed some unconscious resistance to a life of role-playing. But, as he had with persecution and derision, he turned these afflictions into confirmation of his calling. In the midst of trials, the young student was learning to make his anxieties work for him. When the nineteen-year-old Whitefield experienced bouts of insomnia and illness throughout 1734, he convinced himself that Satan was out to wrest his soul. Constant fasting, works of piety, and confrontation with students brought him to the edge of a breakdown: "All power of meditating, or even thinking, was taken from me. My memory quite failed me. My whole Soul was barren and dry, and I could fancy myself to be like nothing so much as a man locked up in iron armour."

Whitefield's condition, though pathetic, was a necessary step in his spiritual odyssey. In fact, alongside his forlorn character as "odd fellow," he was fashioning an education (and a role) of his own making. It was classical and liberal only in appearance — and that only faintly. Whitefield's real inspiration lay in the dramatic accounts of renunciation and conversion recorded in the New Testament. If one were to construct an archetypal script from Pauline accounts of "dying to self" in order to "live for Christ," it would correspond closely to Whitefield's condition in these years. While others were mastering the classics and the habit of command or the theology of Paul, Whitefield was living through the travails of the Pauline "New Birth" so convincingly that he could feel every stage from the depths of despair to the heights of supernatural deliverance.

In fact, Whitefield's self-portrait of the Oxford years seems caricatured from the lives of earlier saints he had read and internalized. Having abandoned "dry sciences" and "books" (save such books "as entered into the heart of religion"), he proceeded to live out a part: "Afterwards, by degrees, I always chose the worst sort of food. . . . I fasted twice a week. My apparel was mean. . . . I wore woolen gloves, a patched gown, and dirty shoes." Thus emerges Whitefield's forlorn self-portrait, much like an eighteenth-century version of Bunyan's Christian carrying a lopsided burden and looking utterly out of keeping with his world. Whitefield had, in fact, read and admired *Pilgrim's Progress,* seeing at its core the story of a character he could embody. Soon the odd fellow became the laughingstock of his fellow students. Having intentionally destroyed his "fair reputation," he was now "set up as a mark for all the polite students . . . to shoot at."

Later Whitefield learned to label this phase of his preparation a "legal obedience" that sought to placate God through good works. Like Martin Luther and the Puritans before him, he found that the more he threw himself into acts of piety and deprivation, the further from God he felt. During Lent, for example, he accelerated his fastings to the point of endangering his health: "I constantly walked out in the cold mornings till part of one of my hands was quite black. . . . I could scarce creep upstairs, I was obliged to inform my kind tutor . . . who immediately sent for a physician to me."

At length, Whitefield's dour condition and avoidance of books came to the attention of unsympathetic college authorities. When Master Matthew Panting threatened him with expulsion, Whitefield interpreted the threat as "persecution" for the sake of the gospel. In fact, it probably represented a timely and well-deserved reminder that college was, after all, at least to some extent, even in eighteenth-century Oxford, about books and science. If the lad did not soon return to his senses, he would not only be out of school but out of health as well. When called to account by his tutor for repeatedly missing classes and failing to complete assignments, a frightened and insecure Whitefield "burst into tears, and assured him that it was not out of contempt of authority, but that I could not act otherwise. Then, at length, he said, he believed I could not; and when he left me, told a friend, as he very well might, that he took me to be really mad."

In fact, Whitefield was not mad. Nor could he "act" otherwise. He was going through a powerful, renovative spiritual experience that was shaping his life and career. His personality may have dictated the extremes of abasement and anxiety, but the experience itself was common to countless saints in the Puritan mode who first had to be humbled and brought low before they could be exalted and purged. In conventional Puritan terminology, he was going through a period of "preparation" antecedent to saving grace. His spiritual experience was at once real and scripted in countless spiritual autobiographies and testimonies.

At the urging of his physician and the college authorities, Whitefield took a temporary leave of absence from Oxford and returned to his boyhood environs in Gloucester and Bristol. By then his situation was desperate. And, as with countless saints before him, it was when the darkness was utterly complete that light finally shone on Whitefield's horizon. Convinced of his own unworthiness and inability to find God, he cast himself on divine mercy, and God found him. While working with the poor and imprisoned in Gloucester and Bristol, he gradually came to "feel" as well as to "see" that grace was free and unconditional. As the denouement of that transition, he experienced the "New Birth." Like Bunyan's Christian before the open sepulcher, he could at last proclaim, "I was delivered from the burden that so heavily oppressed me."

While in many ways Whitefield's conversion was typical of English pietists, it also revealed some distinctive qualities. His outer manifestations of mortification and deprivation were extreme even by Puritan or methodist standards. Whether consciously or not, Whitefield was expressing soul distress and agony through his body with an uncommon directness. In some sense he was preparing himself for a different sort of ministry in which body would be employed to express the agonies of the lost. Later, in enacting the miseries of the damned, he called on his own physical experiences to communicate a lost state.

Also distinctive in Whitefield's spiritual odyssey was the permanence and irreversibility of the conversion experience. Having gone through the pangs and travail of a "New Birth" once, he was to experience no backsliding or loss of assurance.

Unlike countless Puritans before him, beset by ongoing doubts and experiencing "renewed conversion," Whitefield seems never to have doubted. Amazingly, the entire course of self-examination so prominent in his youth virtually disappeared. Henceforth, there were only "casual intermissions" of anxiety that hardly bore mentioning. In place of self-examination and self-doubt, he projected his new self outward in countless performances, enacting for others the convulsive experience of his Oxford years.

During the Gloucester interlude when Whitefield experienced the New Birth, he coincidentally preached his first sermons. Indeed, the two experiences were closely enough related to suggest more than a simple coincidence. For several weeks he preached at the Gloucester county jail, noting with satisfaction that his messages were "well received." At the same time, he found that in addition to benefiting the prisoners, preaching proved the best remedy for his own ills. Gradually he felt restored in body and soul to the point that he could begin thinking about returning to school. Ever thereafter, the combination of crisis, anxiety, and release-through-preaching marked his career. He made illness, anxiety, and persecution work for him in preaching. Inner and outer torment compelled him to place his reliance utterly on God, and with that act of release, he regularly discovered the power to open his mouth in bold proclamation.

Just prior to returning to Oxford, Whitefield addressed the townspeople on the evils of attending plays. Upon hearing that "the strollers were coming to town," he read Law's "excellent treatise" condemning the theater and proceeded to give "a public testimony of my repentance as to seeing and acting plays." By then the new character was complete and the new counterculture publicly demonstrated. Whitefield was ready to complete his studies with the career goal of promoting the New Birth in others, even as he had experienced it in himself. Instead of "acting plays" he would enact the mysteries of the New Birth.

A physically recovered and spiritually regenerated Whitefield returned to Oxford and quickly completed his studies. The odd fellow in woolen gloves and patched gown walking the campus in a spiritual daze disappeared as completely as the young rake. Henceforth he would always dress with dignity and care. The odd-fellow persona had died and was to reappear only in pulpit reenactments of lost souls.

In the spring of 1736 Whitefield graduated from Oxford. At last his schooling was done. The college he had hated as a student, he would later proudly claim in memory. Henceforward, he would sign all letters and publications: "George Whitefield, A.B., late of Pembroke College, Oxford." In fact, Whitefield's campaign to restore his family's lost status had never disappeared, and he reaped a well-deserved triumph to that end on graduation day. Throughout the spring he prepared, by private study, for ordination as a deacon in the Church of England. With unconcealed pride he recorded his new status, "from a servitor to a Bachelor of Arts — from a common drawer to a clergyman."

Exactly where the new clergyman would exercise his gifts and talents was still unclear. One possibility was Gloucester, but that seemed too small. Another was Oxford, but ongoing work with the students there seemed more an interlude than a career. Finally, and most tantalizingly, was the prospect of foreign missions and perhaps persecution in the service of Christ. This much bigger stage engaged his imagination to the fullest extent. The work would be dangerous and call for the strongest masculine virtues. Already the Wesleys had journeyed to the unsettled wilderness of Georgia and written back exciting stories, along with calls for additional laborers. With all of this in mind, a newly ordained Whitefield looked to the future, certain that "God is preparing me for some great work."

3 London Boy Preacher

By the time Whitefield was ordained in June 1736, all traces of the Oxford odd fellow had disappeared. A new, more focused and composed Whitefield appeared, with a presence beyond his years and youthful appearance. Where others generally waited until age 24 or 25 for ordination, Whitefield's piety and works of mercy and exhortation had readied him by the age of 22. With ordination, career decisions had to be made, including choices of location and vocation. It was now time for adult decisions — and destinations — that would determine the course of his life.

Throughout the summer and fall of 1736 Whitefield ministered to prisoners in Oxford and awaited his destiny. His boyhood sense of supernatural direction had not disappeared; to the contrary, it had grown even stronger. Like many in his methodist circle, he believed that beyond the simple call to salvation that all Christians shared, there came more particular and immediate callings — especially to the leaders — that had less to do with salvation than with vocation and career. Often these callings assumed supernatural or extranormal forms such as dreams, impressions, or significant coincidences. The key here was *experience*. Callings, like conversions, had to be tangible and palpable in their immediacy. Without that confirmation, he would act prematurely and miss his moment of destiny.

In fact, Whitefield believed he already knew his destiny and only lacked a sign. From the time the Wesleys first embarked for the "end of the world" in Georgia, the New World mission had captivated his imagination. Georgia was doubly attractive. Besides the mission opportunities for charity and preaching, it represented a great, and potentially dangerous, adventure. The colony was new (founded in 1733) and stood as a barrier against the Spanish. Georgia could prove something to him that no mere pulpit in England could match. Georgia was no place for boys, and it was no place for women. It was romantic, dangerous, and above all manly. There were families — and orphans — to be sure, and these would become increasingly important. But more importantly there was adventure.

Throughout the summer and early fall of 1736, Whitefield and the Oxford methodists received periodic letters from the Wesleys that fired their imaginations. Whitefield longed to join John Wesley, but, "having no outward call" and being "too weak in body," he postponed a commitment.

Finally providence intervened with the needed sign. In July, after returning from an arduous — and not entirely successful — five-month stay in Georgia, Charles Wesley visited Whitefield. The needs were great, said Wesley, and he was sent to "procure labourers" for the New World. Whitefield was his first choice. This seemed to be the direct call that Whitefield sought, and it was sealed several months later when John sent a letter apprising Whitefield of the great needs of Georgia. The message concluded with a dramatic challenge:

> Only Mr. Delamotte is with me, till God shall stir up the hearts of some of His servants, who, putting their lives in His hands, shall come over and help us, where the harvest

is so great and the labourers so few. What if thou art the man, Mr. Whitefield?

Wesley clearly knew what appealed to his correspondent. The dramatic mode, so reminiscent of Whitefield's own earlier decision to attend Oxford, had an immediate effect. No sooner was it read, Whitefield recorded, than "my heart leaped within me, and, as it were, echoed to the call." Here was the sign. Now the only question was when.

Through an unforeseen series of delays and postponements, Whitefield was prevented from embarking for a full year after his decision to become a missionary. In fact, these delays proved as significant (though in this case unacknowledged) to his call as the letter from Wesley. They provided a critical period in which he preached freely and regularly before diverse audiences, discovering the true extent of his prowess. During this period he also discovered the value of newspapers and, for the first time, applied the psychology of public relations to his preaching. In a series of increasingly stiff tests that culminated in London, he learned that he was a dramatic preacher without peer. And he learned that preaching, unlike any other charitable activity or mission, gave him that sense of power that had so far eluded him.

On Sunday, June 27, 1736, the day following his ordination, Whitefield preached his first sermon. There, before admiring family, friends, and local officials, he climbed the pulpit of St. Mary de Crypt, where he had worshiped as a youth, and began to preach on the methodist theme of "The Nature and Necessity of Society in General and Religious Society in Particular." Later, with all the exuberance of triumph, he described the event in his journal:

> Curiosity, as you may easily guess, drew a large congregation. The sight at first a little awed me, but I was comforted with a heartfelt sense of the Divine presence and soon found the unspeakable advantage of having been accustomed to public speaking when a boy at school,

and of exhorting and teaching the prisoners and poor people at their private houses whilst at the University. . . . As I proceeded, I perceived the fire kindled. . . . Some few mocked, but most of those present seemed struck, and I have since heard that a complaint has been made to the Bishop that I drove fifteen mad the first sermon.

The language he used to describe his first sermon is instructive. Later the terms would become formulaic, but in the beginning they were the words of discovery. In this account, he did not simply "instruct" or "edify" or "please" his congregation: he "struck" listeners with a divine "presence" and an "authority" that drove some stark raving "mad." Clearly what impressed him was the power he possessed in the pulpit, in contrast to the powerlessness and inferiority he often experienced in society. All this was heady for one so young, and all the more for one who wanted power and respect so badly.

Whitefield continued to preach and to describe his efforts to any and all who would listen. Repeatedly he called attention to his youthfulness and to his "infant childish" appearance. Then he described the transformed expressions on people's faces as they beheld him in the pulpit. First at Gloucester, then at Oxford and Dummer in Hampshire, he preached to the students, the poor, the prisoners, and the illiterate. All of these engagements were gratifying, and all confirmed his abilities. But the sternest test of his mettle still awaited him in the London metropolis. Once again he waited for the call he had already determined was his.

In August 1736, the call sounded. Whitefield's methodist friend Thomas Broughton invited him to supply his Tower pulpit in London. With some trepidation and an uncontrollable anticipation, he accepted.

Perhaps at no other time in its long and noble history had London represented a more ideal site to launch a preaching revolution. It had grown to be Europe's largest city, leaving Amsterdam and Paris far behind. Within the city limits, it housed one in seven English men and women. And contained in its widely diverse population were the heights of aristocratic privilege and the depths of urban poverty.

Equally important for Whitefield's career, London was the center of commerce and the exporter of culture throughout the British empire. As never before, culture had become a product. London was awash in its goods and services, as were the provinces as far away as Scotland and America. The middle class was expanding rapidly, and with its growth came the rise of a market economy. Suddenly the idea of "fashion" took hold of a vast new segment of society. An ever-growing number of middle-class wage earners consumed an ever-growing number of goods. People flocked to buy their own ceramics and pottery, to include knives with their forks, and to add meat to their daily diet. Hacks and quacks advertised miracle cures and tonics in the newspapers and attracted nearly as many sufferers as did licensed doctors. Hair fashions for men and women as well as for children's dolls all became part of the burgeoning eighteenth-century market economy.

Twentieth-century historians have demonstrated that Whitefield's eighteenth-century London was in the midst of a great consumer revolution that transformed ideas and institutions apparently unrelated to commerce and materials. In fact, London was becoming, in Neil McKendrick's apt phrase, "the shopwindow for the whole country." The effect of this consumer revolution was to insert ever greater numbers of middle-class and even working-class English people into a marketplace world premised on consumption and free-market spending.

Beyond simple economic exchange, the marketplace came increasingly to define social reality and dictate the terms by which society and various subcultures came into existence. The urban marketplace occupied a place apart from traditional institutions and centers of power such as church, state, military, or nobility. It evolved into a morally neutral arena of goods exchanged and services governed by impersonal rules of supply and demand. No one had any special claims on its considerable rewards. Success depended on hustle, and hustle required offering appropriate goods and services in response to particular demands.

Following the example of such business entrepreneurs as Josiah Wedgwood, cultural entrepreneurs began marketing their skills and products to growing networks of paying customers. Increasingly the old patron-client economy gave way to the buyer-seller economy of the marketplace. Books, magazines, and newspapers proliferated and were eagerly purchased by private subscription at lending libraries and London's two thousand coffee houses and taverns. The marketing of the theater was no less impressive. David Garrick, who first played London within a year of Whitefield's first sermons, discovered there an exciting world of unprecedented possibilities. Drury Lane soon generated revenues in excess of £300 a performance, including after-hour performances at cheaper rates for working-class audiences. In 1732 London theaters were attracting fourteen thousand customers per week — a stupendous increase over the Restoration era. Similar successes were enjoyed by artists of other sorts. Music halls proliferated in Piccadilly as well as in smaller inns and taverns throughout the provinces. The effect of all this rigorous commercialization was to create the *idea* of leisure activity and apply that concept to ever-expanding sectors of the English population. Objects and pursuits that had once been the exclusive domain of the aristocracy now came within the reach of great new numbers of people. Even the working class was not exempt from the spending revolution and could be increasingly found at market days and public events. Along with the commercialization of leisure grew the habit of social outings and public events staged for paying customers.

In this dynamic arena it was only a matter of time before religion was marketed alongside these other cultural endeavors. The transition would not become complete for another century, but the seeds were planted by 1730. In economic terms, religion increasingly represented a product that could be marketed. In turn, the public supported its marketers, together with the charitable and religious causes they championed, liberated from past patriarchal relations and freely responsible for making their own choice. This process of commercialization necessarily transformed concepts of religion and religious experience generally: they came to be viewed in more individualistic and subjective terms. "Experience," "taste," and "attraction" became sufficient criteria for purchase.

Before religion could become a marketplace phenomenon, however, it required an entrepreneur — a Wedgwood or Garrick who could offer it in public settings during the week for the general public. Someone needed to conceive of religion, in effect, as another leisure-time activity that could attract customers in the marketplace and promote itself through a full spectrum of advertising and media coverage. Whitefield soon became that entrepreneur, but only after he had familiarized himself with London and its market possibilities.

On August 4, with "fear and trembling," he took the stage coach to London. Later he recalled his excitement at the prospect of preaching "at a place to which, not many years ago, I would have given much money . . . to have gone up and seen a play." Upon arrival he met with several methodist worthies and spent time walking the streets "in a gown and cassock," listening with concealed delight to people commenting on the "boy parson." Then his moment arrived. On Sunday, August 8, Whitefield preached to a large audience at Bishopgate Church. As he surveyed the congregation, he viewed a scene he had enacted countless times in his imagination. At first he suffered some stage fright that "a little dazed me," but then he found his voice and "was enabled to preach with power." Once again, power was the overriding self-perception: "The effect was immediate and visible to all; for as I went up the stairs almost all seemed to sneer at me on account of my youth; but they soon grew serious and exceedingly attentive, and after I came down, showed me great tokens of respect." Once the sermon was completed, much the self-satisfied hero, he "speedily slipped through the crowd."

Here, at last, was the respect and power he had craved

and defined for his destiny. Preaching could do what missions and charity could not: it could make him an unrivaled some-body in the cause of Christ. For two months Whitefield lingered in London building on his successes. He delivered sermons at Ludgate Prison on Tuesdays and at Wapping Chapel on Sundays. All the while his reputation grew, allowing an under-stated confession in the *Journal* that "I began to grow a little popular." Elsewhere Whitefield strained to find language that would accurately reflect his experience. In his assessment, audiences no longer simply "benefited" from the performance or "improved" the message in their life; now they were "startled" at the power so young a preacher could impose through the sheer passion of his preaching.

Whitefield responded to the new audiences and gave the performances of his life. What seemed to him in retrospect intuition or providence was, in fact, also a response to acclaim he had already rehearsed endlessly in his imagination. No stage could provide the sense of power and legitimacy he derived from the pulpit. And no other minister could match his achieve-ment. He was an Oxford-educated Anglican priest who, through the force of his presence and personality, was building a vast following from the bottom up.

Wherever he traveled, news of him spread by word of mouth and crowds materialized out of nowhere. For the first time, religious assemblies became almost frightening in their intensity and enthusiasm. Crowds began to grow, invariably prompting fears of a mob. At St. John's Church in Bristol, the audience was so large that he had to schedule an additional meeting the next day to accommodate the unseated crowd outside. The following day, Whitefield reports, was a repeat of the day before. "I again complied; and the alarm given here was so general, that, on the following Lord's Day, many of all denominations were obliged to return from the churches, where I preached, for want of room. . . . The Word . . . was sharper than a two-edged sword. The doctrine of the New Birth . . . made its way like lightning into the hearers' consciences."

Excited language, irrepressible (if regrettable) pride, surprise, and wonderment punctuate Whitefield's recollection of these years in his *Journal*. He never explored the reasons for his success beyond simple acknowledgments of Providence. Yet alongside Providence was certainly a startling talent, the makings of which can be inferred through an examination of surviving sermon texts and observer's comments.

Whitefield's first published sermon, "The Nature and Necessity of Our Regeneration or New Birth in Christ Jesus," which appeared in London in 1737, contains the all-consuming theme of the New Birth that was featured in one way or another in virtually every sermon he preached. In terms of text (2 Cor. 5:17) and doctrine, the sermon contains nothing exceptional. Sermons on the necessity of a New Birth had abounded in the regular preaching of nonconformist ministers since the seventeenth century and were becoming a staple of the Wesleys' methodism. Whitefield's unique contribution lay in his impassioned manner of presentation and in his single-minded emphasis on experience.

In analyzing Whitefield's novel manner, two considerations immediately present themselves. The first is thematic emphasis. Earlier treatments of the New Birth tended to present the subject in a theological context before turning to personal applications. That context, in brief, was the acknowledgment or recognition of regeneration as a new spiritual and ontological status. Where once sinners had stood alienated from God, after the New Birth they took on the mantle of Christ and became — *in God's eyes* — new creatures. Left unspecified in Puritan sermons was whether and to what extent the new creatures became new in their own eyes. Personal experience was subordinated to considerations of the new status before God. It mattered less that individuals *felt* this new position before God than that they understood what had happened in the spiritual realm and responded to that new status with appropriate acts of praise and thanksgiving.

In Whitefield's sermon, the personal experience was immediate and overwhelming. He preached as though there might be no tomorrow, to an audience who might never again assemble in its present configuration. Throughout, he showed no interest in theology. Instead of doctrine, he explored the feelings of New Birth and through his exploration invited hearers to experience it for themselves. Imagination was central to his presentation of feelings. Repeatedly he asked his listeners to imagine a different state of being, to imagine being birthed into a new creature. What would happen, he asked, if one were consciously to live through "a thorough, real, inward change of heart"? On the level of belief, little might change, since many already had a "head knowledge" of salvation. But in terms of feelings and passions, the effects would be overwhelming.

Puritans, of course, conceded this point emphatically. It was on the level of emphasis that the differences appeared. Whitefield addressed neither the understanding nor the theologically informed and properly aligned "affections"; he spoke simply and overwhelmingly to the passions of the heart. The new creation of which he spoke was not a "mere metaphor"; it was as self-evident and palpable as a "tasteless palate" suddenly brought alive at a sumptuous feast. Salvation was preeminently a personal affair of the heart:

> Every one that has but the least concern for the salvation of his precious, his immortal soul, having such promises, such an hope, such an eternity of happiness set before him, should never cease watching, praying, and striving till he find a real inward, saving change wrought in his heart, and thereby knows of a truth that he dwells in Christ and Christ in him.

To understand the novelty of Whitefield's experiential preaching, we must move beyond the text to the context. And here the most salient point is Whitefield's insertion of the body into his discourse. Even though his first sermons were written out in classic Anglican fashion, his body did not — could not — remain still in the prescribed fashion. From the start of his

39

preaching, apparently without premeditation or guile, he evidenced a dramatic manner that remained a hallmark of his preaching style throughout his career. A sarcastic account of his sermon on the New Birth printed in the Anglican *Weekly Miscellany* called attention less to Whitefield's theme than his bodily manner: "Hark! he talks of a Sensible New Birth — then belike he is in Labour, and the good Women around him are come to his assistance. He dilates himself, cries out [and] is at last delivered." Such histrionics, the account complained, were an affront to good taste and privacy. Moreover, they were an affront to manliness. Again Whitefield played the woman, this time from the pulpit rather than the stage. And again, the results were striking. To a far greater extent than most of his clerical peers, Whitefield took on female as well as male characters from Scripture, finding in them subjects apt for dramatic recreation.

Whitefield was not content simply to talk about the New Birth; he had to sell it with all the dramatic artifice of a huckster. Any churchgoer could understand the theological status of a new creation, but to see a preacher travailing in labor as the new birth took place was to encounter an unprecedented and shocking demonstration. Whitefield not only asserted that the new creation was more than mere metaphor, he embodied it.

To appreciate Whitefield's printed sermons fully, we have to read them less as lectures or treatises than as dramatic scripts, each with a series of verbal cues that released improvised body language and pathos. Words or phrases such as "Hark!" "Behold!" "Alas!" and "Oh!" invariably signaled the pathos Whitefield dramatically recreated with his whole body. The words were the scaffolding over which the body climbed, stomped, cavorted, and kneeled, all in an attempt — as much intuitive as contrived — to startle and completely overtake his listeners. Reading Whitefield's popular London sermon "The Eternity of Hell-Torments" as a script, one can easily picture him moving to the following lines, recreating a sinner's arrival in hell:

O wretched Man that I am, who shall deliver me from the Body of Death! Are all the Grand Deceiver's inviting Promises come to this? O Damned Apostate! Oh that I had never hearkened to his beguiling Insinuations! Oh that I had rejected his very first Suggestions with the utmost Detestation and Abhorrence! Oh that I had taken up my cross and followed Christ! But alas! These reflections come now too late. But must I live for ever tormented in these Flames? Oh, Eternity! That thought fills me with Despair. I cannot, will not, yet I must be miserable for ever.

Whitefield's effective use of his body was accentuated by his cross-eyed stare, the result of a childhood case of measles. It appears in virtually every portrait, and often drew attention in the press. To modern viewers, the cross-eyed stare may appear distracting and unattractive, but, as historian Jon Butler points out, many ordinary eighteenth-century viewers saw in this a sign of power and supernatural presence.

Along with body movement came tears. Tears became Whitefield's homiletical trademark or characteristic psychological gesture. In general, Whitefield was prone to cry often. But to his surprise, tears in public signified something entirely different from tears in private. In private, tears signified weakness and effeminacy. Before his tutors, his tears were pathetic. In public, however, they commanded power. They brought listeners into his world. Cornelius Winter recalled that

I hardly ever knew him go through a sermon without weeping, more or less, and I truly believe his were the tears of sincerity. . . . I could hardly bear such unreserved use of tears, and the scope he gave to his feelings, for sometimes he exceedingly wept, stamped loudly and passionately, and was frequently so overcome, that, for a few seconds, you would suspect he never could recover; and when he did, nature required some little time to compose himself.

41

Winter's description is valuable for the picture it gives of a consummate actor able to express his vulnerable inner self in the pulpit. In Whitefield's sermons, private thoughts and raptures became public renditions. Whereas Puritan preachers were often overwhelmed by passions in their diaries yet composed in public, Whitefield saved his impassioned reflections for enactment in the pulpit. He did not hesitate to employ the personal pronoun in a manner reminiscent more of the diarist than the preacher. Nor did he hesitate to blurt out the feelings he was immediately experiencing. When preaching on grace, he would often interject with "alas" and sympathy: "Oh, who can avoid crying out at the Consideration of this Mystery of Godliness?"

Besides pathos and tears, Whitefield frequently appealed to his listeners' imaginations as he enacted the agonies of damnation and the ecstasy of salvation. Here the leading cue was the word *methinks*. In a sermon on the new heaven and the new earth he invited his hearers to engage their imagination and to

> lift up your Hearts frequently towards the Mansions of eternal Bliss, and with an Eye of Faith, like the great St. Stephen, see the Heavens opened, and the Son of Man with his glorious retinue of departed saints sitting and solacing themselves in eternal Joys, and with unspeakable Comfort looking back on their past sufferings and self-denials, as so many glorious Means which exalted them to such a Crown. Hark! methinks I hear them chanting their everlasting Hallelujahs, and spending an eternal Day in echoing forth triumphant Songs of Joy. And do you not long, my Brethren, to join this heavenly Choir?

Tears, passions, and consolation fused in Whitefield's sermons to produce a new and powerful form of preaching. Although endowed with a voice that was often likened to the "roar of a lion," Whitefield offered a message not primarily of fear and hell-fire but of compassion, suffering, and comfort. At heart, Whitefield's preaching was maternal in tone. The same consolation and comfort he had received from his mother he directed out to his hearers with powerful results. In a sense, Whitefield learned to let the woman in him speak in a lion-like voice that startled hearers everywhere.

As Whitefield's popularity increased, he grew in self-confidence and daring. His career unfolded in a series of dramatic moments of self-discovery that revealed ever-greater talents in the area of dramatic improvisation. But to be wholly freed to exploit his talents, Whitefield needed to be freed from the written sermon text. There could be no document standing between his body and his audience. Like an actor memorizing his script, he had to internalize his text and articulate his message with apparent spontaneity and effortless improvisation.

Extemporaneous preaching had become an accepted innovation among the Oxford methodists during Whitefield's tenure there. In 1735 John Wesley discovered the method by accident, having once forgotten his notes. The ensuing extempore sermon was so powerful that he recommended it to all who could muster the courage. Sometimes the speaker would not even know his text until he rose to preach. Such preaching established a unique bond between speaker and hearer and released the full range of improvisation and inspiration. For dramatic speakers like Whitefield it was the perfect release.

Whitefield's extemporaneous debut came on December 28, 1737, on the eve of his departure for Georgia:

> It happened providentially that a lecture was to be preached that evening at Deptford, and several importuned me to preach it; at first I was fearful (O me of little faith), having no notes. But afterwards (having got consent of the minister), I went up, depending on the promise, 'Lo! I am with you always even unto the end of the world,' and was enabled to preach to a large congregation without the least hesitation.

With that, Whitefield's pulpit arsenal was complete. Where others felt hesitant or at a loss, he discovered release. The longer

43

his voyage was postponed, the more he experimented with extemporaneous preaching. His prodigious memory for character and dialogue enabled him to transform the pulpit into a sacred theater that vitally re-presented the lives of biblical saints and sinners to his captivated listeners.

And as he had mastered the London pulpit, Whitefield eventually mastered the London press. In advance of virtually all his clerical peers, he sensed the potential of the press and exploited it fully. "Whitefield stories" began to circulate in print, quickly assuming the status of legend. Many of these stories were contributed by Whitefield himself and reported in his journal. Self-promotion did not come easily to most clerics, whose sense of self and career was shaped by the local parish and a public reserve befitting their station as venerable prophets and social superiors. But it came naturally to Whitefield. Where more timid souls would leave the descriptions of adoring crowds to others, Whitefield intuitively grasped the emerging science of public relations and never missed an opportunity to promote the "gospel successes" he enjoyed. Such was the extent of his popularity that while speaking in Bristol he reported that "multitudes came on foot, and many in coaches a mile without the city, to meet me; and almost all saluted and blessed me as I went along the street." Besides news of large congregations, Whitefield revealed several "large offers" to remain in Bristol. All of this was grist for a publicity mill that the young preacher did not hesitate to exploit by word of mouth and print. He promoted religion with the same public notice and puffery that others devoted to more mundane products and services.

Mass media and mass consumption were inseparable, and Whitefield took full advantage of both in promoting the cause of religion — and himself. A long and checkered career with the press began in these months of waiting. He noted with satisfaction how his sermon "Regeneration" was published and "sold well to persons of all denominations . . . at home and abroad." Advertisements for his sermons appeared everywhere, including the hostile *Weekly Miscellany*. Soon the offices of Whitefield's publishing friend and fellow Methodist James Hutton were strained to meet the demands. New sermons were called for, and Whitefield eagerly complied. "The Almost Christian" and "The Nature and Necessity of Society" were advertised widely and sold well. Whitefield knew that many Anglicans begrudged his successes, but instead of keeping silence he openly gloated. Appropriating the words of Christ's ancient critics, Whitefield imagined his current critics asking about him "Can any good come out of Nazareth?"

Before leaving for Georgia, Whitefield rushed into print with everything he had. Most of his published sermons date from this period, the early years of his career, before he was twenty-five. Of sixty-three printed sermons, forty-six originated in this period and were reprinted on both sides of the Atlantic throughout his lifetime and after.

Beyond learning the power of advertising his work, Whitefield learned to make *himself* news. In part this was a simple function of his popularity. By September 1737 he noted with satisfaction how "my name was first put into the public papers." Later, following a fund-raising sermon series at St. Swithin's in London, the press recorded the astounding success of a "young gentleman going volunteer to Georgia" who had raised the staggering offering of £28, most of which was collected "in half-pence" from innumerable working-class supporters. Although professing unhappiness that the press dwelt on money instead of message and "would not lose two shillings for anybody," Whitefield was nevertheless pleased. He had made the news.

Whitefield discovered that the press built audiences as effectively as word of mouth. From this point forward, he used the press as much as it used him, to promote and stage his preaching performances. For the first time in the eighteenth century, a preacher joined the ranks of generals, governors, and actors as a news event. "The tide of popularity," Whitefield gloated, "now began to run very high." The obligatory humility required of his profession could not suppress the exhilarating fact that "I could no longer walk on foot as usual, but was constrained to go in a coach, from place to place, to avoid the hosannas of the multitude." So enamored was he of his own successes that contemporaries and later readers had trouble accepting his accompanying methodist codicil that God "gave me to see the vanity of all commendations but His own."

But Whitefield also learned that popularity was only part of the secret for becoming news in a news-starved society. Equally important was controversy and public confrontation with traditional authority. Whitefield was no social radical bent on overturning society, nor was he in the habit of challenging civil authority — indeed, the crown always elicited his highest praise. But bishops were another matter. Whitefield could challenge them on religious grounds without calling the establishment itself into question. And in doing so, he could demonstrate his pulpit power. In fact, he had not gotten over the anger he felt at Oxford, and in his self-righteous contest with the bishops he found a vent for the anger that was both cathartic and, in his eyes, utterly legitimate.

Invariably, Whitefield set his successes alongside the perceived failures of the established church. With controversy and the press in mind, he was learning to stage preaching events in ways that vaulted him to the forefront of public attention. He grasped intuitively the potential for fame whether the notices were praising or damning. In either case, he saw his name set before the public eye, and, as he noted in his journal, "peoples curiosity was stirred up more and more."

In response to Whitefield's criticisms, clerics condemned him for promoting his fame at their expense. They complained that he was not on the mission field winning new souls to the gospel but robbing parish priests of their congregations and offerings. His services competed with theirs, and badly needed offerings were piling up in his coffers while the poor at home suffered.

Soon Whitefield came to the attention of the Bishop of

London. The resulting exchange initiated a round of controversy that was to follow him for the rest of his career. In his journal account, Whitefield created the picture of a young soldier for Christ boldly entering the bishop's chamber, asserting his right to the Georgia mission, and remaining until the bishop "gave me a satisfactory answer, and I took my leave." The language is triumphalist and self-righteous, and was certain to appeal to readers who themselves chafed under the yoke of authority.

The more this controversy was played out in the press, the more Whitefield emerged as the heroic victim. In a technique that would reap endless rewards, Whitefield portrayed any public criticism as "persecution" from on high, fueling popular antagonism to authority and identifying himself as the beleaguered underdog. Throughout it all, one could easily forget that he was a twenty-three-year-old deacon defining his career to his superiors. Through clever manipulation of the press he assumed for himself the best of both worlds: an ordained insider attacking authority as if he was an outsider.

Though vitriolic, the controversy with the bishops was a public relations dream come true. By fall of 1737, with his voyage still postponed, Whitefield reported that "thousands and thousands came to hear. My sermons were everywhere called for." Soon the engravers got into the public act. Like the newspapers, visual arts were moving rapidly into consumer markets with caricatures and satiric renderings identified most dramatically with William Hogarth. A print began circulating showing an ambitious Whitefield "leaning on a cushion, with a bishop looking very enviously over my Shoulder." Whitefield immediately dismissed the print as another attempt at character assassination. Yet, in light of the young preacher's growing but still undefined ambition, it may not have been so far from the mark. In a letter to John Wesley complaining of the bishop, he added the heady note that "I tremble to tell you how I have been continually disturbed with thoughts, that I, a worm taken from a common public-house should ere I die, be

47

one myself." Aware that his confession exceeded all bounds of Christian humility, he quickly closed with the request that "your earnest prayers, surely, will not be wanting for me, that I may not split on that most dangerous of all rocks — worldly ambition."

Whitefield neglected no art or medium as he began the steep climb of self-promotion. To counter the satiric caricaturing circulated widely in the woodcuts, Whitefield sat for a portrait, supposedly for his mother, noting, "if I would not let her have the substance, I would leave her at least the shadow." Portraits were not in themselves out of the ordinary, except in the case of a subject so young. Whitefield was neither an aristocrat nor a politician, yet the portrait placed him in the important category of public figures.

By the eve of his departure, Whitefield had become a bona fide sensation. He had preached to thousands, and his printed sermons could not keep up with popular demand. In freewill offerings and donations for the impending Georgia mission he had raised the extraordinary sum of £1,300 — a figure exceeding the annual incomes of all but the wealthiest bishops. In part he had been helped by others, but mostly he had helped himself, validating Poor Richard's aphorism long before it was written. There had been no models on which to draw. Rather, through intuition and boundless self-confidence, Whitefield had created new conceptions of preaching, ministry, and public relations that others would follow and that he would carry with him to the ends of the earth.

4 Colonial Missionary

No eighteenth-century religious figure lived out more roles more quickly than the young Whitefield. Characters that had once resided in plays, Scriptures, and his imagination now regularly took on reality in his life. The boy preacher no sooner established his reputation as a preacher than he traded it in for that of the aspiring missionary-to-be, loaded with energy and offerings for the orphans and debtors who inhabited the Georgia colony. When Whitefield at last departed on February 2, 1738, he reenacted an adventure English men and women had been staging for over a century of American colonization.

Sailing with Whitefield on the *Whitaker* was General James Oglethorpe, founder of the Georgia colony and commander of a regiment of soldiers sent to protect English interests on the southern border shared with Spain. The soldiers served notice that the New World was dangerous. They also represented a group Whitefield intended to reach for the gospel.

Although the American colonies were over a century old, Georgia was barely five and offered, in many ways, the same primitive environment Europeans had earlier encountered in Jamestown and Plymouth Colony. Whitefield understood the harshness of the conditions he was facing. At best the voyage would take two and a half months in a vessel under fifty tons. The winter departure date meant additional discomforts and insecurities. A contemporary travel account painted a bleak picture of Atlantic crossings: "smells, fumes, horrors, vomiting, various kinds of sea sickness, fever, dysentery, headaches, heat, constipation, boils, scurvy, cancer, mouth-rot, and similar afflictions, all of them caused by the age and the highly-salted state of the food, especially of the meat, as well as by the very bad and filthy water. . . . There are so many lice, especially on the sick people, that they have to be scraped off the bodies." Added to the problems of hygiene and health were the ever-present threats of war with France or Spain and the possibilities of privateering. Such a voyage required youth, stamina, and the strongest motivation. Whitefield did not inherit the strongest constitution, but the adventuresome spirit was there, together with a compelling sense of personal calling and destiny.

Compounding the young missionary's problems was the fact that both Wesley brothers had returned prematurely from America — but not before giving the word *methodist* a bad name. Charles Wesley had come back after only five months in Georgia, ostensibly to raise additional support and volunteers for the Georgia mission, though in fact he was exhausted and disillusioned. John Wesley had returned in December, as Whitefield was departing, the victim of an unhappy love affair that had run him afoul of local authorities. Both Wesleys had denounced slavery in the harshest terms. They had insisted that foreign nationals conform to their methodist liturgy in worship. Neither of these demands had won friends among the inhabitants and, in fact, neither Wesley would ever return to America. One methodist of wealthy background, Charles Delamotte, had been left behind, but his vocation was teaching, not preaching. Clearly, the future of the mission now rested with Whitefield.

With the Oxford odd fellow forever abandoned, Whitefield threw himself into the Georgia mission. To assist him in the work of missions and the possible establishment of an orphan house, Whitefield brought several assistants, of whom the most important was James Habersham, a methodist convert and close friend of the young missionary. Throughout his career, Whitefield proved to be a master at winning friends. The same intensity that had taken him to the brink in confrontation with bishops could, when turned to friendship, win followers and associates whose loyalty and devotion would be lifelong. Habersham was among the first of Whitefield's close friends; he would administer methodist affairs in Whitefield's frequent absences from Georgia and in time become Georgia's leading merchant.

Where others of less determined personality often employed a long voyage to rest and gather resources, Whitefield set about immediately to transform the *Whitaker* into a voyaging mission. Before the ship embarked, he wasted no time appointing Habersham as teacher and himself as chaplain to the crew and soldiers. Certain that there would be shipboard adventures, he also prepared a journal that could be sent back to England like the Wesley's earlier journals, possibly to be published alongside his sermons. For his first entry, he intended to convert the soldiers.

Unlike John Wesley and other methodists who separated private diary from public journal, Whitefield abolished the distinction in ways that anticipated the artful autobiography of his soon-to-be friend and publisher Benjamin Franklin. In the same way he translated inner feelings spontaneously to the pulpit, Whitefield used the journal to move directly from pen to public. In the process, the private Whitefield became lost both to the public and to himself. But to the public Whitefield represented a new religious character that would fire popular imagination and generate unprecedented demands for autobiographical literature.

The Georgia diary and the subsequently written autobiography were Whitefield's first attempts at journalistic self-promotion and, in their own context, were pioneering works of genius. Earlier than most, Whitefield perceived that the journal — once confined to the private and inner world of the diarist — could become an ideal vehicle for creating a public image. One could carefully select entries with a view toward constructing a persona — the person one wanted to be or the person one thought would edify unknown readers — rather than presenting oneself as one "really was." In fact, a journal writer could sketch into his entries any character he wished to be, and that character would become the person an unsuspecting public would see in the document, reading it as if it were a private self-revelation or an open letter to close friends. The writer could even fool himself.

As a teller of tales the young Whitefield had few equals. He had an ear for language and, though never a scholar or polite essayist, he produced colloquial prose ideally suited to the popular press. Reports on weather, course headings, and winds he deftly interspersed with nail-biting accounts of storms at sea, cascading waves, split sails, and imminent danger. Something in the sea released Whitefield's deepest imaginative and descriptive powers, and the repose of the journey gave him time to write. In fact, he could never get enough of the sea, whether motionless in languid winds or racing along "as it were on the wings of the wind." He confessed that often instead of visiting the sick "I stood upon deck, and admired the wonders of God in the deep." As for Puritan writers before him, the ocean crossing became a metaphor for Whitefield of the Christian's spiritual pilgrimage across a dangerous sea to a strange new world. In his journal, it emerged in the language of providence and power.

Throughout the travel portions of his journals, Whitefield invited his reading public to become fellow travelers and co-laborers in the great adventure, friends who shared his terrors and excitements. Most dramatic in Whitefield's accounts were reports of the storms that threatened the lives of all aboard. Readers could easily imagine the situation when "the sea was very boisterous indeed, and the waves rose mountains high;

52

but God was pleased to give Mr. H[abersham] and me an unusual degree of faith, and we went on singing psalms and praising God, the water dashing in our faces all the way." On another occasion, "I went on deck; but surely a more noble, awful sight my eyes never beheld! For the waves rose mountain high, and sometimes came on the quarter-deck. I endeavored all the while to magnify God, for thus making His power to be known. Then creeping on my knees (for I knew not how to go otherwise), I followed my friend H. between decks, and sang songs and comforted the poor wet people."

The picture here of heroic Whitefield magnifying God in the teeth of a gale does not fit comfortably alongside his oft-confessed timidity in the face of physical danger. But for his readers it did create a vivid sense of adventure in which he was at the center. In the account of another storm, readers learned that, "though things were tumbling, the ship rocking, persons falling down unable to stand, and sick about me, I never was more cheerful in my life, and was enabled, though in the midst of company, to finish a sermon before I went to bed." Action was the common theme throughout, whether nature's action erupting in all its savage fury and malevolence or Whitefield's action of praising God and doing acts of mercy. In his journal, Whitefield described no moments of idleness, boredom, self-censure, or passivity, though surely such occurred. Intuitively he knew what common readers liked both in stories and characters, and he did not disappoint them. He sculpted of himself a heroic character whose secret strength was faith in God and whose life testified to the truths he proclaimed.

Whitefield carried both his heroic persona and his theme of action into an accompanying story of even greater excitement and personal legend: the conversion of the crew and soldiers. In fact, ocean, storm, and calm acted in his journal to provide the pace and background for his ongoing efforts to silence and eventually becalm a fierce band of soldiers. The jagged progress of the ship in winter voyage became a meta-

phor for Whitefield's progress with the soldiers. Engaged readers soon learned that the real drama in the journal was not
natural but supernatural.

In the rough-and-tumble world of eighteenth-century
Anglo-America, soldiers and sailors were the ultimate men.
The shipboard life of "Jack Tar" was notorious for its brutality
and the harshness of shipboard conditions. Few fates were
more dreaded than impressment into the British navy. Renowned for their violence as well as their profanity, they were,
in Whitefield's eyes, the supreme challenge. Himself youthful
and somewhat effeminate, he had to believe that nothing
would be more impressive than his successful witness to the
crew. Certainly nothing would more impress him. At the same
time, he desperately wanted God "magnified" in all he did.
Through his faith and the power of his ministry, he determined
to take the sailors on, and in the end he succeed in winning
many to the manly cause of the gospel.

The ongoing saga with the ship's crew occupies the
largest portion of Whitefield's journal. It takes up even more
space than the New World mission. As ship's chaplain, Whitefield had responsibility for overseeing the spiritual exercises of
the ship's captain and crew. As missionary, he assumed for
himself responsibility for changing their behavior. He began
his ministrations to the sailors with ringing remonstrances
against swearing and vain oaths — long the currency of simple
discourse among men at sea. He followed this up with an even
less popular denunciation of "the heinous sin of drunkenness."
Predictably, his words floated aimlessly through the air like so
much sea mist. Instead of reforming their behavior, the sailors
seemed only to swear more whenever they saw the young
parson approaching.

But the missionary-to-be would not be discouraged or
silenced. Undaunted and unintimidated, he continued his remonstrances. "Persecution" was fuel that fed his determination
and drew forth his greatest exertions. Few words occur with
greater frequency in Whitefield's journal than *persecution*, and

apparently no other circumstances so tested his manhood. The more the soldiers scoffed and heaped abuse on him, the more determined he was to win them to Christ — and to himself.

In fact, he succeeded. And the path to that success was less his words than his actions. He knew how to make friends by following a lifelong credo to "be servant-like, but not servile." The shipboard crew soon learned that this included them. In Whitefield they discovered a friend and comforter as well as a rebuker. Alongside his admonitions he filled his time with acts of mercy and compassion that expressed the sentiments of divine love and mercy he proclaimed in his preaching. Morning and evening he visited the sick sailors and shared food from his considerable stores of supplies collected for Georgia. Through sheer will power and determined charity, he broke down the walls of hostility and gradually won a grudging respect.

Throughout the harsh winter voyage he preached daily to the ship's crew and passengers. When not reading from the prayerbook, he preached extemporaneously and sharpened the skills he would bring with him to America. Passions remained at the center of his repertoire. Never one to soften words, he exploited the most frightening passions to achieve the desired effect. A text on John rebuking Herod gave Whitefield the opportunity to proclaim "that great men should not be angry if ministers should reprove them out of love." Two days later he noted that "my subject was, the eternity of hell torments" — a theme he had already developed to great effect in London.

As the voyage progressed ever closer to the New World destination, Whitefield's readers found him moving ever closer to converting his captive audience through the tools of mercy and comfort. He described a gradual alteration in the attitudes and actions of the troops: "I perceived the soldiers were attentive to hear me, when I applied myself to those around the sick persons." If this added to Whitefield's egotism, it also developed a genuine public concern that gave his words meaning. As more of the ship's passengers succumbed to seasickness and other maladies, he was genuinely touched, and busied himself with "furnishing them with sage-tea, sugar, broth etc." His response was direct and compassionate: "At the sight of so many objects of piety, I was sensibly touched with a fellow feeling of their miseries. . . . I had a most comfortable sense of the Divine Presence with me in many particulars, and in the evening joined in intercession with my other companions on deck, in behalf of absent friends and all mankind." In many ways, the young Whitefield was a prisoner to his feelings; apparently the only outlets he could tolerate were either acts of mercy or impassioned preaching that had as its central theme comfort and consolation.

In reading through the journal, it is clear that no one was more aware of Whitefield's heroism than Whitefield himself. Equally clear is the fact that his heroic model was taken from scriptural narratives. In a dramatic rather than literary or exegetical sense, biblical characters became "types" or models that provided a pattern for his own image. His description of the acts of charity and witness he performed outside of the pulpit suggests that in a sense he *became* the apostles he embodied. His actions were not mere "act" but reality. Of the biblical types, none was more important than the apostle Paul. Whitefield probably knew the character and words of Paul as well as he knew himself. The theme of persecution, so ubiquitous in Whitefield's writings, was almost invariably discussed in terms borrowed from Paul's writings. So ingrained was the influence of the apostle's language and peripatetic lifestyle on Whitefield's imagination that he virtually adopted Paul's persona for his own. When rations ran short on board, Whitefield used the occasion to record in his journal how this happened, "so that I can say, with the Apostle [Paul], I am 'in hunger and thirst, cold and fastings often.' Hereafter, perhaps, I may add, moreover in bonds and imprisonment." In fact Whitefield would never be imprisoned like the apostles of old, but he spoke of it often and may have been, one suspects, a little disappointed that the arrests never materialized.

In late February the *Whitaker* stopped over in the military outpost of Gibraltar, giving the young missionary an opportunity to display his preaching talents to a larger audience. Upon landing, he confided to Habersham (and his readers) how "I had reason to think . . . that God had some work for me to do at Gibraltar." His premonitions were soon confirmed when he "preached in the morning . . . before such a congregation of officers and soldiers as I never before saw. The church, though very large, was quite thronged, and God was pleased to shew me, that He had given extraordinary success to my sermon."

In addition to providing an outlet for preaching, Gibraltar presented the young traveler with an unforgettable look at a variety of cultures and peoples. The ethnic, linguistic, and religious diversity of Gibraltar dazzled him. His cultural observations were often as astute as his observations and descriptions of nature. He developed as well an incipient sense of cultural relativism. In observing the diversity of paper currencies in circulation, for example, he was led to reflect "on the stupidity of those who place their happiness in that which has no intrinsic worth in itself, but only so much as we arbitrarily put upon it."

While in Gibraltar Whitefield also encountered a variety of religions. Following a visit to a Roman Catholic chapel he had nothing but lament and repressed hostility: "Oh! who hath bewitched this people, that they should thus depart from the simplicity of Christ, and go a whoring after their own inventions." Like most of his generation, he was to harbor anti-Catholic sentiments throughout his career.

The Jews were a different story. They posed no immediate threat to English Protestants, and in fact represented a mission rather than an adversary. In visiting his first synagogue, Whitefield replaced the language of hatred with that of wonder and evangelical warmth. It certainly helped that the rabbi of the synagogue had heard Whitefield preach in Gibraltar. When the young evangelist visited, the rabbi placed him "in one of their chiefest seats." Whitefield's account gave readers insights both into the outer scene of the Jewish service and the inner scene of his own emotions. Ever the soul winner, he overlayed his description of the service with his internal state "in secret prayer to God that the veil might be taken from their hearts, and that blessed time might come when His chosen people should again be engrafted into their own Olive Tree and all Israel be saved."

Along with preaching and sightseeing, Whitefield enjoyed the company of the ship's captain and governor. Throughout his career Whitefield challenged the bishops and religious critics without ever challenging the idea of social hierarchy or deference. He invariably singled out meetings with important magistrates and dignitaries and recorded them in his journal. If fearless witness to soldiers confirmed his manhood, moments with elites confirmed his social status. In daily luncheons with the governor and military officers he was happy to commend "the regular behaviour of the officers at table."

By the time of his departure, Whitefield was attracting audiences of unprecedented size, among some of the roughest characters in the world. Of the many affected by his preaching, he was most observant of the soldiers, who were generally "the more unlikely to be wrought upon." But wrought upon they were, so that when the time came for farewell, "many wept." This account he followed with a prayer for humility in the face of all his triumphs: "O grant I may, like a pure crystal, transmit all the light Thou pourest over me, and never claim as my own what is Thy sole property!"

Once the voyage resumed, Whitefield encountered more opportunities to minister than he could handle. A fever raged through the ship, draining the young missionary's strength and eventually felling him. In describing his illness he adopted a Pauline sense of "to die is gain" that would recur throughout his ministry: "I earnestly desired to be dissolved and go to Christ; but God was pleased to order it otherwise, and I am resigned, though I can scarce be reconciled to come back again into this vale of misery."

By the conclusion of the New World voyage, Whitefield had a remarkable tale to tell. The transformation of the soldiers was, in many instances, almost complete. These tough men had become softened to the gospel. Many had attended prayers and sermons with miraculous results: "more of the sailors are convinced of sin and others send notes to be prayed for." Once on shore, an emboldened Whitefield could report, "I have no reason to complain of them, for they come very regularly twice a day to prayer, and an oath seems to be a strange thing amongst most of them. Many marks of a sound conversion appear in several on board, and we live in perfect harmony and peace, loving and beloved by one another."

The good relationships Whitefield had developed on board were not immediately replicated in Georgia. John Wesley's scrape with the law and his refusal to bend rules to tolerate other faiths and nationalities had not eased the way for later methodists. Nothing of the Wesleys' work remained, with the exception of Charles Delamotte. Instead of a hero's welcome to match his hero's farewell from the *Whitaker*, Whitefield faced another in a long succession of challenges.

Though weakened by the voyage and a nagging fever, Whitefield immediately set about seeking out "pious souls" around whom he could build a ministry. The task proved more difficult than he had imagined. Here was neither urban population nor captive shipboard audience. He found no bustling streets, no thriving theater, no crowded market stalls. Rather, the Georgia he encountered was literally at the end of the English world. Its largest "city," Savannah, was little more than a trading outpost with a scant population of five hundred. Its only public buildings included a jail, a wharf, and a courthouse that doubled as a church. Whitefield found a total of 140 small frame houses built on creaky pilings that quickly rotted in the termite-infested soil. Georgia was still twenty years away from replacing such impermanent wood structures with more durable brick buildings. In short, everyday life in Georgia was transitory and isolated. Sandy roads often became impassable, so settlement and travel had to focus on the streams and rivers. Beyond the sheer physical demands of the wilderness was the vulnerability to Spanish attack from the south. All that stood between the English colonists and the warlike Spanish "papists" was a small military outpost at Frederica, one hundred miles to the south of Savannah.

In Georgia Whitefield found a polyglot population that included English soldiers, debtors freed from English prisons, German-speaking Moravians, Swiss Lutherans, French Huguenots, and Scottish Highlanders. These inhabitants shared a hardscrabble life far removed from England's consumer revolution. They considered themselves fortunate if they had pewter dishes, one fork, and a roof over their heads. Their "marketplace," in Savannah, consisted of a series of stalls offering a meager selection of imported goods. They could readily purchase wine and beer, but rum was outlawed by the trustee government and had to be smuggled in from South Carolina.

If Whitefield was disappointed with this primitive Georgia, he was careful not to let it show. The fact that Georgians had never heard of the great evangelist and so displayed a lack of enthusiasm about his arrival did not deter him. With typical exuberance, he threw himself into the tasks of ministry and charity. Homes and small chapels replaced crowded cathedrals and massive pulpits, and Whitefield instinctively adapted his ministry to suit the small groups. In fact, he proved himself a born raconteur, at ease in any social situation. He moved from door to door enlisting worshipers and learning about the country's customs and faiths. In a letter to Gloucester he summarized his activities as follows: "I visit from house to house, catechise, read prayers twice and expound the two second lessons every day; read to a houseful of people three times a week; expound the two lessons at five in the morning, read prayers and preach twice, and expound the catechism to servants, etc., at seven in the evening every Sunday."

Whitefield's social skills and his determination not to offend local standards soon won him a much warmer reception than the Wesleys had received. To the evident satisfaction of all the planters, he repudiated the Wesleys' denunciation of slavery in Georgia and in fact urged its legalization. He also petitioned for the importation of rum. In deference to local customs, he did not demand that German, Swiss, or French inhabitants conform to Anglican rituals of baptism but instead incorporated their national traditions into the Anglican liturgy. Here we see the first signs of the ecumenicity and inclusiveness that would come to be such a notable feature of his ministry throughout the transatlantic world.

In addition to engaging in nonstop preaching and prayer, Whitefield addressed himself to the great problems of poverty and deprivation. Like all new colonies, Georgia was inadequately funded and poorly managed. The visionary ideals and philanthropic concerns of the trustees had not been backed up with hard currency. Churches were few, and schools and other charitable institutions simply did not exist. Immediately Whitefield recognized that charity was as needed as evangelism. Everywhere he dispensed supplies and charity to the sick and poor. He carried boxes of food, clothing, and devotional books through Georgia, often door to door, establishing widespread welcome and goodwill among most of the inhabitants. In words that he knew contrasted greatly with the Wesleys' earlier reports, he declared that "I looked for persecution, but lo! I am received as an angel of God."

With an adventurer's taste for travel and an evangelist's hunger for souls, Whitefield wasted no time visiting every settlement in the colony. Along the way he organized schools, supervised the cutting of lumber for church construction, and visited a small orphan house at Ebenezer, which confirmed the need for another that would be open to children throughout America and England.

At the same time, he realized that this small, struggling colony, while beloved, was much too small a canvas on which to paint his life's work. The needs of the people pulled at his heart as had those of the sailors on the *Whitaker*, but neither compelled his will. Like Paul, he needed many places and above all many cities like London, Bristol, Gibraltar, or, in the New World, New York, Philadelphia, and Boston. So, even while he was traveling and ministering, he was thinking. How could he reconcile his Anglican orders and the requirement that he have a particular home base assignment or "living" with the life of travel and evangelism he desired?

In the course of visiting families and orphans an idea began to germinate in Whitefield's mind that would bloom rapidly into a full-fledged plan. Instead of a career in the pulpit or on the mission field, he could take responsibility for a charitable institution that required external funding and support to survive. And what more perfect institution than the orphan house charity first conceived by Charles Wesley? The orphan house would provide Whitefield's home base, while the fundraising needs would require substantial travel to any and every locale that offered potential donors.

The idea for a Georgian orphan house that could be more inclusive than the small Moravian mission had circulated before Whitefield's arrival in 1738. Already in 1737, Charles Wesley, acting as Gov. Oglethorpe's secretary, had outlined preliminary plans for an orphanage modeled on institutions created by Herman Francke, leader of the pietistic movement in Halle, Germany. In Wesley's mind such an institution would serve the cause of both charity and piety. It would be a place that redeemed young orphans in body and soul.

Whitefield took this idea and ran with it for the rest of his life. If Georgia could absorb adult indigents from England, he reasoned, it could also absorb orphan children teeming in England's cities and in the American colonies, and give them a new start. He would found the institution and, through his travels and evident power to raise offerings, would support it with preaching and fund-raising missions throughout London and abroad. The more he tried the idea on, the better it fit. To devote his life to the Georgia orphan house would allow him to develop each of the characters he embodied. It would be located on a far-flung mission field peopled by adventurers and desperados, it would free him up time to be an itinerant "planter" or "pilgrim" like Paul, and it would provide a "family" without the demands of a fixed residence.

By August Whitefield's supplies had run out, and he prepared to return to England. Yet in that remarkably brief period of three months, he had established his reputation and restored goodwill to the name *methodist.* He had provided badly needed supplies of food, medicine, and pious literature; he had encouraged the founding of schools and churches; he had ministered to the sick and needy; and he had announced his interests in founding a charitable orphan house. He had seen the people's needs and realized that further assistance would require outside funding of the sort he knew he could raise in England and abroad.

In a farewell meeting with the Georgia trustees, Whitefield shared his vision for the orphan house and received an enthusiastic endorsement. Already he was loved, and the trustees saw no hint of trouble from the methodist side of his character. He was willing to assume responsibility for establishing an orphan house and mission in Georgia *without* requesting financial aid or a salary from the trustees. At the same time, he would need to travel widely as an ambassador for the Georgia orphan house. The advantages were thus mutual. The trustees would not have to shoulder the burden of supplying funds and teachers, and Whitefield would have to travel to raise support in urban centers. In short, he could be of more use to Georgia away than at home, which suited him perfectly.

Thus began a lifelong commitment for Whitefield. Though Georgia would never be his permanent residence, it would be the only locale he would routinely refer to as home, and he would come to refer to the orphan house as his family.

On September 9, Whitefield left many small groups of friends behind and returned to England. The ocean crossing provided the "retirement" needed to crystallize his plans. His target was the cities because of their potential for great audiences, but from prior experience he knew that he would encounter difficulties and obstacles. He knew, for example, that rival priests and bishops would not take kindly to his invasion of their parishes. And he had some concerns about how he was to preach to the already churched. How was he to transcend traditionally defined parish boundaries to speak to the people at large? In contemplating these problems of access, he recognized the dual advantage of the orphan house: it not only represented a legitimate act of charity in its own right and a "home" of record but also served as a pretext for itinerant preaching. If England was not a mission field open to traveling exhorters, it was a "Christian" nation committed to charity that extended beyond parish boundaries. Here was the entrée Whitefield could exploit in the interest of his urban ministry.

In addition to developing plans for his orphan house, Whitefield used the return voyage to compose sermons for print and to complete his journal entries. While still in Savannah, he had learned that the journal record of his visit to Gibraltar was not only being read by his methodist friends but was being distributed by two publishers, one of whom was his friend Hutton. The news did not disturb him, though he wrote that such publications ought to be "deferred till after my death, or written by some other persons." In fact, he had invented a new use for the medium that broke with convention and created an immediate best seller. The journal went through six printings in the first six months.

Unlike some overnight sensations that are forgotten as quickly as they arise, Whitefield's legend grew with his absence. With nothing but the persona of the *Journal* to fill the public imagination, he became more beloved to his friends and more despised by his foes. As the orphan house would be his vehicle for travel, so the journals would be the medium for building his reputation, maintaining his presence among reading audiences throughout England and abroad. Charity, preaching, and journalism came together in Whitefield to create a potent configuration — a religious celebrity capable of creating a new market for religion. The returning missionary had a sense of what he was to achieve in the ensuing years, and he closed his Georgia journal with a prayer of certain expectation: "He who preserved Daniel in the den of lions . . . will, I hope, preserve me from the fiery trial of popularity, and from the misguided zeal of those, who, without cause, are my enemies."

5 London Field Preacher

In December 1738 a rested and ambitious Whitefield returned to London ready to implement his preaching vision. The voyage had done nothing to dampen his enthusiasm — or his sense of apostolic destiny. Readers of his *Journal* learned this when he described a reunion with his methodist friends outside London, a meeting that "put me in the Mind of St. Paul's Friends, meeting him at the three Taverns, and I like him, was not a little comforted."

By 1738, one might have thought Whitefield had enacted all the characters and scenes there were to be seen. But there remained one more major creation that would complete his redefinition of the eighteenth-century pulpit: field preacher. The part of field preacher was not, strictly speaking, invented by Whitefield. But as we shall see, he so revised and redefined "fields" as to carry field preaching or field "conventicles" from a rural to an urban setting. In the process, he redefined the meaning and significance of the concept itself, and by so doing bequeathed a new, more modern sense to the term *evangelical*.

His field preaching competed not only with the "velvet-mouthed" preachers of his church but also with the vendors, sportsmen, and entertainers of the marketplace.

Whitefield's road to the fields was, in part, inadvertent. Upon returning to London he found that his journals had generated great controversy in his absence. Friends had found ample evidence in them for rejoicing; enemies had found more than enough for offense. While Whitefield had expected rejection and opposition, the depth of clerical antagonism surprised him. But it also compelled him to give serious consideration to other outlets for ministry — among them, outdoor preaching.

As early as 1737 Whitefield was told of the Welsh field preacher Howell Harris, who had been traveling the "fields and valleys" of Wales since 1735. Harris supplied a contemporary model and precedent, but his ministry was limited largely to the outdwellers and unchurched. Could outdoor preaching also work in the heavily churched urban fields of London? Was Whitefield the man who could make it work? Such questions involved not only issues of access and legality but also questions of calling. In short, was his instinct to begin outdoor preaching in fact a call from God?

Before answering these questions, Whitefield needed to legitimate his pretext for itinerant preaching by becoming a fully licensed minister in the Church of England. This legitimation, by definition, required a "living." On January 14, 1739, in the familiar environs of Oxford, he was ordained a priest in the Church of England — a vow he would neither rescind nor renounce throughout his lifetime. Once ordained, he met with the Georgia trustees and the bishop of London and requested assignment to Georgia with responsibility for the orphan house and the surrounding parish. Although no friend to Whitefield or the methodists, the bishop complied, perhaps in part hoping to rid himself of the methodist nuisance. But here he miscalculated. With living in hand, Whitefield was free to seek entry into all the London churches for his orphan-house charity.

What was more, if they refused him, he had a pretext to preach out of doors to any and all who would hear.

Having settled the problem of pretext, Whitefield turned to the question of calling. The dramatist within him recognized immediately how well suited his ministry would be to the out of doors. Lacking any sacred consecration, an open-air urban setting would provide the perfect "stage" for his highly dramatic, sensational weekday preaching performances. By separating himself from the confines of the pulpit, he would free himself to pursue embodied preaching without restraint. What more perfect backdrop for his novel brand of improvised evangelism and extemporaneous response than the secular setting? With no walls to hinder, the audiences would certainly grow, possibly limited only by how far his voice could carry. Individuals uninterested in the church could be sought in the profane spaces of the marketplace and, mixing together with methodist believers, could create "religious" assemblies that represented something entirely new: neither church nor sect, neither sabbath nor festival, neither sacred nor profane, but all, wrapped up in one hybrid event.

An outdoor Whitefield would no longer be competing with the churches so much as with the merchants, hawkers, and stage players of the world. The market centers and fairs would attract thousands whom Whitefield could divert through his powerful ministry. In economic terms, religion would compete in the marketplace for its own market share. In religious terms, it would be going out to the hedges and highways to convict sinners. Everything about the idea seemed both right and irresistible. But it was also potentially illegal. Churchmen would undoubtedly balk at a preacher appearing in their own back yards.

Before Whitefield would pursue such a ministry, he felt the need for a clear call to do so. He would not move alone on so innovative an idea. To this end he initiated a correspondence with Howell Harris that soon grew into a strong, mutually supportive friendship. As early as December 20, 1738, on the eve of his ordination, he wrote to Harris introducing himself as one "unknown to you in person, yet I have long been united to you in Spirit." After praising Harris's ministry and seeking a personal meeting, he closed, "my dear brother, I love you in the bowels of Jesus Christ, and wish you may be the spiritual father of thousands, and shine, as the sun in the firmament."

Predictably, Harris replied in kind: "I should blush to think the name of such an ignorant, negligent, unprofitable servant should reach your ears." Harris did not know of Whitefield's interest in the fields, but he had already heard of his successes in London, which led him to exclaim, "O, how ravishing is it to hear of such demonstration of the divine love and favour to *London*." With that interchange, the two itinerants forged a relationship for mutual counsel and support. Whitefield later confessed that "a divine and strong sympathy seemed to appear between us, and I was resolved to promote his interest with all my might."

In presence and personality the two differed greatly. Unlike Whitefield, who was slight, of moderate height, affected, and easily frightened, Harris was large, aggressive, and fearless — known to back down mobs through the sheer force of his will. He was, in eighteenth-century terms, a man's man. One account of his preaching in the streets at St. Davids in Pembrokeshire noted that "every particle of his speech flashed and gleamed so vividly, as lightning, on the consciences of the hearers, that they were terrified, and feared that the day of judgment had overtaken them: yea so powerful were the effects accompanying his words, that bold and hardy men, being seized with fainting fits through fear and terror, fell as corpses in the street." In contrast to his fearsome presence, Harris adopted a pattern of intimate speech that was almost sensual in its appeal to the believer's "union" with Christ. He converted the language of love, courtship, and even romance from earthly connotations to heavenly metaphor in ways that anticipated the erotic revivalism of the Nova Scotian itinerant Henry Alline in the 1770s.

But for all the differences in style, personality, and presentation between Whitefield and Harris, there were important similarities that bonded the two together and ultimately provided Whitefield with the support he sought in his call. Both were born in 1714 and had attended Oxford, where each had given evidence of more concern for his soul than his books. Whitefield barely graduated, and Harris dropped out shortly after matriculation. Both traveled widely and envisioned their ministries more in terms of planting the seeds of grace than of watering what others had already sown. Both had strained relations with the Church of England, Whitefield remaining at its margins, Harris leaving it altogether. In the course of their travels, both were drawn to the methodist style of extemporaneous prayer and preaching even though their theology remained strictly Calvinist. And both ratified their unique ministries with appeals to experience and spiritual impressions. Whitefield spoke often of dreams and leadings in his journal, while Harris became known as "the man from South Wales who had seen a vision." Harris's calling to field preaching came in scriptural terms. While agonizing over his call to the fields, Harris recalled, "these words forcibly came into my mind — 'Behold, I have set before thee an open door, and no man can shut it.' And by the effect produced on my soul, I am persuaded that the passage was applied to me by the Holy Ghost." Whitefield later adopted these terms for himself as well.

If internal experience confirmed that Whitefield had an "open door" to the fields, however, he still required the pretext of closed pulpits to "compel" his outdoor ministry. Such a pretext soon materialized in the "St. Margaret's Affair." According to Whitefield's ingenuous account, he preached in St. Martin's parish in London on February 4, only after being invited by unnamed "friends" who, he had assumed, had the permission of the local rector. According to the equally innocent but contrary account in the *Weekly Miscellany*, however, these friends turned out to be "several lusty fellows" who led Whitefield to the pulpit "while the proper Preacher was lock'd into his pew." Outraged by this illicit "intrusion" into one of their pulpits, the rectors at St. Martin's and other London churches proceeded to close their doors to Whitefield's ministry.

News of the St. Margaret's incident soon spread in the press, launching an intensive war of print between the friends and enemies of the Whitefield forces. But instead of working to ease the tensions so that closed doors would be opened, Whitefield proceeded to inflame the issue by attacking his "persecutors." In a printed "Letter to the Religious Societies," he let fly the accusation that "it is most certain, that the Generality of our modern Prophets or Preachers, even the most *zealous* of *them*, are no better than the Pharisees of Old, or the *Papists* of the present time." Elsewhere, he averred that instead of letting good gospel ministers preach, "the clergy subscribing to the Articles of the Church of England was the key to Ecclesiastical Preferments; and when they got them, they then put the key in their pockets."

Words like these not only pitted clergy against people but class against class. They had the calculated effect of ensuring that closed doors would remain closed. This, in turn, provided the pretext for which Whitefield had been waiting. With church doors locked, he could now pursue his new living in the only way that remained — in open-air services. Instead of retreating, he could boldly inform his readers that such rejection was the "certain sign that a more effectual door will be opened, since there are so many adversaries."

Within days of the St. Margaret's affair, Whitefield began planning in earnest for his outdoor campaign. It would require careful practice and preparation outside London, much as a touring company might perfect its performance in smaller outlying theaters before playing Drury Lane or Covent Garden. There were many unanswered questions that had to be addressed before London. Would a dramatic, extemporaneous style work in the fields? Who would attend the performances? Would his listeners be attentive or disruptive? Could his voice project? Did he have the courage? Contained in the marketplace environment was an arena of free speech. But free speech and open space could be brutal. The same *Weekly Miscellany* that carried the news of Whitefield's controversy also carried the story of a recent tragedy in Soho, where a mob "seiz'd an Informer in Dean-Street and after dragging him thr' the channels, they threw him into a Horse-pond, after which they pelted him in so cruel a Manner that he died on Sunday morning." Only time and experience would reveal the fate of a field preacher.

Beginning on February 17, 1739, Whitefield embarked on a six-week voyage of discovery, a journey that answered his fears and uncertainties with such resounding success that even he was surprised. His experimental preaching began with a trial by fire in the rough Kingswood coal-mining district near Bristol in southwest England. The area was familiar to him and ideally suited to what lay in store in London. The men, women, and children of Kingswood labored long hours in the 150 coal pits that pocked the countryside. They were a violent, short-lived people who were regarded as some of eighteenth-century England's most desperate inhabitants. The area itself was forbidding, and not apt to attract attention from churchmen, who had shown an inclination to stay away. It was the perfect testing ground.

To provide encouragement and support, Whitefield persuaded another friend, William Seward, to accompany him. Seward, scion of a wealthy English family and recent convert to methodism, proved a most fortunate choice. He had both the accouterments of aristocracy and a methodist's humility and desire to serve the cause of the gospel. Together Whitefield and Seward traveled to Bristol, where they requested the use of the local pulpit, knowing full well that it would be denied them.

Immediately following news of the closed pulpits, the two drove through Kingswood in Seward's carriage announcing a service later that night. The sight they created was intriguing, to say the least: two low-life methodists riding in a gentleman's carriage and announcing a sermon in the fields. That night, following dinner, they went outdoors to preach to whoever would come. The chosen spot was Hanham Mount, site of earlier sermons by a methodist sympathizer named Richard Morgan. Ever sensitive to his surroundings, Whitefield used the location as an opportunity to preach on Christ's Sermon on the Mount. By Whitefield's standards, the audience was small. But the enthusiasm of their response and his own of freedom in expression promised far greater successes in the future.

Despite the small numbers, Whitefield recorded the event with all the excitement of a smashing success: "There were upwards of two hundred. Blessed be God that I have now broken the ice!" Once begun, the Kingswood campaign generated a clear momentum, fueled largely by word of mouth among the working-class population. From Hanham Mount, Whitefield traveled locally and preached everywhere but in the churches, exploiting ladders, roofs, and market spaces. He was particularly effective at the "Glass House" — an open space located in the yard of each glass factory. The working classes proved so eager for his ministry that he concluded that "this *field* preaching is particularly comfortable to the poor; whenever *field* preaching is stopped, farewell to the power of religion."

On Wednesday, February 21, Whitefield returned "amongst the miners," and this time he found nearly two thousand patient colliers waiting outdoors to hear him preach. A new world was opening before him. On February 25, he noted with unconcealed excitement that "at a moderate computation, there were about ten thousand people to hear me. The trees and hedges were full. All was a hush when I began; the sun shone bright, and God enabled me to preach for an hour with great power, and so loudly, that all, I was told, could hear me."

For some time the fields had maintained a mysterious hold on Whitefield's imagination much as the sea had; now he was learning why. Where the sea had calmed his spirit, the fields inflamed him and produced unprecedented preaching performances. With the unconcealed delight of life-defining discoveries, he confessed that "the fire is kindled in the country;

and I know, all the devils in hell shall not be able to quench it." As in the past, the themes of power, majesty, and comfort dominated his vocabulary. Whatever feelings of might had overtaken Whitefield in the pulpit were multiplied out of doors where the excitement of uncertainty and the unprecedented crowds brought forth his ultimate efforts.

While preaching to the miners, Whitefield stepped up his attacks on the established clergy, further ensuring both popular acclaim and closed pulpits. He also continued to work on his journal entries and had them printed regularly. If churches would not open their pulpits to his appeals for the orphan house, then he would take those appeals to the fields. When Bristol's Bishop Baxter repeatedly refused requests to let him preach, Whitefield described their meetings in condescending words certain to further incense the clergy. Upon meeting the bishop, Whitefield "confided" in his journal that he dismissed the cleric before he himself could be dismissed. Then, "to shew how little I regarded such threatenings, after I joined in prayer for the Chancellor, I immediately went and expounded at Newgate as usual." Despite clerical resistance, Whitefield reported that "thousands went to hear me." The bishop's disapproval "rejoiced me greatly. Lord, why dost Thou thus honor me?"

The lessons Whitefield had learned in the churches found even better application in the fields. The louder he jousted with the bishop, the larger his audiences grew. At length the bishop relented and allowed Whitefield the use of Bristol pulpits to appeal for his orphan house. But by then the outdoor campaign had utterly taken over. By Whitefield's estimate, the audiences had grown from four to fourteen thousand, and eventually to twenty-three thousand. Allowing for exuberant exaggeration by a factor of two, it is still reasonable to suppose that he attracted crowds of ten thousand or more.

Size was the confirmation he needed. Throughout his travels, Whitefield legitimized his novel and challenging ministry with numbers. His ubiquitous audience estimates — recorded even when Scripture texts were not — constituted not only evidence of hubris but a badge of legitimacy. If his ministry was unlawful, would God bless it with such numbers and changed lives?

Whitefield settled other questions as well in these early days. Clearly the extemporaneous style worked well. Indeed, it worked better out of doors than it did in churches. With no notes and no pulpit, he could move freely, encumbered only by the gown that remained his last visible tie to the established church. The outdoor setting elevated his novel techniques to near perfection. Equally important was the discovery of his vocal range and ability outside. Whitefield was surprised to learn that "those who stood farthest off could hear me very plainly." An unsurpassed sense of power accompanied the realization that voice and body were released to their utmost in the field. Whitefield the timid soul on the street became Whitefield the powerhouse without rival in the outdoor pulpit. And with power came assurance: "my preaching in the fields may displease some timorous, bigoted men, but I am thoroughly persuaded it pleases God, and why should I fear anything else?"

In fact, Whitefield's fears were always greater than he let on in his journal. Mass preaching inevitably elicited feelings of anxiety and illness, but he managed to make these feelings work for him. Unlike the tropical maladies he had contracted in Georgia, the illnesses in England were more nervous and reminiscent of the Oxford odd fellow. Invariably before preaching, he would feel weak or sick. Sometimes he would feel hoarse, certain that his voice was going to fail him. At other times he would be unable to catch a breath — all classic signs of the anxiety attacks faced by many great performers. And, as with all great performers, Whitefield's symptoms disappeared as soon as he made his appearance on the boards.

For inner strength Whitefield relied on prayer and spiritual meditation, and he interpreted freedom in speaking as a divine "deliverance." Such exercises served not only the needs of his spirit but also the needs of his nervous disposition. Time in prayer — usually right up to the moment of preaching — allowed him essential repose and self-collection before he exploded into speech. On one such occasion, he noted that before speaking at St. Helen's, all "on a sudden I was deserted and my strength went from me. But I thought it was the Devil's doing. . . . Accordingly, though I was exceedingly sick in reading the prayers, and almost unable to speak when I entered the pulpit, yet God gave me courage to begin, and before I had done, I waxed warm and strong."

In addition to stage fright, Whitefield experienced the fears of an extemporaneous speaker. With no written text before him, he could never be certain what — if anything — would come next in the discourse. Whitefield confided to his Scottish friend and biographer John Gillies that his extemporaneous preaching "often occasioned many inward conflicts. Sometimes, when twenty thousand people were before me, I had not, in my apprehension, a word to say either to God or them." But this fear too helped to produce great performances. Despite crippling fears, he continued, "I was never totally deserted."

As long as he lived, Whitefield suffered the dilemma of his anxiety-filled and anxiety-releasing preaching. Even as he feared performance, he craved it. The only deliverance he could imagine was death. Death — the greatest fear of all — became in Whitefield's thinking a great friend that would end his illness and anxiety and reunite him with his Savior. In the end this would be his undoing, because he disregarded all illness as a result. But such a perspective also steeled him to adversity and invariably produced the words and passions that enlivened his listeners and transformed the way they thought and felt about life, death, and eternity. And through it all, Whitefield learned never to allow fears or sickness of any kind to silence him.

Having seen and conquered Kingswood, Whitefield began thinking in earnest of London. But first he had to talk to Harris. On March 7 the two friends met at Cardiff, sharing experiences and preaching together, Whitefield in English and

Harris in Welsh. To Whitefield's eye the meeting was providential, and "my heart was still drawn out towards him more and more." Whitefield then preached with Harris at the Cardiff town hall and again on April 4 in Monmouthshire. At Usk, Whitefield noted, "the pulpit being denied, I preached upon a table under a large tree to some hundreds." The opposition of a local clergyman simply fueled the martyr's rhetoric: "Poor man! He put me in mind of Tertullus in the Acts; but my hour is not yet come. I have scarce begun my testimony." The following day Whitefield and Harris traveled to Abergavenny accompanied by thirty enthusiasts, reminding Whitefield of Joshua and his small band of conquering horsemen.

Besides visiting Harris twice in Wales, Whitefield continued practicing outside London. Faced with another closed pulpit in Bath, he invoked his self-proclaimed right to the fields and preached in heavy snow "to a much larger audience than could reasonably be expected." Wherever Whitefield found closed pulpits, he rejoiced and took to open spaces in markets, open windows in courtyards, public halls, and the fields. On March 18, while preaching in Bristol, he "was taken ill for about two hours, but, notwithstanding, was enabled to go and preach." Again at Elberton the pulpit was closed, "so I preached on a little ascent on which the Maypole was fixed."

By mid-April, Whitefield and Seward were ready for London. From Gloucester he confided to his Welsh friend, "Oh dear Mr. Harris, My heart is drawn towards London most strangely." His arrival on April 25 was announced in advance, and he quickly elicited the clerical rejection he needed to move outdoors. At St. Mary's in Islington, the church warden forbade him the use of his pulpit. In a peacemaking guise that concealed his evident satisfaction at the rebuff, Whitefield assured the warden that he would no longer trouble services within the church. Outdoors, however, was another story. Immediately following the communion service, Whitefield adjourned to the courtyard adjacent to the church and began to preach, "being assured my Master now called me out here, as well as in Bristol." Then, with a perfect blend of persecuted resignation and righteous indignation, he announced his decision to enter the fields of London: "let not the adversaries say, I have thrust myself out of their synagogues. No; they have thrust me out. And since the self-righteous men of this generation count themselves unworthy, I go out into the highways and hedges, and compel harlots, publicans, and sinners to come in, that my Master's house may be filled." If the boy preacher and Georgia missionary had invoked Pauline language, the field itinerant brought forth language that verged on the messianic.

Whitefield's London campaign left nothing to doubt. For his first performances he settled on the location at Moorfields, a public park frequented by crowds seeking entertaining diversions. He deliberately set the time for his self-confessed "mad trick" in the early morning, when he knew he would be at his best. Because the time preceded the scheduled morning prayers, he could not be accused of competing with the churches.

The first sermon was a small but immensely significant success. Neither church nor mob moved to silence him. Immediately following the sermon, Whitefield attended matins at Christ Church, where, he later gleefully recorded, he heard the rector "preach most virulently against me and my friends." The blast had the desired effect of arousing popular curiosity and expanding audience size.

That evening Whitefield traveled to his second major target at Kennington Common, a twenty-acre urban park that was the site of frequent executions. As in his first outdoor sermon on the mount at Bristol, Whitefield employed his outdoor setting to reinforce his message. There, standing beside a permanent scaffold, he preached a startling sermon on the inevitability of death and the eternity of hell's torments. Although he lacked Harris's physical strength, Whitefield's dramatic instinct placed him in a category by himself. With an actor's sense of informed improvisation, he drew on the physical landscape to enliven his message. Mounts, scaffolds, snow, or thunder —

he used them all instinctively as props and background for whatever words came to his mind.

Before long Whitefield had the staging of his outdoor performances down to a science. From the start, he relied heavily on his methodist friends to supply the inner core around which the event could grow. In a typical performance, friends and curious onlookers would gather through advance word of mouth, forming a circle around a predetermined spot convenient for assembly and projection. Soon Whitefield would arrive in Seward's handsome coach and join the circle in prayer and song. A crowd would swell around this center without attention to "seating" or social rank. Unlike the churches, where careful attention was paid to rank and defer ence, the field assemblies were socially unstructured. Traditional rules did not apply here. It was first come, first served.

While the crowd swelled and enthusiasm rose, Whitefield would wait for the right moment to begin, generally signaled by the singing of a psalm or a spiritual hymn written by Isaac Watts or the Wesleys or a sacred tune adapted from one of the tavern folk songs. Whitefield used the music to mobilize his audience, to transform them from passive viewers to participants. Indeed, it is here that the theater analogy finally breaks down, because these listeners became actors as well as audience. At the effective moment, Whitefield would turn the focus on them, describing them as actors in a divine drama and challenging them to play their roles.

Following a period of song, Whitefield would launch into a spontaneous prayer, which would set the context for his extemporaneous sermon. In fact, of course, many of Whitefield's sermons were extemporaneous only in the sense that he had no notes. Where other preachers recorded their notes and repeated favorite sermons three or four times in a pulpit career, the itinerant Whitefield repeated some favorite sermons thirty times or more, adapting the details and improvising on a core character or theme to suit immediate settings and circumstances.

In opening his sermons, Whitefield displayed the servitor's genius for ingratiation to establish a bond with his audience. As often as not this meant passing over his Oxford connections to emphasize his identification with the working classes. In his sermon "What Think Ye of Christ?" he observed that Jesus was ignored by the "governors and teachers" of the Jews while "the generality heard him gladly." By drawing this link between the early Christians and the people he was addressing, all the while speaking of "us" and "them," he established the emotional bond he needed.

Whitefield relied heavily on characters and experiences from his varied past in crafting the field sermons. He also met with prisoners, and read the papers for news of executions. Executions were intensely popular affairs, and by making use of them, Whitefield combined poignancy with a shrewd nose for what drew huge crowds. In one sermon he portrayed a prisoner awaiting execution, using words that may have been quoted from the Kennington scaffold as a "midnight call" to hard-hearted sinners to repent:

> I have heard that the present ordinary sits up with them all the night before their execution. . . . If they find any of them asleep, or no sign of being awake, they knock and call, and the keepers cry, awake! and God help thee to take care thou dost not sleep in an unconverted state to-night.

Having set the context, Whitefield went on to press his application:

> The prisoners tomorrow will have their hands tied behind them, their thumbstrings must be put on, and their fetters knocked off; they must be tied fast to the cart, the cap put over their faces, and the dreadful signal given: if you were their relations would not you weep? don't be angry then with a poor minister for weeping over them that will not weep for themselves.

80

At this point, Whitefield himself was undoubtedly in tears that were both genuine and contrived, releasing innate feelings that in public he could acceptably shed only in the pulpit. Few had seen such a compelling spectacle of pathos before. And few could stay away.

Word spread in short order both about the clerical opposition to Whitefield and his dramatic outdoor meetings. Soon, by Whitefield's estimate "no less than thirty thousand people" gathered in hushed silence to hear his message of the New Birth. With a director's eye to detail, he situated himself so that the wind would carry his voice to the outermost circle of listeners, and noted with satisfaction that the people remained silent and attentive. They, like him, had never been part of such an event; "all agreed it was never seen on this wise before."

In bringing his dramatic preaching to the marketplace, Whitefield recognized that he was opening a pandora's box. Sensitive to the potential of evil in what he was doing, he felt that he needed further confirmation of the basic rightness of his way. It came on May 1 when word of his preaching at a private house drew such a crowd that it was impossible, without considerable danger, to contain the people indoors. "Now know I more and more that the Lord calls me into the fields," he wrote, "for no house or street is able to contain half the people who come to hear the word." He had made a brilliant — if circular — progress to the fields. He used adversity to create his outdoor crowd, then used that crowd to justify the necessity of his outdoor preaching. He confided almost apologetically that "I find myself more and more under a necessity of going out into the fields."

Just as closed pulpits worked to increase Whitefield's popular appeal, so the opposition press swelled his audience. The harsher the condemnation, the greater the public curiosity. Leading the way was the Anglican *Weekly Miscellany.* On May 5 the paper reported the ominous news of an "extraordinary *Itinerant,* who lately made a Progress into the Western Parts of

England, and some parts of Wales, where, from Tomb-stones, and Market crosses, on Commons and mountains, he preached to vast numbers of ignorant People, and, since his Return, in a wide Place near a Building which would suit him better. This is a method quite as *new* with us, as it is *irregular and illegal."*

Alongside the *Miscellany* came a barrage of anti-Whitefield tracts that soon numbered in the hundreds. In one particularly influential pamphlet entitled "The Nature, Folly, Sin, and Danger of Being Righteous Over-much," the bishop, classicist, and playwright Joseph Trapp challenged the legitimacy of Whitefield's field preaching:

> we have heard of Field-Conventicles in Scotland among the Enthusiasts of that Country. . . . But for a Clergyman *of the Church of England* to *pray* and *preach in the Fields*, in the Country, or *in the streets* of the City, is *perfectly new*, never heard of before; a *fresh Honour* to the *blessed Age* in which We have the happiness to live. . . . To pray, preach, and sing Psalms, in the Streets and Fields, is worse, if possible, than *intruding into Pulpits* by downright *violence* and *Breach of the Peace;* and then *denying* the plain Facts with the most *infamous prevarication.*

The "irregularity" and "illegality" of Whitefield's preaching stemmed, it was maintained, from his "antinomian" claims to an "inspiration and assistance from the Holy Spirit." The *Miscellany* argued that if Whitefield could have demonstrated a true supernatural, apostolic gift, such as the ability to perform miracles, then his claim to preach without a license could be validated. But Whitefield produced no miracles. In fact he was no different in terms of supernatural gifts than any simple country priest. And for that reason, his critics insisted, he had no right to invade other preachers' precincts or compete for their congregations.

The clergy's case against Whitefield made sense in theory. As long as he did not renounce his ordination, he was, in effect, competing with his own church — at least according to the old parish rules. But traditional arguments were crumbling in the face of Whitefield's novel methods and in the context of the new marketplace mentality. It was a changing world, and among a people already accustomed to the impersonal, mass setting of the marketplace, his "revivals" were not only acceptable but obviously successful.

Besides condemning the illegality of preaching where he had no license to go, the *Weekly Miscellany* censured Whitefield's style, which was dangerously "enthusiastic" and apt to arouse the "illiterate Vulgar" into a methodist "mob." In its May 12 issue, the *Miscellany* complained, in reference to St. Margaret's, that Whitefield's followers had "threatened to pull down *Churches* because their Master and his Brethren were not suffer'd to preach in them." If not stopped, the insurrection would simply grow. "If they are permitted to hold their Conventicles at pleasure, and to ramble up and down, singing Psalms, and preaching in the open streets, or in more open Fields, wanton Curiosity will carry thousands to see and hear such new Things."

Central to the offense of Whitefield's enthusiasm was his theatricality. Unlike the dissenters, Anglicans did not object to theater per se, but they did object to theatricality in the pulpit. If methodists like Whitefield criticized the actor for being a hypocrite who "acts that part he is not," Anglicans criticized Whitefield for portraying saints and biblical characters he most emphatically was not. The whole thing was a sacred ruse. Most offensive was Whitefield's willingness to impersonate Christ or God the Father judging errant sinners. An outraged essay in the *Miscellany* complained that "the Gentleman that on Sunday morning succeeded the Montebank in MoorFields . . . exhibits himself to publick view every day (but Sundays) from the *Wall;* instead of a *Stage,* harangued his Congregations and by the Choice of his Text most blasphemously compared himself, after his usual Custom, to our Blessed Saviour." A later issue reiterated the charge of theatricality: "The next Winter the town may promise themselves a new Entertainment on the Stage, of

Harlequin turned Methodist, by way of Reprisals, since the Methodist has certainly this summer turned Harlequin."

Unlike other vulgar entertainers, Whitefield drew even his enemies and detractors to his performances. No one could stay away. By July an increasing number of carriages could be seen at Moorfields, indicating a rising curiosity among the upper classes. The more his enemies roared, the more his popularity soared. He drew an estimated eighty thousand people to a sermon at Hyde Park. Even discounting that number substantially leaves a staggering total, a crowd the size of which had not been seen in all England since the great battles of the Civil War. Whitefield himself marveled that it was "by far, the largest I ever preached to yet." The "yet" is instructive for revealing how in the first flush of unprecedented success, neither Whitefield, his friends, nor his enemies had any clear sense of where it would all end.

More evidence of his effectiveness showed in the offerings he collected for the Georgia orphan house. Indeed, this was the most tangible intersection of pulpit and marketplace. While personal income never ranked high on Whitefield's list of priorities, fund raising for charitable missions was paramount. Whitefield himself did not hesitate personally to urge contributions with shameless pathos, and he often stood by exiting crowds with hands outstretched. He did not collect offerings at every sermon, but when he did, he routinely reported collections of forty or fifty pounds, much of it from commoners who contributed their half-pence in such volume that it took "more than one man [to] carry [it] home." Though hardly wealthy, working-class people did enjoy a level of discretionary income that was unknown a century earlier. Over the summer, Whitefield received over £1,000 — a figure equal to a city priest's annual income. All of the offerings were fully accounted for and disbursed in Georgia.

Before long, other enterprises appeared on the fringes of the Whitefield scene. If competitors could not beat him, they determined to join him. Ambitious vendors of one sort or another plied their trades on the outskirts of the crowd. Locals rented out scaffolds, wagons, and seats to eager viewers, and of course pickpockets had a heyday. By the same token, Whitefield often selected preaching locations near merchant stalls, theaters, and other events to catch the overflow. At Hackney Marsh, he timed his preaching to coincide with the horse races there, convinced that "the common people go to these diversions for want of knowing better." His forte was making use of profane time, not sacred time. He selected moments outside of traditional religious meeting times, and spaces that drew crowds, exploiting both to the full.

With a genius for self-promotion and the energy of youth, Whitefield preached relentlessly, seizing every moment to build on the momentum. He shuttled back and forth between Moorfields, Kennington Common, Hyde Park, and outlying towns such as Hampton Heath, Hertford, and Northampton, preaching from table tops, open windows, courtyards, hills, wagons, and marketplaces. In a six-week span he delivered at least forty field sermons to audiences numbering in the tens of thousands. In all, outdoor summer audiences numbered somewhere between eight hundred thousand and one million — a figure without precedent in the annals of English preaching. When not preaching, he worked at preparing over twenty sermons for print and writing hundreds of letters to correspondents throughout Scotland and America describing the wondrous events of his itinerant ministry. Never again would he experience quite the sensation that came with his first exposure to the "fields." Nor would the thousands who saw him and participated with him in what was being labeled a great "revival."

For one so attuned to the power of self-promotion, Whitefield remained remarkably unselfconscious about his spectacular pulpit innovations. In fact, his identification with Paul made it clear that he viewed his ministry more in terms of the early church than as some entirely new and modern phenomenon. How else was one to explain the stupendous results? If, to modern eyes, marketing techniques and dramatic pathos were critical to Whitefield's success, they went largely unrecognized in the press and in Whitefield's journals and letters. It was all too new. Intuition and experience outpaced theory and self-consciousness. Whitefield was so caught up in his Pauline part that he could not possibly see that his brilliant — if instinctive — promotion could in itself be accelerating this miraculous work of the Spirit.

The summer of 1739 belonged to Whitefield. In a remarkably short period of time his questions were answered and his destiny revealed. Besides preaching to thousands, he received a grant of five hundred acres from the Georgia trustees for his orphan house. In addition, he received invitations from both England and America, which he intended to honor. On August 14 he embarked for America on board the *Elizabeth* to test his calling and destiny in other settings in America and Scotland. Soon Americans would get their first exposure to the "field phenomenon," and their churches would never be the same again.

6 American Awakener

Whitefield arrived in Lewes, Delaware, on October 30, 1739, almost exactly a year after his last departure. As the Georgia missionary, he had been little known to colonial audiences outside the South. But a year later, as the author of the Georgia journals, Calvinist critic of Anglicans, and tireless letter writer, he had achieved a certain fame. Moreover, the most exciting news — of the London outdoor revivals — was just reaching American newspapers when he arrived. The timing was perfect. At virtually the same moment Americans learned that Whitefield had taken London by storm, they learned he was about to preach in Philadelphia.

On the voyage over, Whitefield had developed a clearly defined plan of action for his American tour that was novel and audacious. The orphan house was only a small — if necessary — part. More ambitious was his plan to build on the techniques and momentum of the London preaching and transform his Calvinist revival into an international event with himself at the center. Such an event would have been unthinkable in the localistic, traditional culture of seventeenth-century Anglo-America. But not in 1739. All of the pieces for an international, interconnected revival were uniquely in place. In looking at the changing relationships between England and her colonies, eighteenth-century historians have described a process of "Anglicization" in which the empire was becoming increasingly more unified under British influence. The explosion of goods and trade under the comprehensive umbrella of the Navigation Acts integrated the English empire as never before. In the American colonies this economic integration was reinforced by new charters and royal governments designed to establish a political integration as well. And at the same time, American colonists were increasingly exposed to British culture and learning: intellectually and culturally they were growing more rather than less "English," as they were in matters political and economic.

In the midst of this cultural anglicization, Whitefield's plan was brilliantly simple. He would promote a religious anglicization — an integration of common religious experience around the new revivals. Just as he had adapted the marketplace to religious ends in England, so he would adapt new international linkages of transportation, trade, and communications to a self-conscious, intercolonial "Calvinist connection" built around the revival. Similar to the integrating power of Georgian politics, the East India Company, or Wedgwood pottery, Whitefield's revivals would forge a new, potentially powerful religious market around the key trading centers of Philadelphia, New York, Boston, Edinburgh, Glasgow, London, and Bristol. And from there the revivals could move inland.

Along with colonial-style imitation of English ways, Whitefield would add a wrinkle of his own to the emerging Anglo-American network. Economic and political anglicization originated in London and migrated exclusively one way. London was the core and all else the dependent periphery. Whitefield's revivals, on the other hand, could in time reverse the cultural exchange. Scotland and America could become centers of religious piety that would reverse the direction of anglicization. This was a heady enterprise that Scottish and American Calvinists were prepared to embrace and one that would endear Whitefield to his "periphery" audiences. It would reinstitute America's "Puritan errand" to a wayward Europe in the modern guise of mass revival and transdenominational, open-air appeal. To be sure, not all of this was fully clear to Whitefield in 1739. But the outline was fixed and the plan set in motion from the moment he stepped on American shores.

Whitefield selected Philadelphia as his first American stop. It was a wise choice. Although founded later than other northern cities, Philadelphia had already grown to be a major port city with a thriving market economy. The Quaker-dominated, pacifistic government was relatively untouched by the latest colonial war with France, so it was able to concentrate its energies on economic growth and the cultivation of ever-expanding markets. Its expansive mood comported well with Whitefield's energies and ambition.

Besides its geography and economic advantages, Pennsylvania also evidenced a unique cultural climate that fit Whitefield's ecumenical appeal. In its ethnic, religious, and linguistic diversity, Pennsylvania was in many ways the most American of all colonies, and Philadelphia the most cosmopolitan city. Its rich farmlands and its policy of religious toleration together attracted a heterogeneous population of Catholics, Jews, and Protestants, all of whom were tolerated and none of whom were powerful enough or, in the case of the Quaker founders, intolerant enough to stifle the others. By the same token, most of these groups had established separate islands of identity. Whitefield would strive to bring them together under the banner of revival.

If Whitefield's plan was simple in conception, it nevertheless called for tremendous human resources and intense labor. Here again, friends became important. Just as Habersham had assisted with the orphan-house ministry, so William Seward joined Whitefield on the second American trip to provide full-time assistance with travel, funding, and above all publicity. In the early years, Whitefield relied heavily on letter writing as a crude public relations medium to spread the word of his revivals in personalized ways that both built anticipation and enlisted local helpers sympathetic to the cause of international Calvinist revival. Here Seward was essential. His job was to stay one step ahead of Whitefield. Some days he never left his lodgings, "sometimes writing a hundred letters a day." Other days he traveled by horse, spreading the word by mouth that Whitefield was coming.

Before Whitefield began in William Penn's model city of brotherly love, his way had been carefully prepared by Seward's announcements and his own meetings with local clergy of all denominations. In discussions with them he outlined his orphan house ministry and shared his vision for revival. To his great surprise, all were enthusiastic, including Philadelphia's Anglican commissary Cummings. Indeed, Cummings was so appreciative that he turned the church over to his young colleague.

On November 6, 1739, Whitefield began his Philadelphia ministry by reading prayers and preaching at Christ Church to a "numerous congregation." Following the service, hundreds urged him "to preach in another place" that could accommodate larger crowds. With that incentive he moved out of doors, and the revival was on. On November 8, Philadelphians saw the real Whitefield preaching extemporaneously from the courtyard steps to an estimated audience of six thousand curious onlookers — nearly half of Philadelphia's urban population. The results were spectacular and ensured successes in America that would equal or exceed anything he had seen in England. Benjamin Franklin was in the audience that day, and he marveled at how far Whitefield's voice carried. No less impressive was his charismatic power. It was, Franklin later confessed, a "matter of speculation to me who was one of the Number, to observe the extraordinary Influence of his Oratory on his hearers."

Though Whitefield could not have predicted it, he and his American audiences were a perfect match. In Whitefield, American colonists found a speaker who embodied their own uncertain and highly ambitious status as English provincials. In time preacher and audience would discover many commonalities: both coveted English praise and legitimacy at the same time they chafed against authority and arbitrary powers; both were at their righteous best when challenging authority in the name of the popular audience; both craved recognition from the very authorities they loved to challenge; and, most important, both leaned toward creative, extrainstitutional solutions to entrenched problems of liberty and order — solutions that by-passed traditional authority and sought new principles of association, exchange, and order.

Pennsylvanians, like Londoners earlier, discovered that the out-of-doors location was the perfect environment for Whitefield's popularly oriented, extrainstitutional message. Indeed, in Philadelphia, where the social chasm separating rich from poor was less dramatic (there really were no rich on the level of England's aristocracy), Whitefield's appeal was even more inclusive. Outdoor preaching both expressed and encompassed social reality for Americans in a more comprehensive way than it ever could in the more stratified, hierarchical environs of England.

Whitefield's revival was peculiarly American in other ways as well. At base, his outdoor appeal and legitimacy rested on public opinion. While depending on all the local support he could get, he spoke in the name of no denomination and enjoyed no state support. His movement — if it was to become a movement — transcended traditional institutions and depended solely on the voluntary goodwill of the people. And yet the authority of public opinion was not recognized by English law. True legitimacy was conferred from above; legitimate power traveled from the top down. By the sheer location and circumstances of his ministry, Whitefield challenged these time-honored axioms of social order and hierarchy.

Before Whitefield, no one had fully tested the ability of public opinion to build a movement that was intercolonial and even international in scope. Or, to put it differently, no one before Whitefield had sufficient popularity to found an intercolonial movement. In a circular logic that would in time come to define modern America, appeals to public opinion required public access, and public access depended on popularity. As the first intercolonial religious celebrity, Whitefield paved the way for extrainstitutional movements that would reverse traditional order and travel from the bottom up.

Such movements were virtually irresistible in the "free aire" of the New World. In fact, Americans' connections to traditional authority were always tenuous. For a century they were virtually self-regulating. If theorists had not yet emerged to tell them that this was the way society *ought* to be organized, experience had taught them that this was in fact the way American society *was* organized. And it worked. Whitefield's contribution was to take this logic one step further, to move from America's already tenuous institutional ties to a situation with no institutional underpinning at all save public opinion. Shared religious experience was both spiritually regenerating and a form of power that, once experienced, was never forgotten.

Every stop along Whitefield's trip from Philadelphia to New York and back was marked by record audiences, often exceeding the population of the towns in which he preached. From eight thousand in Philadelphia to three thousand in the village of Neshaminy, Pennsylvania, he won over an ever-increasing constituency. Chief among his friends and allies was the influential Tennent family, especially the elder William and his charismatic son Gilbert. They had recently begun a "New Side" Presbyterian "Log College" — over the objections of other "Old Side" Presbyterians — intended to train ministers for evangelical ministry. Soon after meeting the elder William Tennent, "an old grey-headed disciple and soldier of Jesus Christ," Whitefield identified him with the Presbyterian Erskine brothers in Scotland as part of a new Anglo-American united front of piety. Gilbert Tennent, something of an American Howell Harris, was so enamored of Whitefield's ministry that he and another admirer, James Davenport, followed him to New York and Philadelphia, observing his manner and hoping to imitate his successes in travels of their own.

In fact, a coterie of prorevivalist dissenters was already active in Pennsylvania, so Whitefield's efforts there were as much reinforcing as pioneering. Ever since the preaching of the Dutch Reformed pastor Theodore Frelinghuysen in the 1720s, Pennsylvania had experienced religious revivals. The Tennents had built on these in the 1730s and been joined by such others as the Presbyterian minister at Elizabethtown, Jonathan Dickinson, and John Rowland of New Brunswick. Whitefield became the catalyst who drew together many of these voices for "heart religion."

In America news traveled rapidly, and Whitefield was often surprised to discover how crowds "so scattered abroad, can be gathered at so short a warning." The advance work of Seward and the cooperation of local enthusiasts served him well. Not only were the crowds unprecedented in size, they were unusually quiet — virtually spellbound. "Even in London," Whitefield remarked, "I never observed so profound a silence."

As in England, Whitefield's field preaching relied heavily on imagination and dramatization. In one particularly favorite New World sermon, "Abraham Offering His Son," he created a series of scenes. The first scene opened with "the good old man walking with his dear child . . . now and then looking upon him, loving him, and then turning aside to weep." At this point in the narrative Whitefield himself may well have wept and momentarily halted the discourse, allowing the pathos to sink in. Then followed a second scene at the altar where Abraham was barely prevented from taking his beloved son's life in a profound moment of faith and obedience. By now the audience would be locked into Whitefield's performance and they would see with Abraham's eyes what Whitefield wanted them to see: "Fancy that you saw the aged parent standing by weeping. . . . Methinks I see the tears trickle down the patriarch Abraham's cheeks . . . adieu, my Isaac, my only Son, whom I love as my own soul; adieu, adieu." Here, as elsewhere, White-field's sermon in print appears melodramatic. But when performed live, with all the body language and pathos of a great actor, the lines receded into the passion and the hearer was locked into a dramatic world from which there was no easy exit. Doctrines, uses, proofs, and applications all receded into the background as the passions took over.

In the third and climactic scene, Whitefield bridged the gap separating Abraham from Christ through the passions:

> Did you weep just now when I bid you fancy that you saw the altar? Look up by faith, behold the blessed Jesus, our all-glorious Immanuel, not bound, but nailed on an accursed tree: see how he hangs crowned with thorns, and had in derision of all that are round about him: see how the thorns pierce him, and how the blood in purple streams trickles down his sacred temples! Hark! And now where are all your tears? Shall I refrain your voice from weeping? No, rather let me exhort you to look to him whom you have pierced, and mourn, as a woman mourneth for her first born.

It is not unreasonable to assume that Whitefield's dramatic mode of preaching had an even greater impact on American audiences than it did in London or Bristol for a very simple reason. Theater was a familiar — if controversial — institution in eighteenth-century England, but it had not yet reached American shores. Apart from occasional plays in Philadelphia, New York, Charleston, and Williamsburg, Americans had no organized drama. There were no professional companies or permanent stages until late in the eighteenth century. In seeing Whitefield preach, many Americans were for the first time in their lives seeing a form of theater. Until then, public performance — whether civic or religious — had been governed by classical canons of speech established by Cicero and Quintillian. Magistrates gathered on Courthouse Day in Virginia and ministers proclaiming election sermons in New England all followed models of "gravity" and "decorum" that precluded body and passion. Even New Side revivalists in the middle colonies found much to learn in the impassioned oratory of Whitefield.

Invariably audience responses were both delighted and confused. Here was someone impersonating characters, but he did not seem to be indulging in the "hypocrisy" of the stage: his characters were not fictional but real and familiar. It was biblical history in a theatrical key. After hearing Whitefield preach, New York Presbyterian minister Ebenezer Pemberton confessed, "I never saw or heard the like." In describing what he saw, Pemberton instinctively drew on dramatic terminology. Noteworthy was Whitefield's "clear and musical voice." Even more striking was his use of body: "he uses much gestures," such that "every accent of his voice, and every motion of his body, speaks, and both are natural and unaffected." All of this, moreover, was conducted in so "natural" a way that if it was the "product of art," it was "entirely concealed."

The more successful Whitefield was, the more he antagonized Anglican colleagues who shared his affiliation but invariably found themselves the butt of his biting sarcasm. If Whitefield's ministry was ecumenical, it was an all-inclusive ecumenicity that was explicitly "Calvinist" in theology and opposed to all forms of "Arminianism." In fact, Whitefield's Calvinism and anti-Arminianism became more and more strident as he traveled through Calvinist America and Scotland and met with the eagerly supportive descendants of the "old Puritans." American Anglicans were willing to meet him halfway — even South Carolina's Commissary Garden welcomed the Georgia missionary on his first visit. But Whitefield showed an obvious lack of interest. Confrontation, as Whitefield knew, aroused curiosity, and his own Anglican Church was his favorite target. Soon Anglican churchmen throughout the

American colonies joined their London brethren in opposing Whitefield. And, as in England, their opposition simply fueled popular enthusiasm for the young critic who fearlessly denounced clerical "formality" and Arminian preaching.

As he traveled from Philadelphia to New York, Whitefield attracted the majority of inhabitants even as he lost Anglican support. This was the one denomination to which he was formally tied, and the one from which he had to distance himself in order to maintain his interdenominational appeal. On hearing of "a disturbance in Philadelphia," New York's Commissary Vesey closed all Anglican pulpits to Whitefield and urged his congregations to boycott the sermons. With the battle thus joined, Whitefield had the opposition that he needed to establish "persecution" and plead for popular sympathy. Wherever he traveled, he checked the newspapers for criticism, recognizing "the advantage of the things my adversaries have inserted in the public papers: they do but excite people's curiosity, and serve to raise their attention." With characteristic bluster he excited his readers with accounts of standing the commissary off. When told his field preaching was illegal, Whitefield replied that so too was the commissary's time spent frequenting "public houses." There were times when Whitefield could be utterly enamored of authority figures, but when dealing with commissaries and bishops, he would confidently proclaim that "I was no respector of persons; if a bishop committed a fault, I would tell him of it" — though always, he added, "with a spirit of meekness."

With his own denomination closed, friends multiplied from the dissenters. In fact and spirit, most Americans were dissenters, at odds with traditional, hierarchical ways. This, combined with their historic Calvinism, elicited strong bonds of sympathy and support in response to the news of Whitefield's persecution. At each stop he found strong allies whom he integrated into his ever-expanding network of pro-revival sympathizers. Ebenezer Pemberton quickly got over his confusion and eagerly opened his meetinghouse to Whitefield's indoor preaching. A wealthy merchant, Thomas Noble of New York, agreed to work with Seward in promoting Whitefield's tours and serving as a conduit for the ever-expanding letter-writing network. These, together with the Pennsylvania New Siders, formed the nucleus of a transatlantic evangelical alliance.

When not mesmerizing audiences with his "heavenly cadence" and biblical characterizations, Whitefield was outraging Anglican clergy with his denunciations of an "unconverted ministry." In an oft-repeated sermon entitled "The Lord Our Righteousness," he launched into an attack on all clerical enemies of revival. Invariably, he used the rhetoric of the "jeremiad" — a ritual lament for lost piety, familiar to all Americans — but instead of directing it against the people, he turned it on the clerical opposition to his revival. To startled audiences he would proclaim the new orthodoxy that

> many ministers are so sadly degenerated from their pious ancestors, that the doctrines of grace, especially the personal, all-sufficient righteousness of Jesus is but too seldom, too slightly mentioned. Hence the love of many waxeth cold; and I have often thought, was it possible, that this single consideration would be sufficient to raise our venerable forefathers again from their graves; who would thunder in their ears their fatal error.

The adversarial voice, so familiar to colonial preachers, sounded quite different when directed at them.

In America, the inverted jeremiad was perfectly matched to Whitefield's novel delivery in outdoor settings. Just as the setting upset traditional social rankings and seating, so the rhetoric reversed accusations and assured the people that spiritual declension was not their fault. Through setting and rhetoric he forged a potent message capable of uniting ordinary people in a transatlantic array. Together, Whitefield and his new audiences would challenge the seats of ecclesiastical authority wherever they appeared in churches, colleges, and the press. At the same time, however, that challenge stopped short of civil authority and the "gentlemen" who embodied it. By inclination and temperament, Whitefield remained the proud Oxonian. His confrontational rhetoric was more anti-clerical than antihierarchical, though popular audiences (and critics) heard both emphases in it.

On November 28, Whitefield delivered his farewell sermon to the people of Philadelphia. The meeting was to be held at Christ Church, but the audience was so large that he adjourned "to the fields," where he preached for one and a half hours from a balcony overlooking the crowd. Assembled in the audience were listeners of all classes, including local magistrates at the top and a growing cadre of slaves at the bottom. Included also was the printer-entrepreneur Benjamin Franklin, who was to become an advisor and friend of the young evangelist. Then followed a farewell dinner with the governor and proprietor Thomas Penn. Dinners like these not only boosted Whitefield's popularity and satisfied his craving for recognition among the elite but insulated him from the charge of being an incendiary bent on overturning the social order.

With the first leg of his tour a resounding success, Whitefield moved south to attend to the orphan house project that had ostensibly brought him to the New World. He had much to celebrate. He had attracted audiences that no preacher before him enjoyed. In addition, he had created a nucleus of influential contacts in Philadelphia and New York pledged to promote the cause of revival in its new outdoor setting. A new Anglo-American movement had begun to take shape. All that remained was to complete the tour and then perpetuate it with follow-up ministries and native imitators gifted with a charismatic flair for drama and spiritual sensation. Through his travels, Whitefield became the voice and symbol of a movement that transcended local boundaries and denominations and appeared poised for massive growth.

In America as in England, "revival" itself took on a new meaning as a staged, translocal event, held outdoors on weekdays in open competition with more secular entertainments and diversions. In the past, revivals were local, mysterious events that occurred once or twice in any generation and that remained within local communities. With the New Birth as his product and the promise of a transatlantic market, Whitefield introduced religion to a dawning consumer age. Wherever he encountered a "thriving place for trade," he would set up shop and market his revival.

On January 10, 1740, Whitefield arrived in Savannah, completing a forty-three-day journey of some 1,200 miles by horse, foot, and canoe. He had preached often, and he recorded the stops along the way in his journal. Few men had undertaken such a journey, and his reports were filled with all the adventure and excitement of his earlier ocean-crossing experience. He recorded days spent traveling through "uninhabited woods" in the perpetually reborn and unsettled American wilderness. Letter and journal readers thrilled to stories of converts and confrontations with authority. They also marveled at New World sights seen through the itinerant's eyes: "We observed a variety of birds; and in the evening, heard the wolves howling like a kennel of hounds." Ever the devotionalist, he went on to note that the sound of wolves "made me reflect on what the Psalmist says, 'The lions roaring after their prey do seek their meat from God.'"

Once in Georgia, Whitefield immediately took steps to construct a new orphan house. To that point, the small band of orphans and their schoolmaster James Habersham had lived in a rented house. The land for an orphan house had already been allocated and funds had been raised in England (though not yet in America) for the purpose. Whitefield had had architectural plans drawn up in London. The plans were ambitious and costly, yet with his offerings and the support of his friend Seward, Whitefield believed the feat to be possible.

Possible or not, it constituted a formidable challenge. In view of that, Whitefield abandoned his parish responsibilities in Georgia and lived in the orphan house. Despite a scarcity of labor and materials, he began work on a dock, a highway connecting the orphan house to Savannah, an extended fence, housing for the children and Whitefield, and a meeting room. On January 24, he named the cleared lot and foundation "Bethesda" — a "house of mercy." A month later, the first brick of the "great house" at Bethesda was laid, and twenty acres of land were cleared for planting. The number of orphans grew to forty and, together with local laborers and staff, represented "nearly a hundred mouths" to feed and clothe. All were dependent on Whitefield.

Besides the construction of the physical plant, Whitefield devoted considerable attention to the actual operation of the orphan house. As he envisioned it, James Habersham would preside over an institution that would inculcate methodist piety among the children and at the same time prepare them for manual trades. The boys would learn farming and other manual skills, while the girls would learn to spin cotton and maintain a household. In time, Whitefield hoped to include a Latin master who could identify promising males and prepare them for college and a career in the ministry. Each day would include regular work hours together with worship services and devotional readings in morning and evening. In theory, the worship was to be Anglican, though in practice Whitefield adopted the extemporaneous mode preferred by methodist exhorters.

Although he rejected permanent residence in the South as a colonial missionary, Whitefield retained a lifelong concern with its inhabitants, especially the slaves. He had early endorsed slavery in Georgia — and throughout his ministry he never repudiated it — but in time he did condemn the planters' refusal to reach the slaves with the gospel of the New Birth. This, he asserted, was worse than irresponsible. It reflected a mentality that denied the slaves a soul — a pernicious assumption that Whitefield meant to undo with his preaching. Already he had attracted considerable interest among the slaves in his Philadelphia audiences, and he intended to do more, even if that meant facing the "whip" of the southern planter. Ever on the lookout for "acts of mercy," he began to think of a residence for slaves that would complement the orphan house. While in North Carolina he noted,

> I went, as my usual custom . . . among the negroes belonging to the house. One man was sick in bed, and two of his children said their prayers after me very well. This more and more convinces me that negro children, if early brought up in the nurture and admonition of the Lord, would make as great proficiency as any among white people's children. I do not despair, if God spares my life, of seeing a school of young negroes singing the praises of Him Who made them, in a psalm of thanksgiving. Lord, Thou has put into my heart a good design to educate them; I doubt not but Thou wilt enable me to bring it to good effect.

Whitefield and Habersham eventually went so far as to own slaves themselves. Yet, paradoxically, they did more as southern planters to bring Christianity to the slave community than any of their contemporaries in Georgia or Charleston.

Throughout the winter sojourn at Bethesda, Whitefield continued his torrent of letter writing and followed events closely both in England and in Philadelphia. In February, he published a series of letters in the Charleston press that escalated his newspaper war with the Anglican hierarchy and southern slave owners. In one, especially noxious to Anglican authorities, he accused the highly popular and respected John Tillotson, a revered Archbishop of Canterbury at the end of the seventeenth century, of having never experienced the New Birth and of knowing no more of saving grace than "Mohamet." In another, equally abhorrent to American slave holders, he attacked the insensitivity of slave owners to their slaves and upbraided them for refusing to look to their spiritual and physical needs. Such behavior, he warned, would not go unnoticed. Indeed, he contended that "God has a quarrel with you" for treating slaves "as though they were Brutes." If these

101

slaves were to rise up in rebellion, "all good Men must acknowledge the judgment would be just." Immediately other
newspapers and journals picked up on these articles and, in
the case of the slave letter, discussed the souls of slaves in print
for the first time.

On other fronts, Whitefield worked closely with publishers and printers publicizing his two favorite subjects: the
New Birth and himself. In Philadelphia, he contracted with
Benjamin Franklin to print his journals. But Franklin would not
have the field to himself. Alongside his *Pennsylvania Gazette*
was Andrew and William Bradford's *American Weekly Mercury*,
which devoted front-page coverage to Whitefield from his first
visit in November 1739 throughout the next year. For the fledg-
ling American newspapers, whose primary subjects had been
largely limited to political and economic commentary, Whitefield represented a new avenue of inquiry. For the first time,
religion become part of the exchange of information in the
secular press. It became, in effect, news. The press was so
generous in praising Whitefield that Commissary Cummings
complained openly — and correctly — that the printers con-
spired with Whitefield to trumpet his name at the expense of
established religious and economic institutions.

In the meantime, Whitefield watched with particular interest events in Philadelphia following his tour. Since his departure in November, the forces for revival grew steadily
stronger, and with them instances of confrontation and controversy. Unlike past "seasons" of renewal or "harvests" of
young members, this new revival seemed to work against the
churches as much as for them. Even as it threatened competing
entertainments, it also threatened established churches based
on traditional authority and communal norms. And in the more
work-centered American context, where laborers were many
and the unemployed few, it also threatened to draw workers
away from their weekday labors. In the new revival, religion
was becoming less a matter of family birthright or communal
habit than an arena of choice based on personal preference and

individual experience. Along with the intense piety of the New Birth was a rival vision of religious association and meaning that could not help but provoke confrontation.

On March 8, 1740, an incendiary sermon by Gilbert Tennent entitled "The Danger of an Unconverted Ministry" helped the Presbyterian pro-Whitefield New Siders challenge the traditional order. Tennent urged followers to leave their churches if they were not organized around the experience of the New Birth. The theme was a familiar one in Whitefield's preaching, but such rhetoric had institutional consequences. In the aftermath of Whitefield's and Tennent's blasts against an unconverted ministry, Presbyterians, Congregationalists, and Anglicans found themselves bitterly dividing over the centrality of the New Birth. A movement that had begun innocently enough outside of institutions now threatened to turn back on them and rip them apart.

Whitefield's return to Philadelphia in April coincided with the furor set in motion by Tennent's New Side manifesto. To arouse things all the more, Franklin reprinted Whitefield's blast against Tillotson in the *Pennsylvania Gazette* Publicity and Whitefield's own charismatic and controversial presence soon made him a cause célèbre. Even Whitefield could scarce describe "the joy many felt when they saw my face again." Clearly he was well on his way to becoming an American hero, and he reveled in all the attention attending his return. He played the role of pious celebrity to perfection, careful never to offend civil authority, and invariably recording lunches and meetings with governors, proprietors, and other local dignitaries. Only the Church of England felt the sting of his criticism, and it returned the favor by closing its pulpits. Such was the case with the commissary, in contrast to their first amicable meeting. Seward explained that the change was the result "of Mr. Whitefield's writing against Archbishop Tillotson." The refusal was predictable, leading a triumphant Whitefield to gloat, "little do my enemies think what service they do me. If they did one would think, out of spite they would even desist from opposing me."

The day following his meeting with the commissary, Whitefield preached out of doors. In the morning he spoke from a scaffold built on Society Hill to an audience of five thousand. That afternoon Seward reported a sermon "from the Balcony on Society-Hill to the largest Congregation we have yet had in America, computed at Ten or Twelve thousand." The next day he traveled to Abington and preached from a horse block to three thousand. Similar crowds appeared among the Germans in Germantown and in Whitemarsh. When the commissary preached against him from James 2:8, Whitefield preached on the same text to ten times the audience. As he reported, "Religion is all the talk; and, I think I can say, the Lord Jesus hath gotten Himself the victory in many hearts."

For the most part Whitefield's outdoor sermons were ones he had perfected in England. Benjamin Franklin was in attendance at most of the Philadelphia sermons and soon learned to distinguish new creations from repeat performances:

> By hearing him often I came to distinguish easily between sermons newly composed and those which he had often preached in the course of his travels. His delivery of the latter was so improved by frequent repetition, that every accent, every emphasis, every modulation of voice, was so perfectly well turned, and well placed, that without being interested in the subject, one could not help being pleased with the discourse: a pleasure of much the same kind with that received from an excellent piece of music.

Besides the sermon on Abraham, another favorite in these months was a sermon on Zaccheus, which Seward recorded several times in his journal. The story of Zaccheus was no doubt familiar to most Philadelphians, and Whitefield's popular retelling gave it a peculiarly American flavor. Because Zaccheus was short of stature, he climbed a tree to see Jesus better. Like every insignificant person who is suddenly taken seriously, Zaccheus rejoiced when Jesus spotted him in the tree and called him by name, saying, "make haste, and come down; for to day I must abide at thy house."

With this story as his centerpiece, Whitefield delivered a sermon he turned both to social commentary and evangelical exhortation. To the wealthy of the world he warned, "let not therefore the rich glory in the multitude of their riches." For the most part, he continued, it was "the common people [who] heard our Lord gladly, and the poor [who] received the gospel." In words certain to please ordinary hearers, he pointed out not only that the rich were often insensitive to the gospel message but that sometimes they were openly hostile. For "true" gospel preachers such as himself and the Pennsylvania New Siders he warned, "let not the ministers of Christ marvel, if they meet with the [persecution] from the rich men of this wicked and adulterous generation. I should think it no scandal . . . to hear it affirmed, that none but the poor attended my ministry."

Having assured his hearers that "the poor are dear to my soul," Whitefield returned to Zaccheus, this time for evangelistic purposes. First he enacted a frantic Zaccheus running to hear Jesus, and then climbing the sycamore tree. Where Scripture did not record Zaccheus's thoughts, Whitefield filled in the lines with an imaginary monologue: "Surely, thinks Zaccheus, I dream: it cannot be; how should he know me? I never saw him before." Then followed the imaginative rejection: "besides I shall undergo much contempt, if I receive him under my roof." More polite "scoffers" would never demean themselves by running after Jesus; they no doubt thought he was just another "enthusiastic preacher." But Zaccheus would not be denied, and for his efforts he was rewarded with salvation. In closing, Whitefield took on the personality of Christ, urging his hearers to "come, haste away, and hide yourselves in the clefts of my wounds; for I am wounded for your transgressions; I am dying that you may live for evermore."

So caught up was Whitefield in his daily sermons, each with multiple sermonic roles, that he confessed, "I have scarce had time to eat bread from morning to evening." In Philadelphia, as in London, he was becoming lost to all but his public self in the pulpit. Once again, his experience appears more analogous to the actor on tour than to the settled preacher. Unlike ministers who preached only once or twice a week and could more easily separate their "roles" as pastor, father, husband, and community pillar, Whitefield lived in his own self-embracing world of dramatic reenactment. Just as the public self dominates his journals, so it dominated his day-to-day life in ways that were not common to other preachers.

In characterizing the nether world of the actor, Jean-Christophe Agnew observes that "he certainly never claimed to represent himself on the stage. . . . Nor, finally, did he represent his 'character.' He *was* the character as long as the action of the play went forward, and he could expect to be taken as such by his audience." In very similar ways, Whitefield *was* the biblical characters he portrayed. These characters were more than historical renditions or readings from Scripture. Through his interpretation, they took on lives of their own and became a form of revelation unique to him. In fact, in the time of the sermon he was neither Whitefield nor Zaccheus nor Herod nor Christ: he was all of them brought together in one cathartic vortex of experience and passion common to all great drama.

And so Americans discovered the Whitefield who had earlier taken London by storm. At the same time, Whitefield discovered through his preaching the passions within him and gave them true expression. He was not "acting" as he preached so much as he was exhibiting a one-to-one correspondence between his inner passions and the biblical saints he embodied. He was most complete in the pulpit, where his private and public self came together in body, voice, and gesture to be an open window into his own deepest personal response to the gospel accounts. Such performance required courage to let the self within be seen fully from without. And, like all displays of courage, it brought power and attention.

Along with many "hopeful" conversions, Whitefield collected overwhelming offerings on his return engagement to Philadelphia. In one meeting he received £100 sterling, a figure that Seward accounted "more than ever we had at once" in England and more than many colonial ministers received in a year.

Franklin attended these sermons and recorded a classic account of Whitefield's power over the purses of his listeners. Franklin had come to the sermon "resolved he should get nothing from me." But then, "as he proceeded I began to soften, and concluded to give the Coppers. Another Stroke of his Oratory made me asham'd of that, and determin'd me to give the Silver; and he finish'd so admirably, that I emptied my Pocket wholly into the Collector's Dish, Gold and all." Whitefield himself rejoiced at the outpouring of money, even greater than "what God had done for me at Moorsfields and Kennington Common." In all, he collected over £500 in his spring tour, virtually all of which was returned to the inexhaustible needs of the orphan house.

Whitefield now turned to give increasing attention to the needs of the slave community. Despite his outspoken plea for the legalization of slavery in Georgia, he increasingly sought out audiences of slaves and wrote on their behalf. Gary B. Nash, in his study of the Philadelphia slave community, dates "the advent of black Christianity" in Philadelphia to Whitefield's first preaching tour. Nash estimates that perhaps a thousand slaves heard Whitefield's sermons in Philadelphia, both at Christ Church and out of doors. They heard from him that they had as surely souls as the white folk who had enslaved them and that their master owed them the freedom of religious conscience.

William Seward recorded frequent meetings with slaves in Whitefield's quarters, a sight Seward interpreted "as a good omen that God intends the Salvation for the Negroes, while he passes by their despisers, and worse than Egyptian Task-Masters." All the while, Whitefield's vision of white cruelty to slaves grew, so that finally he determined to supplement preaching and conversion with more tangible assistance. Until this time, Whitefield's every dream seemed to materialize. Now he added one more. Along with his preaching, Whitefield announced his intention to create a school for blacks in Pennsylvania that would both train them in crafts and nurture them in spirit. On April 22, Seward paid £2,200 for five thousand acres of land outside Philadelphia and named it "Nazareth." It is not clear whether Whitefield intended that the blacks at Nazareth be slaves or free (or both), but he certainly intended that in Nazareth the blacks would meet with "the best usage."

So effective was Whitefield's plea for the slaves that Philadelphia's most prominent dancing master, Robert Bolton, renounced his old vocation and turned his school over to blacks. By summer's end, over fifty "black Scholars" had arrived at the school. Tragically, the progress stopped there. Financial setbacks and the lack of personal supervision prevented Whitefield from establishing the momentum necessary to entice others. His noble experiment failed. In time, the land was given over to a Moravian community. Yet despite his failures (institutional and personal), his voice of compassion for the slaves continued to ring out and win their enduring adoration.

While Whitefield and Seward worked in the middle colonies, they were also planning ahead to the South, New England, and Scotland. Seward's journal provides a glimpse of religious publicity in the making. On April 22 he received news of a sloop going to Georgia. Immediately he sat down and "wrote letters to Savannah, Charlestown, Frederica, Virginia, Cape-Fear, New Brunswick, and New York." In that day alone he sent out over a hundred letters containing news of the tour. In many letters, he "Inclosed our Brother's Letters against Archbishop Tillotson, and about the Negroes, and also sundry News-papers [accounts]." Along with reports on Whitefield's successes in Philadelphia, Seward "wrote paragraphs for the News, where our Brother was to preach and had preached." A widening network of correspondents was being created even as Whitefield traveled from place to place.

Following a farewell sermon to twenty thousand at Philadelphia, Whitefield returned again to the orphan house. There he fought two battles that would keep his name in the news. The first was with the Georgia trustees over the question of ownership and control of the orphan house. His anti-Anglican bursts had not endeared him to the trustees, and many began to suspect he intended to transform the school into a methodist seminary. In response they moved to tighten controls.

Whitefield, buoyed by his hero's welcome in the middle colonies as well as by the financial security of large offerings and Seward's wealth, dismissed the trustees' offer of financial support. He serenely declared that he and his wealthy friend William Seward would see to all the financing of the orphan house. In that way, he would have total ownership and direction. He added that trustee support was minimal, and everywhere he mentioned them "it . . . met with contempt."

Stung by Whitefield's arrogance — recorded in the ubiquitous *Journal* and published for the English-speaking world to read — the trustees and the secretary of the colony responded by holding Whitefield to public account for all moneys disbursed at the orphan house. They also insisted that ownership of the deeded lands belonged ultimately to them and that Whitefield could not bequeath them in his will. As a further slap, they insisted on the rights of regular visitation and inspection, along with payment of a quitrent for the five hundred acres earlier ceded.

The gauntlet was thrown down, and Whitefield eagerly entered the fray. In a widely reprinted letter to the trustees, he challenged their right of ownership in terms that left little doubt about his contempt for their authority. As for accountability, he owed them no explanation. There would be an accounting to be sure — but to *his* public — the poor and dissenting "fools for Christ," not the trustees. Secretary Stevens's claims were preposterous, Whitefield went on, especially when everyone knew that virtually all of the fund raising, planning, and staffing was "owing chiefly to my own particular interest, and therefore I have a right to the sole disposal of it." Whitefield's bombast succeeded in eliminating the quitrent and leaving open the question of inheritability (eventually resolved in his favor). At the same time, it made him the darling of American colonists who also chafed at authority and relished confrontation. This would be reinforced when he fought his second battle with Commissary Alexander Garden.

As clerics throughout America had before him, Garden played perfectly into Whitefield's hand. He denied his pulpits to the outspoken itinerant and sought to censure him. Central to Garden's grievance was Whitefield's "railing Accusation against the clergy of the *Church of England* in general, and the present *Bishop of London* in particular." Equally offensive was Whitefield's theatricality, which especially infected the common and the ignorant. To bewitched American listeners Garden offered stern counsel:

> [Whitefield's sermons] were preached midst the Sound of that Gentleman's Voice in your ears; — that enchanting *Sound!* The natural and alone Cause, which produced all the Passion and Prejudice, that prevailed 'mong some (the weaker some indeed) of you, in his Favour, against them and every thing else that opposed him; and which would equally have produced the same Effects, whether he had acted his Part in the Pulpit or on the Stage. . . . It was not the Matter but the Manner, not the Doctrines he delivered, but the Agreeableness of the Delivery, [that] had all the Effect upon you. . . . Take away this Cause, no more Multitude after the Preacher!

While Garden had clearly pinpointed a partial explanation for Whitefield's success, he utterly missed how completely his criticism played into Whitefield's hands. Few Americans cared about the Church of England or its bishop, let alone theatricality, except to the extent that they enjoyed Whitefield's blasts against the former and his indulgence in the latter.

When Garden threatened to suspend Whitefield from the ministry, Whitefield replied contemptuously (and publicly) that he would regard such a suspension "as much as I would a Pope's bull." In response Garden summoned the young itinerant to an ecclesiastical court, hoping to silence him. But this move served only to further the "persecuted" Whitefield's popularity.

Whitefield continued to criticize Anglican authorities and demand that slave owners acknowledge that their slaves had souls. With the case of Nazareth fresh in his mind, he prevailed on a recent convert and well-to-do Charleston planter named Hugh Blair to "erect a Negro school in South Carolina" to teach the slaves basic Christianity. Blair and his brother Jonathan hired another Whitefield convert, William Hutson, a former "stage player," as the first master of their school. Eventually Hugh Blair's emotional instability unraveled the whole enterprise, but for a time it stood as another tangible and widely publicized token of Whitefield's concern for the souls of black folk.

Throughout June, Whitefield preached to record audiences in Charleston and attracted newspaper coverage in Philadelphia, New York, and Boston. His account of his "trial" before Garden's "court" read like Stephen before an unconverted Paul and the Jewish Sanhedrin. As Garden railed against Whitefield, the young itinerant invoked the martyr's identity: "I pitied, I prayed for him; and wished, from my soul, that the Lord would convert him, as He once did the persecutor Saul, and let him know it is Jesus whom he persecutes." On August 14 the Charleston *Mercury* described Garden's trial and Whitefield's response in terms that left no doubt where the paper's loyalties lay. It described a badly put upon Whitefield who

> recommended submission to authority, and love to enemies, in such a manner that he allay'd the resentment of the People against his Prosecutors, acquired the love and esteem of some who before were his opposers, and remov'd strong prejudices conceived against him by many who never before heard him.

111

Words like these were too much for Garden to bear. Too late he realized he had been taken in. The more he tried to expose Whitefield's theatricality and hubris, the more Whitefield turned accusations into a "persecution" he would willingly endure for the sake of the gospel and the multitudes who should hear it. Whitefield had the press in the palm of his hand, and no authority would ever win a confrontation in that medium.

The triumphs continued, and so did the coverage in northern newspapers. Reports of a fall tour in New England raised great expectations. Despite fears that his daily preaching had dealt an "irrecoverable stroke to the health of my body," Whitefield rejoiced to see how "many seemed to sympathise with me." He would take that assurance with him to New England, where the heart and soul of his beloved Puritanism still lived.

7 A New Religious History

On September 14, 1740, Whitefield arrived in Newport, Rhode Island, en route to Boston. His New England tour would not last as long as the two visits to the middle colonies, but the advance notice and built-up anticipation released a wave of popular enthusiasm that equaled or exceeded anything he had seen.

Whitefield was no scholar, and revivalism, as a field of inquiry, could not be found in the colleges. Yet Whitefield understood the history of modern revivals as well as anyone — and New England's central place in the emerging mythology. Revivalism enjoyed a popular history, partly written and mostly oral, carried through newspapers, letters, and word of mouth. In spirit and constituency, it functioned as a popular alternative to the Enlightenment rationalism of Locke and Newton, and, like the growing international community of scholars linked into a "Republic of Letters," it transcended local institutions and hierarchies. In George Whitefield the movement had its catalyst and floating center, and in New England it had its chief intellectual proponents.

113

These proponents of the eighteenth century's "New Religious History" (all found on the margins of the more intellectually respectable Enlightenment) made a formidable list: Lady Selina, Countess of Huntington; Howell Harris in Wales; the Erskine brothers in Scotland; Theodore Frelinghuysen and the Tennents in Pennsylvania; Josiah Smith in Charleston; and Solomon Stoddard in Massachusetts. Above all the rest, however, stood Stoddard's grandson Jonathan Edwards. The Northampton of Stoddard and Edwards was not the first town to be revived, but it was certainly the most important, for out of a convulsive revival there in 1734, Edwards produced a classic literary account of revivals entitled *A Narrative of Surprising Conversions*. This treatise stood as the *textus receptus* for the New Religious History promulgated by Whitefield and his allies. Edwards's *Narrative* began as an extended letter to Boston's venerable Benjamin Colman. Colman immediately recognized its value and recommended its publication. Without delay, the work became a best-seller that was widely reprinted in America, England, and Scotland. And as more and more communities experienced revivals, they looked to that account as the benchmark and point of comparison for self-understanding. Through Edwards's history, the revivals were made intelligible as a "work of God" according to the most current knowledge of the age.

Already in Philadelphia, Whitefield had been reading Edwards's account, as well as Stoddard's revival manual, *A Guide to Christ*, published twenty years earlier. New England would be the last stop on his tour, yet in symbolic ways it would be the most important, for it would link him to the birthplace of the modern revival. The science of revival was already in place. With the arrival of Whitefield, letters and newspapers would be joined with local clerical support to ensure success. A little controversy and some advance news were all that was required to whet the public appetite.

Newspapers and ministers were Whitefield's best advance sources, and New England had both in abundance. Bos-

ton alone boasted four newspapers, and other chief cities from
Hartford to New London had papers of their own. As before,
the papers rallied behind Whitefield and built on the growing
myth of his powers. Long before scholars and historians had
time to do their work, the New England press chronicled the
New Religious History. Even more effective as Whitefield's
advance agents were the New England ministers. Through the
agency of Harvard and Yale, the region included over six
hundred classically educated Congregational clergymen,
placed in virtually every town throughout Massachusetts and
Connecticut. The ratio of minister to population was the lowest
in the Western world, and as public voices the clergy had few
competitors. Indeed, the ministers controlled public communications so effectively that in most communities they simply were *the* voice of authority and corporate meaning. For
generations they had spoken of, prayed for, and experienced
"revival," always in a local communal setting, as a reaffirma-
tion of local institutions and authorities. These revivals continued to appear in 1739 and 1740. Yet they were destined to
be redefined in the wake of Whitefield's mass meetings.

Throughout the summer, Whitefield's triumphs and confrontations in the south and middle colonies continued to receive full coverage in New England's newspapers. In an age
that had not yet established copyright laws, accounts were
borrowed verbatim from Philadelphia and New York newspapers and from letters that Whitefield and Seward had sent
to prime the media pump. As early as April, the *New England
Weekly Journal* carried front-page coverage of Whitefield's attacks on Tillotson and southern slave owners and applauded
both. New England readers already anticipated seeing "a man
of middle stature, of a slender body, of a fair complexion, and
of a comely appearance." He was "sprightly" and "cheerful"
in temperament, and they understood that he moved "with
great agility and life." The *Boston Gazette* described a Whitefield
sermon at the Philadelphia courthouse in which "the pulpit
seem'd almost to be the Tribunal, if the comparison may be

pardon'd, of the great Judge, clothed in Flames, and adjudging a guilty world to penal Fire."

Soon the Boston printers got into the act. Samuel Kneeland and Thomas Green printed Whitefield's *Account* of orphan house management and disbursements, which he had written to allay public suspicion concerning his offerings. The major Boston publishers Draper, Rogers, and Fowle picked up Whitefield sermons, while booksellers such as Daniel Henchman imported Franklin's edition of the *Journals* to meet widespread public demand.

As always, controversy was Whitefield's best friend, and New England accommodated with at least one outspoken skeptic, the conservative and thoroughly anglicized publisher Thomas Fleet. Fleet's audience aspired to gentility, so he chose as his journalistic model those fashionable London magazines that heaped abuse on the "field preacher," identifying him with methodism and mayhem. Fleet maintained a staunch antagonism in his *Boston Evening Post* throughout Whitefield's early tours of New England. But, like other opposition, he simply fueled public curiosity. After reading Fleet's reprinting of Commissary Garden's harsh strictures against Whitefield, audiences became all the more intent on seeing the field preacher for themselves.

New England's clergy expressed as much excitement about Whitefield's arrival as the newspapers. As he had with the press, Whitefield prepared them carefully. Already in February, while working at the orphan house, he had received an invitation from Edwards to preach in Northampton. Edwards had begun the letter by reminding Whitefield how his Northampton pulpit had once been "distinguished with Light." Recently, however, the town had fallen on "more hardened" times. Could Whitefield visit and fan the embers of a waning piety? The results, Edwards dared to think, could be stupendous and involve more than Northampton. A mighty reformation could be kindled that would signal "the dawning of a day of God's mighty Power and glorious grace to the world

116

of mankind." With so irresistible a proposition, Whitefield immediately accepted the invitation — and challenge.

While Edwards's international reputation was important, his help was not as central to Whitefield's New England designs as that of Benjamin Colman. If Edwards was America's greatest theologian, Colman personified America's genteel but still orthodox Congregational establishment. His English ordination and cosmopolitan manners fitted him perfectly to serve Boston's most anglicized elite at the wealthy and innovative Brattle Street Church. At the same time, Colman remained staunchly Calvinist in theology and a friend to the new evangelical revivals.

Colman first learned of Whitefield through reading the *Journals* and newspaper accounts. In July he received a letter from Whitefield expressing hopes for revival in New England. Borrowing his image from Edwards, Whitefield announced that "surely our Lord intends to put the whole world in a Flame." He indicated that he planned to visit Colman and New England "some time next month" and hoped that he would lend him support by opening his pulpit and allowing him to preach. In closing, Whitefield mentioned the ongoing needs of the orphan house at Bethesda and his hope of raising support in New England for its ministry: "Leave it to God. He hath the hearts of all men in his hands, and I am fully persuaded will provide for [the orphans] some way or another. Oh the blessedness of living by faith!" Colman was happy to comply with Whitefield's request, and he forwarded copies of the letter to other ministers, including Jonathan Edwards, to be read from their pulpits.

Whitefield's careful preparations and advance publicity paid handsome dividends. By the time word spread that he had arrived in Newport and would soon be in Boston, the country was in a turmoil. In Newport, the Anglican rector James Honeyman resolved not to allow "the noisie Mr Whitefield" to preach in his parish, but the "chief" people in his church overruled him and opened their pulpit. Whitefield

117

promptly preached his signature sermon "The Nature and Necessity of Our Regeneration," and with that the New England revival was on.

In Boston, Colman, together with William Cooper, eagerly shared the news of Whitefield's arrival with the New England press and offered their pulpits. This in turn set up a flurry of invitations throughout Boston and into the countryside. Before setting foot in Boston, Whitefield had a full-blown itinerary from which to choose. His only rejection came from Commissary Timothy Cutler, which gave him the opportunity to declare that the Anglicans "should not have an opportunity of denying me the use of their pulpits." Instead, he proclaimed, he would take his message into the much larger Congregational meetinghouses and into the fields.

Whitefield's inaugural sermon from Colman's pulpit attracted an overflow crowd estimated at four thousand. By all accounts, it moved the audience as though they were hearing the message of regeneration for the first time. According to one excited account, "he uses much gesture, but with great propriety: every accent of his voice, every motion of his Body, speaks, and both are natural and unaffected. If his delivery is the product of art, 'tis certainly the perfection of it, for it is entirely unconcealed." By the following day at Joseph Sewall's South Church, the crowd had grown to an estimated six thousand. From there Whitefield traveled in the afternoon to his beloved fields and, in his first sermon on Boston Common, attracted a rapt audience estimated by the *Weekly Mercury* at five thousand.

The next day was Sunday, and, in keeping with his policy, he refused to speak in the morning, instead attending Brattle Street church to hear Colman preach. Colman was at his evangelical best, prompting an enthusiastic Whitefield to praise his preaching for its warmth and zeal. He also had good things to say about New England preaching generally, though in fact he attended only one other sermon during this trip through New England.

That Sunday afternoon, Whitefield preached at Thomas Foxcroft's Old Brick Church. So vast was the gathering that the audience had to adjourn to the common. There, in the outdoor market center, Whitefield held eight thousand listeners spellbound with his full-bodied enactment of the horrors of sin and the raptures of undeserved grace. Freed from the restrictions of walls, he roamed around his portable field pulpit at will, amazing his audience with the sheer pathos and passion of his delivery. For his own part, Whitefield experienced the typical performer's anxiety, feeling weak and hoarse at the start, but he was soon "enabled to speak, and could have spoken, I believe, till midnight."

Despite a population of only seventeen thousand, Boston was producing crowds that rivaled Whitefield's field preaching in London. Unlike London, however, many of these crowds gathered in meetinghouses never intended for such volume. A tragedy was virtually inevitable. Word had spread that Whitefield would preach at Mr. Checkley's meetinghouse the next day, and predictably the crowd poured in, filling the building beyond capacity. As Whitefield was still making his preparations, someone in the gallery broke a board to make a seat. The sound triggered a panic. As described later by the *Mercury*,

> the word was soon given by some ignorant and disordered Persons, that the galleries gave way; upon which the whole Congregation was immediately thrown into the utmost confusion and Disorder, and each one being desirous to save themselves some jump'd from the galleries into the pews and allies below, others threw themselves out at the windows, and those below pressing hard to get out at the porch Doors, many (especially women) were thrown down and trod upon by those that were crowding out, no regard being had to the sensible screeches and outcries of those in danger of their lives, or others.

Before the panic subsided and the building cleared, five people

119

had died. Such a tragedy accompanying a preaching event was unprecedented in the annals of colonial preaching and testified in a particularly powerful, if gruesome, way to Whitefield's popularity. Whitefield himself remained bent on preaching. To the amazement of all, he did not cancel his sermon but instead removed to the common, where he drew from the event powerful applications. Death was the primary consequence of sin, and with so powerful and immediate a reminder, Whitefield preached through a driving rainstorm. No one in the audience left. Later Whitefield made no reference to the tragedy, except to say that "Satan had a hand in this."

As long as Whitefield confined himself to the theme of the New Birth, his message met with almost universal acceptance. But there was another, more polemical strain to his preaching that would soon arouse familiar controversy. As in Pennsylvania and the South, he stepped up his clergy-baiting with inflammatory accusations against established ministers. They were, Whitefield claimed, caught up in the "formality" of their office and, quite possibly, "unconverted." In fact, he could not possibly have known more than a handful of ministers — most of whom were friendly to his visit, and he had attended only two services in New England. But his pulpit rhetoric required antagonists. If religious apathy was not the fault of the people, as Whitefield insisted it was not, then it must be laid at the feet of their spiritual leaders. This inverted jeremiad had worked well in England and the middle colonies, and it would work in New England.

But Whitefield did not stop with criticism of the New England clergy. At Cambridge, after speaking before Harvard students and faculty, he made a powerful enemy by recording in his *Journal* for all to see that the college "is scarce as big as one of our least colleges at Oxford; and as far as I could gather from some who knew the state of it, not far superior to our Universities in piety." He went on to complain that spiritual discipline was neglected and "bad books" such as Tillotson's and Samuel Clarke's deistical volumes were being read instead of the Puritan Thomas Shepard, Stoddard, and "such-like evangelical writers." If this was any indication of a lack of grace — and Whitefield claimed it was — one could reasonably assume that many of the Harvard graduates in New England pulpits were unconverted. Predictably, Whitefield's words enraged the Harvard tutors even while they fanned the fires of his popularity. Attacks on the more secular Enlightenment learning would not win friends in academia, but they would confirm enduring popular resistance to anglicized intellectual pretensions and at the same time feed a sense of popular superiority.

On September 26 Whitefield took a short trip to Roxbury, where he preached to "many thousands" from a "little ascent" in the center of town. In the afternoon he returned to Boston. By then the tragic lessons of overcrowded buildings had been learned, and the preaching site was relocated from Mather Byles's meetinghouse pulpit to a large scaffold erected in the town common. There, before fifteen thousand people, Whitefield preached on the New Birth and marveled in his *Journal*, "Oh, how the word did run!" For their part, New Englanders were equally spellbound. Neither clergy nor laity had ever seen such pulpit performances as these, and they certainly did run to hear the young itinerant. The Rev. Nathan Bucknam of Medway interrupted the standard entries in his private diary to record an extraordinary trip to Boston to hear Whitefield. From October 6 to 9 he attended every Whitefield sermon, dutifully recording both the text and the excitement it generated. In these first halcyon days, no one was immune to the contagion of enthusiasm. No one could believe — or wanted to believe — that Whitefield's performance was the product of art. Even Whitefield refused to believe it was art. Like Paul and the apostles, he believed he simply preached the ancient gospel and that God did the rest: "Wherever I go people will follow me," he wrote, "and I now, almost hourly, receive letters from persons under convictions." The results were purely and sublimely the work of the Holy Spirit working as in apostolic times.

Unlike Philadelphia, where Whitefield had taken no offer-

ings until his second visit, in New England he planned immediate collections. By now his integrity was established, and the
needs of the orphan house were pressing. Seward had returned
to England to preach, leaving Whitefield solely responsible for
the orphan house. The acute need for money committed him
to a fund-raising mission — one that would last the rest of his
life. On September 23, he reprinted his orphan house account
in the *Boston Weekly Journal* along with a letter outlining the
needs. The letter went on to praise New England's reputation
for generosity and the "liberal" offerings already received from
the friends of piety and charity in Philadelphia, New York, and
Charleston. The letter closed, "if God should incline you or
your Friends to promote this good work, I shall be thankful,
and the blessings bestow'd on my lambs thro' your means, I
hope, will much rebound to the glory of God. I have given
myself to this work; and if I die in endeavoring to advance its
welfare, it will be a matter of rejoycing to George Whitefield."

The response to Whitefield's plea exceeded even his own
expectations. In the outlying towns, Whitefield averaged about
£70 Massachusetts currency per offering. In Boston, however,
the figures were staggering: £555 (Massachusetts currency) in
Joseph Sewall's meetinghouse; £470 in Colman's Brattle Street;
and £440 in Joseph Webb's. In all, the *Weekly Journal* reported
collections in excess of £3,000 local currency, or £600 sterling
— a figure far above any reported in Philadelphia, Charleston,
or London.

Whitefield's astounding offerings are significant less for
any personal gain they gave him (there was little) than for the
way in which they confirmed that religion could be marketed
in open-air settings and generate revenue like any other service.
In a single afternoon, Whitefield had raised far more money
than New England's clergy earned in a year. No one in New
England had ever seen such offerings before. The Rev. Moses
Parsons of Byfield was so staggered by reports of Whitefield's
offerings in the *Weekly Journal* that he copied the totals into his
diary — a unique entry in an otherwise conventional diary

filled with entries on weather, preaching texts, and local events. The lesson was clear. Religion need not rely on tax support and established institutions. It could survive — and survive very well — in outdoor settings *if* it was presented in terms that would attract eighteenth-century crowds.

Of course, as the recent history of American television evangelists has shown, the rich potential for offerings can easily be abused. But in Whitefield's case, money and possessions held minimal allure. His peripatetic lifestyle discouraged acquisitions, and his ascetic personal appetites, fixed at Oxford, had never changed. Apart from a taste for Madiera wine, which his friend James Habersham supplied from Savannah, he had no extravagances. Fame was far more compelling a temptation than money. And the more money he raised — and gave away — the more famous he became.

Clearly, on his first tour of New England Whitefield reached "the people" as no one before him ever had. And the people he reached included slaves. As in Philadelphia, he specifically sought out their attendance at his meetings and addressed them directly. At Benjamin Colman's meetinghouse there were so many slaves present that after the service he "went and preached to a great number of negroes at their request." His text was on the conversion of the Ethiopian eunuch, and, as before, it centered on the doctrine that slaves had souls. Whitefield's letters on the slaves had already won widespread attention in New England and prompted novel debates on the souls of black folk. In fact, the letters represented the first journalistic statement on the subject of slavery. As such, they marked a precedent of awesome implications, beyond anything Whitefield could have imagined.

From Boston, Whitefield took his message to outlying settlements. He traveled the familiar pattern of concentric circles begun in London and Philadelphia, stopping at "central places" along the way. There was not a wasted motion. Virtually every day he delivered two sermons along with private meetings and "exhortations" at his lodgings. Attracted by printed itineraries in the newspapers and by word of mouth, audiences of unprecedented size gathered at each stop, many of them exceeding the population of the host community. At seaport towns such as Marblehead and Salem, and in suburbs such as Charlestown and Roxbury, he generated an enthusiasm verging on panic as crowds "elbowed, shoved, and trampled over themselves to hear of 'divine things' from the famed Whitefield."

Most of the time he preached on the common or "in a broad place in the middle of the town." At each stop he recorded the event for others in an expanding network to read. As in earlier journal entries, he paid little attention to exactness in date or travel details. Nor did he bother to mention either preaching text or doctrine — common fare for virtually all other ministerial diaries. His purposes were less historical than promotional and mythological. He was in the business of making a new religious history, replete with its own marvels and divine triumphs, in which audience size and offering totals became supremely noteworthy. He rarely omitted mention of either, for both legitimated God's pleasure in the new religious movement. The Whitefield that emerges in these pages is wholly emptied of self and worldly concerns and utterly absorbed in his Pauline character. In fact, anything else would have detracted from his central purpose of marvel and mythmaking.

Predictably, Whitefield was often ill with "exhaustion" or "vomiting" before performing, only to find that once in the pulpit, "the power of the Word" took over and empowered him to preach for hours. The piety here was no doubt sincere. Equally clear, however, was a pattern of anxiety that most performers experience. And Whitefield knew it. Preaching, he recognized, "is a constant remedy against all indispositions." In an eight-day period he traveled 178 miles outside Boston and preached sixteen times. Yet, he rejoiced, "I was not in the least wearied."

Whitefield returned briefly to Boston, where popular enthusiasm had actually increased. The crowd so thronged Joseph Sewall's meetinghouse that he had to climb in through one of the windows. Then, once again, he prepared for his farewell sermon. Like "revival," "farewell sermon" was a familiar term that had taken on new meanings in Whitefield's itinerant world. What was reserved by other preachers for once or twice in a lifetime became in Whitefield's itinerancy a staged event at every significant stop. In this case, the audience at his farewell sermon on Boston common — estimated at twenty thousand — was all-inclusive. Magistrates and Harvard students, almshouse residents and slaves, friends and enemies all attended. None could stay away. By Whitefield's own account, "numbers, great numbers, melted into tears when I talked of leaving them." All in all, it was a great sight, "perhaps never seen before in America." In fact, there had never been a larger crowd in America to that date.

With Boston behind him, Whitefield moved into the second phase of his New England tour, traveling the rugged ground of the region's hinterland with all the enthusiasm of a pioneer. As always, he carefully selected central places that would attract the largest audiences. Chief of these was Northampton, where, on October 17, he had his long-awaited meeting with Jonathan Edwards. For all of their shared importance to the eighteenth-century revival (and perhaps *because* of it), the two had little in common. Edwards's interests were philosophical theology and the mind, whereas Whitefield's were preaching and the passions. When Edwards spoke of the centrality of the "heart" and the "affections," he did so in highly technical, epistemological ways that Whitefield found personally distracting, if necessary. And so the two came together around the cause of revival, but in such different ways and with such different gifts that they never established the sort of personal chemistry that Whitefield enjoyed with Harris, Tennent, or Franklin.

Still, Edwards was an international figure in the emerging Calvinist network, and Northampton was on the tip of every revivalist's tongue. The meeting carried significance for both Edwards and Whitefield, and each spoke warmly of it. Whitefield later confessed, "I have not seen [Edwards's] fellow in all New England." In all, Whitefield preached four sermons from Edwards's pulpit. The text for the opening sermon does not survive, but the theme dealt with "the consolations and privileges of saints, and the plentiful effusion of the Spirit upon believers." Throughout, he reminded his hearers of their long association with revivals and Northampton's pivotal place in the emerging Calvinist evangelical order. Both speaker and listeners frequently "wept much."

The following afternoon he again preached with great success and confessed,

> I began with fear and trembling, but God assisted me. Few eyes were dry in the assembly. I had an affecting prospect of the glories of the upper world, and was enabled to speak with some degree of pathos. It seemed as if a time of refreshing was come from the presence of the Lord.

In the audience, Edwards felt "weak in body" and was visibly affected by the preaching. Such was Whitefield's power that by the third sermon he could report that "good Mr Edwards wept during the whole time of exercise." Just as exciting, "the people were equally affected, and in the afternoon [sermon] the power increased yet more."

It was important that Whitefield exhibit "power" in Edwards's pulpit, both for the revival of Northampton and for his own position in the international movement. In fact, he met with complete success. Edwards himself reported that as a result of Whitefield's preaching, Northampton was again revived, and "in about a month there was a great alteration in the town."

Five days after Whitefield's visit, Sarah Edwards wrote her brother a remarkably insightful letter describing Whitefield and the recent events. In terms of method, she wrote, "he makes less of the doctrines than our American preachers generally do and aims more at affecting the heart. He is a born orator." The effects were spectacular:

> It is wonderful to see what a spell he casts over an audience by proclaiming the simplest truths of the Bible. I have seen upwards of a thousand people hang on his words with breathless silence, broken only by an occasional half-suppressed sob. . . . A prejudiced person, I know, might say that this is all theatrical artifice and display; but not so will anyone think who has seen and known him.

For his part, Whitefield was much taken with Sarah Edwards, whom he found "adorned with a meek and quiet spirit." He would subsequently look upon her as a model for the type of wife he hoped to find.

Throughout western Massachusetts and the Connecticut River Valley, Whitefield kept up his grueling pace of twice-daily preaching, discoursing often on grace, election, and the dangers of an unconverted ministry. Along the way he encountered clerical admirers and would-be imitators such as Eleazar Wheelock, Benjamin Pomeroy, Andrew Croswell, and James Davenport (whom he had met in Philadelphia, and who shared his suspicions about unconverted elders). All of these young men found in Whitefield's stirring denunciations the rhetoric they needed to challenge authority and encourage lay separations.

Inevitably, these young imitators threatened established authority and strained relations between congregations and their local pastors, and suddenly the potential for conflict in these revivals became vividly apparent. Whitefield's dramatic characterizations were one thing, but his confrontational, us-against-them rhetoric contained the seeds of trouble that even he would live to regret in the deranged ministry of James Davenport.

For the moment, however, all remained relatively calm as churches focused their enthusiasm and zeal on Whitefield's preaching. In Hartford, the pastor Daniel Wadsworth looked forward to Whitefield's visit with great anticipation. Already in February he had received a copy of Whitefield's sermons with prefatory letters by Benjamin Colman and Josiah Smith. The advance publicity had whetted his appetite and that of his congregation, who heard Whitefield at Hartford in the morning and at Wethersfield in the afternoon. Whitefield's afternoon sermon was a favorite from 2 Corinthians 5:17 on regeneration in which he enacted the birthing of a "new creature" transformed by saving grace. Wadsworth had never witnessed such a performance. The truth of the doctrine of the New Birth could not be doubted, but the manner of presentation was a different story: "What to think of the man . . . I scarcely know." Two months later, Wadsworth was still struggling, this time over the *Journal:* "met with the famous Mr. Whitefield's life and read it. But what is it?"

If the clergy were both moved and uncertain, there were no such reservations on the part of ordinary men and women. In Middletown, Connecticut, as Whitefield addressed a moderately large crowd (for him) of four thousand, a local farmer named Nathan Cole described the event in his private diary. His words would be discovered years after his death and widely reprinted in the twentieth century. Scholars find in his account a perfect description of the popular enthusiasm and frenzy that accompanied a Whitefield sermon.

Reports from Philadelphia that Whitefield preached "like one of the apostles" had raised Cole's interest, and he eagerly followed the course of Whitefield's itinerancy, "hoping soon to see him." Word of Whitefield's preaching in Hartford and Wethersfield raised hopes that he would also appear in Middletown. Sure enough, on the morning of October 23, a "messenger" raced through Middletown with news that Whitefield would preach out-of-doors that morning at ten o'clock. Cole's response was frantic:

> I was in my field at work. I dropped my tool . . . and ran
> home to my wife, telling her to make ready quickly to go

on and hear Mr. Whitefield preach at Middletown, then ran to my horse with all my might, fearing that I should be too late. Having my horse, I with my wife soon mounted. . . . We improved every moment to get along as if we were fleeing for our lives, all the while fearing we should be too late to hear the sermon, for we had twelve miles to ride.

After a furious ride, the Coles made it to the Connecticut River by Middletown. Cole struggled later to describe the novel scene before him:

I saw before me a cloud of fog arising. I first thought it came from the great river, but as I came nearer the road I heard a noise of horses' feet coming down the road, and this cloud was a cloud of dust made by the horses' feet. . . . When I came within about 20 rods of the road, I could see men and horses slipping along in the cloud like shadows, and as I drew nearer it seemed like a steady stream of horses and their riders, scarcely a horse more than his length behind another, all of a lather and foam with sweat, their breath rolling out of their nostrils every jump. Every horse seemed to go with all his might for the saving of souls. It made me tremble to see the sight.

Once Cole had stationed himself and his wife in the crowd, he turned back to the river where he saw "the ferry boats running swift backward and forward bringing over loads of people, and the oars rowed nimble and quick. Everything, men, horses, and boats seemed to be struggling for life." The sermon that followed did not disappoint an expectant Cole. When Whitefield climbed the scaffolding assembled for his visit "he looked almost angelical: a young, slim, slender youth, before some thousands of people with a bold undaunted countenance." Soon Cole was caught up in the moment by a master of gesture and presence who "looked as if he was clothed with authority from the Great God." So powerful was

129

the sermon, Cole concluded, that it "gave me a heart wound. . . . I saw that my righteousness would not save me."

It is easy to see why Cole's description is so widely reprinted. It captures, as no ministerial diary could do, the popular impact that Whitefield exerted on ordinary listeners. There was no pretext of analysis or critical description but rather a language that strained to reproduce a novel experience in powerful, image-filled words. The references to shadowy figures, thunderous noise, and clouds of dust all point as no official account could to the powerful emotions evoked by Whitefield's preaching.

In two short months, Whitefield had become the darling of New England. Such was the inherited piety of ordinary New Englanders that his preaching was like "putting fire to tinder." Their long tradition of local revivals fed into a mass event of nearly universal proportions. And for once, Whitefield learned as much as he gave. Never before had he seen such uniformly high levels of popular piety and Calvinist knowledge. Family worship, he observed, "is generally kept up," and "the negroes are better used than in any province I have yet seen." "On many accounts," he concluded, New England "certainly excels all other provinces in America; and, for the establishment of religion, perhaps all other parts of the world."

Yet if all was promising with the people, the same could not be said for their pastors and the colleges that trained them. Even as young admirers followed Whitefield and sought to extend the revival, others grew increasingly cautious. Between his first arrival in New England and late October, word surfaced that ministers such as Wadsworth and Boston's Charles Chauncy were having second thoughts about the character of his ministry. Added to these critics was the *Boston Evening Post,* which began openly to question the effects of Whitefield's preaching. In a series of printed letters, the *Post* praised "the great Archbishop Tillotson" and criticized Whitefield's theatrical methods. Too often, the *Post* complained, Whitefield "captivated by sounds and gestures only." Beyond that, he was making solid, local preachers seem boring and detached by comparison. More "sober-minded citizens" who sought "to attend the ministrations of their own pious and laborious pastors, in quiet peace and orderly Manner" were "stigmatiz'd as atheists, profligates, or very irreligious Persons." Finally, Whitefield threatened to divert scarce resources to his orphanage when "we have much more Need of one among ourselves."

Predictably, Whitefield responded to the accusations in kind. So certain was he of the rightness of his words that he viewed any attack on his ministry as prima facie evidence that it had come from an enemy of the gospel. The ominous warning against an unconverted ministry continued to sound in his oratory. And just as this rhetoric had worked in England against the Anglicans, it was effective in New England when used against Anglicans and critical Congregationalists. Judging from private conversations with younger ministers such as Pomeroy and Davenport, he concluded that many clergymen "rest in a head-knowledge, [and] are close [to] Pharisees, and have only a name to live."

Upon his return to Boston on October 7, a highly confident and combative Whitefield prepared to close out his New England tour on a note of challenge. On October 9, he entered the pulpit at Joseph Sewall's meetinghouse with no text in mind; but, seeing many ministers in attendance, he turned to the account of Nicodemus and Jesus' stern injunction to the wise Pharisee that he must be "born again." Following the sermon, Whitefield wrote: "I am persuaded the generality of preachers talk of an unknown and unfelt Christ. The reason why congregations have been so dead is, because they have dead men preaching to them. . . . How can dead men beget living children?"

The lesson to be drawn from Whitefield's chilling accusations against clerical piety was obvious. If New England was to be revived, the people would have to take the lead. The people would have to be the central characters in the new religious history. This note had been sounded before in England and the southern colonies. Now it was applied, with equal success (and unanticipated consequences), to New England Congregationalists.

Whitefield was not in New England long enough to see the divisive consequences of his rhetoric, but they came nonetheless. Along with new births came wrenching divisions, pitting clergy against clergy and the people against their ministers. This "awakening" was as much an awakening *against* the established churches as it was for them. Communal revivals became translocal events orchestrated by traveling strangers who appealed to individual experience rather than corporate responsibility. Though Whitefield's intent was not social upheaval, that would be the inevitable result of his adversarial rhetoric.

But with the divisions also would come positive lessons. The same power that Whitefield felt in the outdoor revival was felt by his audiences as well. In his brief but unforgettable New England tour he had delivered 175 sermons "besides exhorting very frequently in private." Although he was only an individual, the sheer frequency of his address had left an unforgettable imprint on both the clergy and the people. As elsewhere, New England audiences would learn that their voluntary assemblies could be orderly and constructive.

Whitefield could now survey his New World experience as a whole with the knowledge that the more he traveled in America, the more popular he became. His electrifying manner struck resonant chords with a colonial people that nothing in England could match. As he returned south in preparation for his return to England, Whitefield found himself strangely warmed to the New World and confessed that "all things concur to convince me that America is to be my chief scene for action."

8 Scottish Stranger Preacher

Whitefield's American tour convinced him that a truly transatlantic revival was possible and that he could be its symbolic center. Upon returning to England, he set about building a preaching "Tabernacle" at Moorfields. But he soon learned that standing-room-only crowds depended upon his presence. To succeed there, he would have to give it full-time attention and abandon his vocation as the traveling spark for an international revival. This he refused to do. Not only would a permanent "home" weaken the revivals, it would also lessen his effectiveness. If he were to stay in one place week in and week out, his "art" would be discovered in repetition and his unique impact would fade.

Besides, the competition with Arminian Anglicans on the one hand and Arminian Methodists on the other was too stiff. Already the Wesleys had moved in perfectionist directions and warned their hearers not to follow Whitefield. Whitefield responded by publishing an open letter to John Wesley condemning his denial of predestination in favor of "universal redemp-

133

tion" even as he confessed his ongoing "love and honour" to his Oxford friend. Whitefield could preach in London to be sure, but a permanent base would require him to found a rival movement, which he refused to do. Clearly a transatlantic movement could not be centered in England.

The future, Whitefield was convinced, lay in the provinces and colonies. Revivals there could create a pincer movement capable of closing back on England itself. While politics, economics, and learning were spreading fast from the metropolitan core to the provincial periphery, Whitefield envisioned the Calvinist revivals creating an opposite pattern, from the periphery inward. The principal cities of the periphery — Philadelphia, Boston, and Edinburgh — would be the enlightened nodal points from which true revival would spread through England and, from there, throughout Europe and the world. The groundwork had already been done in Philadelphia and Boston. That left Edinburgh and Scotland.

Among the provinces, Whitefield was always interested in Wales and Ireland and occasionally visited them. But his central interest was Scotland, for obvious reasons. Scotland in many ways resembled America, particularly the middle and New England colonies. Like America, Scotland emerged from the English Reformation with a strong dislike of episcopal government, Anglican ritual, and Arminian theology. Doctrinally the Scots continued to adhere to the Westminster Confession. Institutionally they organized themselves into a national Scottish Kirk following the Presbyterian blueprint of John Knox. As with American Puritans, so with Scottish Presbyterians — Calvin's Geneva had established forms of faith that created a perfect environment for Whitefield's novel presentation. In addition, Calvin's frequent usage of theatrical images and metaphors in his writings fit perfectly with Whitefield's own instincts.

The Scottish Kirk permeated all levels of society, creating a people who were highly literate and theologically sophisticated. Though respectful of a learned and settled ministry, they could and did do battle with their ministers on the clergy's own terms. Surviving lay confessions and testimonies confirm a literate population that regularly read the Bible and devotional manuals. In fact, Scottish lay religiosity was probably more informed and systematic than that in New England. While American Puritans paid lip service to the Westminster Confession, they never accorded it the centrality in their culture that it enjoyed in Scotland. Scottish Presbyterians internalized the larger catechism and could quote entire passages by memory. Total depravity, imputation, original sin, predestination, and effectual calling were common tokens of their everyday discourse and the terms they used for self-examination and understanding in private spiritual exercises and prayer.

Throughout the seventeenth and eighteenth centuries, revivals struck the Scottish Kirk with a cyclical regularity not unlike that of the New England town. Most of these were local and communal affairs that reinforced local authority and the church. They differed from those in England or America, however, in that some were led by "stranger preachers" or itinerant "field" preachers who toured the "mountains and valleys" sowing the seeds for local revival. Where American revivals were most dramatically registered in suddenly expanded church membership rates, Scottish revivals were even more immediately registered in on-the-scene "action sermons" that brought long lines of newly awakened to the communion table — and subsequently into church membership. The greater emphasis on the communion service in Scottish piety fit well with the comfort Whitefield derived from sacraments and rituals.

Along with revival, Scotland had its share of divisions. Often as not, these came less from deists or Arminians than from purists whose call for reformation sometimes led to schism and separation. As Whitefield contemplated his Scottish tour, he was aware of two major schismatics, the Erskine brothers, Ralph and Ebenezer. Both had been ordained ministers in the Scottish Kirk but had come to renounce the established church in favor of a new "Associate Presbytery" or "United Secession." Like their "Separatist" counterparts in America who were steadily gaining in numbers in Whitefield's absence, the Scottish Seceders were militantly Calvinist in theology and jealously protective of their lay prerogatives. They opposed the "tyranny" of presbyteries and synods and insisted that each congregation be free to choose and ordain its own pastor. They also required conversion narratives of all members and encouraged separation from local churches if spiritual needs were not being met.

While Whitefield was certain that his future lay with Calvinist revivals, he was not sure which strain of Calvinism he would endorse. Should it be the Calvinism of the established Congregational and Presbyterian churches or the radical separatism of a James Davenport or the Associate Presbytery? Initially his sympathies seemed to lie with the more radical dissenters. They, after all, best embodied the anti-institutional rhetoric he employed so effectively against the Anglicans. But did he want to extend that rhetoric against the Calvinists? Did he want, in other words, to become a social as well as religious radical? Scotland would prove to be decisive in altering his first instincts and drawing him closer to "moderate" Calvinist establishments.

Initially, the Seceders had Whitefield's loyalty. Already in March 1739, he had initiated a correspondence with Ralph Erskine. At this point, the Erskines had still not heard of Whitefield, and Ralph waited to reply "till I heard more about him." After reading the *Journal*, Erskine responded, setting in motion a series of mixed signals between the two that nearly destroyed Whitefield's ministry before it began.

Whitefield assumed that the Erskines would introduce him to their churches and, from there, to audiences of all denominations, as others had in America. The Erskines' assumption was quite different. Given Whitefield's initiation of the correspondence, they mistakenly assumed he understood their polity and sided with their secessionist doctrines, including an uncompromising insistence that separatistic Presbyterianism was the only true polity and that all other orders and ordinations must be renounced.

Whitefield and Seward meanwhile confidently continued correspondence, expecting to find in the Erskines the same base of support they had enjoyed in Tennent, Edwards, and Colman. Ever the promoter, Whitefield mixed news of his revivals with advertisements of his sermons. In February 1741, he wrote from on board the *Minerva*,

> thanks be to rich and sovereign grace, I have experienced much of the Spirit's influences in making nine Sermons, which I intend to print by subscription towards carrying on a Negro school, I am going to settle in Pennsylvania. The price of them will be four shillings. If you or your friends would take few, it might be for the glory of God. My Journal, which I bring over, will acquaint you how the work of God goes on abroad.

He requested information as well: "my ignorance of the constitution of the Scotch church, is the cause of my writing. . . . I should be obliged to you, if you would be pleased to recommend to me some useful books." The Erskines interpreted this as a sign of cooperation among friends. They decided to educate Whitefield further on the full extent of their separatism and rejection of all other churches.

In April 1741, on the eve of Whitefield's first visit to Scotland, Ralph Erskine wrote inviting him to join the Associate Presbytery. Such a move, he explained, would be exclusive. No Seceder could retain Anglican ordination, nor could he appear in nonsecessionist pulpits. At this point, almost too late, Whitefield realized what he had encountered in the Erskines. For the first time, he glimpsed the logical culmination of separatist leanings. Full alliance with the secessionists could only mean alienation from all other audiences. In a hastily composed reply to Ebenezer Erskine, he politely but firmly refused the offer: "This I cannot altogether come into. I come only as an occasional preacher, to preach the simple Gospel to all that are willing to hear me, of whatever denomination." With that he assumed he had ended the debate and that he would be welcomed on those terms.

On this assumption of goodwill, Whitefield arrived in Scotland in August to inaugurate his Scottish campaign. In keeping with his promise to the Erskines, he began his tour at Ralph Erskine's Dunfermline meetinghouse, where overflow audiences thrilled to his signature sermon on the nature and necessity of a New Birth. But trouble ensued. Immediately following his sermon, Whitefield was summoned to a formal meeting with ministers of the Associate Presbytery. They asked him to justify his Anglican ordination and habit of preaching in all pulpits. Dissatisfied with his explanation, the presbyters enjoined him to renounce his ordination and identify solely with them. This Whitefield would not do.

Soon the dialogue moved from ordination to questions of Scottish polity — an area Whitefield neither understood nor cared about. When asked how his views conformed to the Solemn League and Covenant — Scotland's ecclesiastical constitution — Whitefield replied contemptuously that he had no view at all, "being too busy about matters of . . . greater importance." As for preaching only in secessionist pulpits, the demand was unreasonable and counter to the whole transdenominational thrust of his message. Indeed, Whitefield continued, "if the Pope himself would lend me his pulpit, I would gladly proclaim the righteousness of Jesus Christ therein."

The meeting came to an impasse. The Erskines were willing to let well enough alone, but other Seceders were not so accommodating. Their purity would brook no compromise with those outside of their fold. In a widely circulated pamphlet entitled "A Warning against Countenancing the Ministrations of Mr. George Whitefield," the secessionist minister Adam Gib likened Whitefield to a "false Christ" whose great end in life "is to publish and celebrate himself." By refusing to renounce his Anglican ordination, Gib complained, Whitefield "has yet vomited that spiritual poison" of episcopacy on unsuspecting audiences. Whitefield had heard words like these before, but not from fellow Calvinists — and purists at that. Good theology did not guarantee Christian forbearance.

Whitefield wisely chose not to respond to Gib's pamphlet, instead promising a tolerant and ongoing "love and honour" for the Associate Presbytery as he had for the Wesleyan Methodists earlier. But he would attach himself to neither of them. With that declaration, a drift toward separatism was suddenly reversed. For the first time in his career, Whitefield had carried his barbs and rejection to the purists. Henceforth he would align with Calvinist moderates who held to tolerant Reformed theology and an educated ministry but did not require denominational identification. Neither Whitefield's ecumenical theology nor his actor's instinct for center stage would allow him to be preempted by local concerns and interests, whether Presbyterian, Methodist, Baptist, or New World Separatist.

The irony of the secessionist attack was not lost on Whitefield. In fact, it altered the shape of his ministry in profound ways. Suddenly, his closest allies were the moderate established Presbyterian clergy, such as William Macculloch of Cambuslang, James Robe of Kilsyth, Alexander Webster of Edinburgh, Thomas Gillespie of Carnock, John Willison of Dundee, James Ogilvie of Aberdeen, John Erskine of Edinburgh (no relation to Ralph), and John Gillies of Glasgow. They offered him their pulpits, and he in turn offered them a reinforcing revival that helped to stem a substantial secessionist drift before it ever really began. The Scottish revivals were *not* revivals against the churches. For the rest of his career Whitefield spoke against separatism and sought to inspire evangelical revivals within local established churches. No longer a fiery outsider condemning unconverted ministers, Whitefield became, instead, a sympathetic "stranger preacher" sent to reinforce Calvinist revival wherever he saw it.

Throughout the summer of 1741, and again in the spring of

1742, he traveled widely through West Scotland and Edinburgh, realizing successes as large as, if not larger than, any he enjoyed in Philadelphia or Boston. He began in Edinburgh, a bustling port city that boasted a population of seventy thousand. Although it did not compare with London, it was far larger than any American urban center and geographically central to many communities in southern Scotland. As in America, overflow audiences soon pushed Whitefield to the open fields. In his customary fashion, he preached daily outside of regular worship hours and collected badly needed offerings for the Georgian orphans, already over £1,000 in debt since the American tour.

One young admirer in the crowd was the moderate Scottish preacher John Gillies. In time Gillies and Whitefield became close friends (Gillies later prepared Whitefield's earliest biography), but on this visit they were strangers. As Gillies recalled, he could not help but notice Whitefield's "theatrical talent" and his "perfect self-command." Above all, Gillies was struck by the face. Whenever Whitefield spoke, he would preface his discourse "with a solemnity of manner, and an anxious expression of countenance." Once begun, his "actions" captivated hearers: "every accent of his voice spoke to the ear, every feature of his face, every motion of his hands, and every gesture spoke to the eye; so that the most dissipated and thoughtless found their attention involuntarily fixed." Throughout, Gillies continued, his "elocution was perfect." Even apparent losses of self-control, such as faltering speech or cascading tears, proved to be artistic and served to reinforce the delivery.

Whitefield's oft-repeated adaptation of a condemning English judge pronouncing final sentence on a capital offender was a particular favorite with Gillies. A solemn Whitefield would turn to his audience, eyes brimming with tears, voice shaking, and say, "I am now going to put on my condemning cap. Sinner I must do it: I must pronounce sentence upon you!" And then, repeating the words of Christ, he would declare: "Depart from me, ye cursed, into everlasting fire, prepared for the devil and his angels."

140

Gillies noted how the itinerant Whitefield moved with "such vehemence upon his bodily frame" that his audience actually shared his exhaustion and "felt a momentary apprehension even for his life." Where other congregations would leave uplifted or convicted, Whitefield's congregations left drained and emptied of all emotional resources. There was energy left for neither audience nor speaker.

From Edinburgh, Whitefield carried his message to outlying areas and rejoiced to find that the work of revival had already begun there among the local pastors. In the towns and villages of Perth, Dundee, Fintray, and especially in Glasgow and Aberdeen, he encountered enthusiastic audiences, which, he observed, were "much like that in New-England."

The parallel to New England is revealing, for in both places Whitefield was dealing with theologically informed popular audiences, and he adjusted his preaching accordingly. The drama remained, to be sure, but alongside it he injected a theological vocabulary and doctrinal emphasis that presupposed a knowing — and sympathetic — audience. In Glasgow, his inaugural sermon was the heavily doctrinal "The Lord Our Righteousness," in which he inveighed against all deniers of total depravity and imputation: "Come then, ye Arians, kiss the Son of God, bow down before him. . . . And as for you Socinians, who say Christ was a mere man . . . you are accursed."

Having established his doctrinal credentials, Whitefield proceeded in familiar fashion to address the passions. A divine Christ who is "an unapplied Christ, is no Christ at all." Then followed a set of questions framed in technical theological language but directed to personal experience: "Were you never made to abhor yourselves for your actual and original sins, and to loathe your own righteousness? Is Christ your sanctification, as well as your outward righteousness?" From fear of condemnation he turned abruptly to hope and the experience of regeneration: "Were you never made to see and admire the all sufficiency of Christ's righteousness, and excited by the spirit

141

of God to hunger and thirst after it? Could you ever say . . .
nothing but Christ! nothing but Christ! Give me Christ, O God,
and I am satisfied! Was this, I say, ever the language of your
hearts?"

The questions over, he turned to the application. In a
voice choked with sobs, he openly reflected on the state of his
hearers' souls:

> Alas, my heart almost bleeds! What a multitude of pre-
> cious souls are now before me! How shortly must all be
> ushered into eternity: and yet, O cutting thought! was
> God now to require all your souls, how few, compara-
> tively speaking, could really say, *The Lord our righ-
> teousness.*

Finally, in the persona of Christ, he pleaded, "Come then, poor,
guilty prodigals, come home. Indeed, I will not, like the elder
brother, be angry. No, I will rejoice with the angels in heaven."
As always, comfort, and not terror, proved to be the final word
in Whitefield's preaching. Part of the explanation for this is
clearly his own personality, but part may also be found in the
strong influence his mother exerted in childhood. The same
comfort his mother had provided him in youth, he would
dispense to his sin-sick audience. He was, after all, enacting her
destiny for him as well as his own.

Clearly Whitefield knew his audience's needs and
delivered the appropriate remedy. In a subsequent testimony
taken by William Macculloch, it appears that women were
especially receptive to his ministry. One "young woman about
nineteen years" saw Whitefield preach in the Glasgow courtyard. She declared his message was so powerful that "when
that minister spoke of the Prodigals going into a far country, I
thought that he was exactly describing me." Following the
sermon, the young woman proceeded to the communion table
and into active church membership.

Another young woman, Mary Scot, wrote Macculloch
about her experience of Whitefield at Glasgow. The letter re-

veals both Whitefield's power and the way in which he used print and speech to reinforce one another:

> Before Mr. Whitefield came to Glasgow my time was spent in nothing but madness and Vanity. . . . When I went to church it was only to se and be seen. . . . In reading Mr. Whitefield's two leters to Bishop Tillotson I was much afected with the last, so I had a strong inclination to hear him as he came. The first text I heard him preach on was The Lord our Righteousness, and according to his viserall freedom he said he could say, that the Lord was his Reighteousnes, which I was strangly afected with, and stayed so closs with me that I durst not be what I had bene before. Prayer then was a pleasure to me. I stayd no more on dresing my self as formerly. I heard nine sermons of him in Glasgow and fouer in Paisly and could no more take up with carnall mirth I was so impressed with Spiritual things and the medetation of what I had heard or read.

Yet another "young woman of 20 years" described a similar experience. She first became attracted to the idea of revival when "about five or six years ago, I heard Mr. Edwards Narrative of the Surprising Work of God at Northampton read; I was very glad to hear that there was such a work of conversion in these far and grand places." Later, "when I read Mr. Whitefield's Journals before he came to Scotland, I was glad that God had raised up so remarkable an Instrument of good to many . . . and I thought that if I might hear him, I might get good also." Upon news of Whitefield's arrival in Glasgow, she rushed to the courtyard and heard "him preach his first Sermon on these words — the Lord our Righteousness and was made sensible of the vanity and insufficiency of all righteousness of my own. . . . I continued to hear him from day to day . . . and thought every Sermon I heard greater than another."

As Whitefield continued to issue his stirring calls to repentance and regeneration, he collected a steady stream of much-needed offerings for Bethesda. General offerings totaled

£500 for the orphan house. Most of these came from ordinary men and women attracted to the evangelical revivals. But the nobility also took part, led by the Marquis of Lothian and Lord Ray. Again, older women proved especially helpful. Lady Mary Hamilton, Lady Frances Gardiner, Lady Jane Nimms, and Lady Dirleton all contributed substantial sums to his ministry. Together these provided Whitefield with a horse for his travels in Scotland and additional offerings for the orphan house.

The unprecedented enthusiasm and support of Scottish audiences convinced Whitefield that the transatlantic revival had become a reality. He returned to London and the Moorfields Tabernacle brimming with enthusiasm and planning for an imminent return engagement to Scotland. In the few intervening months, he labored in London to shore up his Tabernacle ministry and coordinate transatlantic communications.

Earlier than most, Whitefield recognized that any effective transatlantic movement required sophisticated communications and publicity. Letter-writing networks were important, but the movement had already grown too large to be effectively canvassed by circulating letters. Other means would have to be devised.

Of all the possibilities, Whitefield was most taken with the idea of a religious magazine. His *Journals* taught him the value of popular print. A magazine could do all his *Journals* had done and more. Already in April 1741, on the eve of his departure for Scotland, he had taken over a magazine entitled *The Weekly History; or, An Account of the Most Remarkable Particulars Relating to the Present Progress of the Gospel.*

The first issue appeared on April 11, 1741. It bore the name of Whitefield's printer friend John Lewis on the masthead. But in reality it was a Whitefield production, filled with news of his revivals and charitable enterprises. And, as in his itinerancy, it anticipated trends that would become commonplace in subsequent generations. In format, the paper appealed to a popular audience with anticipated features geared to popu-

lar interest. Unlike more elite magazines sold by annual subscription, *The Weekly History* was sold on a cheap-for-cash format not unlike that of the nineteenth-century penny press.
Distribution came through local societies and Whitefield's pre-
existent letter-writing network. For those unable to afford even
the low cost of an issue, Whitefield provided a lending service
where interested readers could "repair to the Printer's House
to read 'em gratis."

Besides using the press to record the new history of revival, Whitefield used it for advance publicity. Already in the
spring *The Weekly History* published accounts of his upcoming
visit to Scotland. In addition, it reprinted letters Whitefield
received from other ministers in the transatlantic network, including Josiah Smith in Charleston, Thomas Noble in New
York, the Tennents in Pennsylvania, and Benjamin Colman and
William Cooper in Boston. News from the orphan house also
figured prominently. Regular reports from superintendent
Habersham described the building projects and the inhabitants.
Alongside these accounts, the paper included conversion narratives penned by the ten- and eleven-year-old residents of the
orphan house. To lend authenticity and poignancy, their testimonies were "spell'd precisely as they wrote them."

Whether through letters, reports, or sermons, the magazine's subject matter was taken up exclusively with the cause
of worldwide revival. Having already led the way with field
preaching and fund raising, Whitefield now pioneered with
religious journalism. All articles were of a piece and made
perfect promotional sense. With everything so new and exciting, a sense of great happenings and imminent glories grew
apace. Whenever reports or correspondence trickled in, the
magazine picked up the stories and disseminated them to
hundreds of readers simultaneously.

Besides learning of the triumphs of the revival, readers
learned of its trials. As persecutions gathered strength, the
revival's friends were urged to speak out against them. John
Cennick reported an attack at Wiltshire during Whitefield's

145

Scotland preaching tour, when thirty ruffians fell on the out-door audience:

> [all] on a sudden came a Company, with weapons, clubs, and staves, into the orchard, crying out, *knock him down! knock him down!* I broke out of my sermon, and began to exhort the dear Flock to steadfastness, and constancy. O what shrieks and cries were heard among them! They soon got round me, and thrust at me. . . . Others of both Sexes, but chiefly Women, they dragged away by their Hair, and having thrown them down, trampled on them.

Sensational stories like Cennick's filled the spaces between ac-counts of mass revivals, keeping the readers' energies vitally focused on the life-and-death struggles of the new revivals.

Whitefield recognized a good idea when he saw one, and he urged his Scottish and American co-laborers to begin journal-istic endeavors of their own. Almost immediately, widely dis-tributed imitators appeared. The first was the *Glasgow Weekly History,* begun by William Macculloch in December 1741. Most of Macculloch's stories were lifted directly from *The Weekly History,* with special emphasis on items of interest to Scottish readers. James Robe established a similar imitator in Edinburgh with the *Christian Monthly History.* In America, Thomas Prince's *Christian History* began publication in Boston in 1743, through the publishing offices of Kneeland and Green.

Although short-lived, all of these creations served the indispensable function of recording a new history in the making. At the same time, they reinforced a popular sense of international significance. For the first time, ordinary men and women were taking actions that placed them at the forefront of *news.* Like Whitefield and his clerical associates, they were all "somebodies" in a glorious cause. Their first halting steps in the direction of a religious journalism transcended their immediate impact, however, for they represented the founda-tion of an evangelical publishing empire destined to dominate Anglo-American print culture in the next century.

Throughout the winter of 1741-42, Macculloch's *Glasgow Weekly History* and Whitefield's *Weekly History* printed endless letters recording the happy results of Whitefield's first Scottish tour. Not only were communities revived, it was reported; they were also driven to reform. Whitefield described with particular satisfaction the disastrous effects of his preaching on the Edinburgh theater. He reproduced one letter reporting that "the first Night a Play was acted here this Season there were but about six ladies at it; the second two: and the third and last none at all."

By early spring 1742, Macculloch had strange and exciting news of his own from the small village of Cambuslang. Through letters and press, an international audience began following the progress of a "great awakening" that sounded like another Northampton in the making. That winter Macculloch had been preaching regularly on the necessity of regeneration. He had followed his sermons with informal meetings at which magazine accounts of current revivals were read and prayed about. His parishioners had shown special interest in stories of mass conversions that had taken place in New England under "Mr. Whitefield's ministry."

Already in February lay leaders observed that the prayers and readings had produced a greater-than-normal interest in religion among the town's two hundred families. Macculloch began holding evening services during the week with recurrent accounts of dramatic conversions. Soon neighbors began to flock to the sermons. On Thursday, February 18, Macculloch preached a sermon on the famous Whitefield theme "The Lord Our Righteousness." The sermon text does not survive, though it undoubtedly followed the conversionist theme of justification by faith alone that Whitefield had preached earlier. The effects were similar as well. Many burst into tears and became so agitated they could not sit still. Others followed Macculloch into his dining room after the sermon to inquire what must they do to be saved. In all, fifty inquirers remained, and fifteen embraced Christ and got "relief from their soul distress."

Throughout the spring of 1742, news of "The Cam'slang Wark" spread throughout southern Scotland, attracting people from other towns and villages. On March 4, Whitefield heard of the "great awakening" in progress and wrote Macculloch a letter of encouragement, urging him to continue daily preaching. By April the awakening showed no sign of abating, and Macculloch wrote Whitefield that "in less than three Months past, about 300 Souls have been awakened. . . . Some have computed the Hearers, these two last Lord's-days, to have been Nine or Ten-thousand." He closed the letter by saying, "I long much to see you here. Let me know by the first opportunity when you think to be with us."

Words like these had the desired effect. In no time Whitefield determined to return and be a part of the great event. In late spring he turned the Tabernacle over to his English associate John Cennick. This time there would be no preliminary meeting with the Seceders. Nor did Whitefield welcome their obstructionism. To head off trouble, he reprinted a letter on toleration, urging the Scots to "let not Bigotry or Party-Zeal be so much as once named among you." He went on to encourage all to participate in revival: "uniting in Heart and Spirit with all that is *holy* and *good* in all Churches, we enter into the true Communion of Saints, and become real Members of the holy Catholick Church."

Whitefield arrived in Scotland on June 3, just in time to catch the revivals at their peak. En route to Cambuslang, he stopped at Glasgow and preached to an enthusiastic audience of twenty thousand. Many of his listeners had been dividing their time between Glasgow and Cambuslang, and now they carried the exciting news of Whitefield's arrival to Macculloch. Again, Whitefield proved to be less the creator than a powerful catalyst and symbol of success, bringing a sense of international significance and culmination to the local work.

By June 6, Whitefield was at Cambuslang. He began immediately to preach that morning and evening. His evening service attracted thousands and continued until 2:00 A.M. The excitement was unforgettable: "there were scenes of uncontrollable distress, like a field of battle. . . . All night in the fields, might be heard the voice of prayer and praise." Such was the excitement that he concluded, "it far out-did all that I ever saw in America." Once begun, events gathered ever-increasing momentum. On Saturday, Whitefield preached to an estimated twenty thousand people in services that stretched well into the night. On Sunday, at a special communion service celebrated in the fields, over 1,700 communicants streamed alongside long communion tables set up in preaching tents. Following the sacrament, Whitefield preached again in the evening on Isaiah 54:5, a sermon entitled "Thy Maker Is Thy Husband." By many accounts, this was the most powerful sermon of the revival. Later he recalled that wherever he walked "you might have heard persons praying to, and praising God. The children of God came from all quarters."

An examination of this sermon reveals its power. He enjoined his hearers, in passionate terms generally reserved for husbands and wives, to be "married to Jesus Christ." The timing for such a whimsical, almost romantic sermon was perfect. Many in his audience had heard protracted sermons on sin and condemnation that left them emotionally distraught; they were ready for a message of love and divine passion. Often Whitefield invoked maternal images of comfort to assuage punished souls. This time he turned to romantic love.

To set the mood, Whitefield began in the persona of a divine messenger sent on a mission "to take a wife for his Master's son, asking if there was any there that wanted to take Christ for their husband, and bidding them come and he would marry them to Christ." Instead of donning the cap of the condemning Judge, he impersonated the marriage agent for Christ. One convert recorded the sermon's effect, describing how "after . . . he laid out the terms [of marriage to Christ] I found my heart made Sweetly to agree."

Printed accounts of the Cambuslang awakening quickly appeared in the journals, magazines, and newspapers. Other more elaborate accounts were prepared by clerical friends of this and other revivals who sought to confirm their lasting impact. In style, their accounts were modeled directly on Edwards's *Narrative of Surprising Conversions*. First the writers provided a physical description of the town and a general summary of manners and morals before the revivals. These they followed with accounts of the revivals and descriptions of lasting changes in piety and morals. Ecstatic behavior alone, they knew, could not legitimate Cambuslang. As in Northampton, it had to be followed with a reformation of manners and morals.

In James Robe's *Faithful Narrative of the Extraordinary Work of the Spirit of God at Kilsyth,* readers learned how an entire town had been transformed almost overnight. They read of audience enthusiasm that bordered on uncontrollable passion: "the Bodies of some of the Awakened are seized with Trembling, Fainting, Histerisms in some few Women, and with Convulsive-Motions in some others." They learned as well that all of these manifestations had already been seen "in our *American* colonies . . . that hath occasioned the Rev. and Judicious Mr. Edwards . . . to preach and publish a sermon upon the distinguishing Marks of a Work of the Spirit of God."

The moderate Presbyterian minister Alexander Webster confessed his initial skepticism about the revivals but reported that after having visited the meetings at Cambuslang he had changed his mind:

> a solemn profound Reverence o'erspreads every Countenance; — They hear as Creatures made for Eternity, who don't know but next Moment they must account to their great Judge. Thousands are melted down into Tears; — Many cry out in the Bitterness of their Soul. . . . Talk of a precious Christ, ALL seem to breathe after him. — Describe his Glory, how ravished do *many* appear! — How captivate with his Loveliness! — Open the Wonders of his Grace, and the *silent* Tears drop almost from *every* eye. . . . These, *Dear Sir,* are the visible Effects of this *extraordinary* Work.

Webster conceded that some conversions might be "transient." But in the main, he believed, the converts were "sincere" and their feelings were no mere "passing conviction." Rather, there ensued a permanent alteration in character that confirmed the occasion of it as a work of God.

William Macculloch also prepared an elaborate handwritten collection of conversion narratives, gathered over a period of several years, with the intention of publishing them. In all, it included the accounts of 106 converts, filling two volumes and over 1,300 pages of closely written manuscript. The chronicle of conversions was never published, but it is preserved in Edinburgh's New College and stands as one of the most remarkable testimonies of eighteenth-century lay piety ever compiled. In many respects it represents a microcosm of the people most strongly attracted to the revivals. The majority of converts were young, between the ages of 16 and 25. Females outnumbered males by a ratio of two to one. And most were ordinary people without connections or major political office; only one "gentleman" appears in the accounts. For the most part, the revivals were an ordinary affair, attracting those on the margins of respectability and social status: tenant farmers, craftsmen, colliers, and, throughout, women.

Many of Macculloch's transcriptions were taken down years after the Cambuslang revival, yet the subjects remembered the events with an immediacy that confirmed a life-transforming experience. Throughout, the influence of local ministers is clear, as well as Whitefield's role as inner accelerator. One unmarried woman, "aged 32," heard Whitefield's sermons on "Elisha multiplying the widow's oil" (1 Kings 17:10-16) and confessed that the imagery was so sharp "that I could almost repeat the whole of these two discourses, and that I repeated the most of the first of these, applying it to my self, and saying that I was the empty soul the Lord was filling and pouring the oil of his grace into."

Other accounts confirm Whitefield's power to evoke vivid images. After hearing the marriage sermon, an unmarried

woman recalled parts of Whitefield's dialogue: when he said,
" 'I'll tell you one thing that hinders your marriage with Christ,
and that is your unbelief' this came with power and melted me
down, and I was made to see, that this was just the thing that
had kept me from Christ." Hearing the same sermon, a young
unmarried man confessed,

> I felt love to Christ in my Soul, and so much joy that the
> sweet offers of Christ as a husband to my Soul that the
> joy of my heart had almost made me to cry out among
> the people, that I was ready to strike hands on the Bargain.
> And after sermon meeting with a Lad of my acquaintance,
> who I knew had been under Exercize, I just flew with my
> Arms about him, and said, such a minister has marrieed
> my Soul to Christ. And I lay down on the Brae, and I was
> so filled with the Love of Christ and contempt of the
> World, that I even wished, if it were the Lords will, that
> I might die on the spot.

Another unmarried man, "aged 28," confessed that, at
first, he was indifferent to the revival, "and thus I continued
till hearing a minister [Whitefield] concerning the woman with
the Bloody issue, that came behind Christ for a touch of the
hem of his garment; I thought I would have given all the world,
if I had had it, for one touch of Christ by faith."

With the joy came tears. Whitefield did not hesitate to
pronounce sin and guilt in Calvinist terms that enacted graphi-
cally what all knew doctrinally to be true. One particularly
articulate and doctrinally informed young woman recalled
how quotations from the Larger Catechism frequently crossed
her mind, "particularly the answer to that Q. 75 wherin consists
the sinfulness of that Estate wherein man fell? The sinfulness
of that Estate . . . is the guilt of Adam's fall . . . whereby he is
wholly disabled. . . . This account of original Sin I felt . . . to
agree exactly to what I was by nature, when I looked back on
my former ways."

By enacting sin and guilt, Whitefield placed almost unbearable strains on his hearers. A woman "about 30 years of age" recalled how Whitefield said, "ye wonder what makes these people cry so: but if the Lord would be pleased to open your Eyes, as he has done theirs, ye would see your hearts all crawling with Toads of Corruptions, and surrounded with Legions of Devils." This image, she continued, "did not affect me much at the time, yet when I came home I took on a Strong apprehension that it was so, and imagined that I felt them within me crawling up my Throat to my mouth, and turned away my eyes that I might not see them coming out of my mouth."

Often Whitefield's graphic imagery incited images or visions in Scottish audiences that had few immediate parallels in Northampton's experience. Behind the images, one almost senses the tortured imagination of the long-abandoned Oxford Odd Fellow. One forty-year-old man confessed how, while hearing Whitefield at Cambuslang,

> I fell under great Terror, and thought I would certainly perish for ever: and while I was hearing in this condition, with my hand over my Eyes, Hell was represented to my mind, as a Pit at the foot of a Hill, and a great drove of people marching into it, and I along with them, and when I was got very near it, I thought I looked over my shoulder, and saw a very beautiful man, who smiled on me and made a motion to me with his hand to come back at which I was very glad.

Whitefield's preaching in Scotland encouraged these powerful visions to a far greater extent than it had in America. Following one of Whitefield's evening sermons on the preaching brae, a young man recalled,

> I fell into a swoon, (tho I did not cry any) a horror of great darkness coming over me. . . . And in the middle of this Swoon, my bodily eyes being shut, I thought I saw a clear light all at once shining about me as when the Sunshines bright at Noon, and apprehended that I was in a very

large room. There was represented to my mind a very large scroll of papers, let down as from the roof above filling the breadth of the room . . . and it appeared to be all printed over in large distinct lines and letters. But when I thought I essayed to read I found I could not read. . . . Only it was impressed on my mind that was a scroll containing all my Sins that were all marked and recorded before God. And after a little the Scroll was drawn up again, and I recovered out of my swoon.

Such was the envisioning power of Whitefield's sermons that many ministers were led to thoughts of apocalypse. The incidence of mass conversions, dreams, and visions put one and all in an eschatological mind. While Jonathan Edwards was actively speculating on an American millennium, his Scottish colleagues were doing the same in Scotland. The young John Erskine was so convinced not only of the permanent effects but of their significance that he went on to predict the millennium. In a widely circulated sermon entitled "The Signs of the Times Considered," he pointed to the evidences of the last days. One prophecy of the end days was preaching of unprecedented power: "And have we not seen the Rev. Mr. *Whitefield* preaching the Word, instant in Season and out of Season, and willing to *spend* and *be spent* for the Gospel?" Clearly, even greater things were in store.

Perceived similarities between Scotland and Northampton had their significance too. In a letter to Benjamin Colman published in the Boston press, the Rev. John Willison of Dundee compared "the work" there to Northampton and noted how "the Lord hath been pleased to begin a work much like that in New England." Besides supplying news, letters like this had the effect of cementing the Scottish-American evangelical connection that would thrive throughout the remainder of the eighteenth century and beyond.

Along with great audiences and enthusiasm came stupendous offerings, rivaling any Whitefield had seen in London or New England. In his study of revival offerings, Arthur Fawcett found that offerings that averaged £3-12 per service swelled to an unequaled £194 at Whitefield's second communion service. All told, annual giving for Bethesda jumped from a respectable £146 in the 1741 tour to an astounding £1,445 in 1742 — a tenfold increase. Through their gifts as well as their prayers, magazines, and correspondence, Scots and Americans were being drawn together into a transatlantic evangelical fellowship that had also become a big business.

Whitefield's "great awakening" in Scotland convinced him that his strategy of reaching England by working from the periphery inward was correct. As social and political elites looked increasingly to England for models of polite literature and taste, Whitefield inverted the process of "Anglicization" and made England a religious province of Scottish-America. Through his preaching and publications, he helped to create a strong sense of continuity binding America (especially Boston and Philadelphia) to Scotland (especially Edinburgh and Glasgow). Youthful American leaders such as Tennent, Davenport, Edwards, and Wheelock, together with their Scottish counterparts John Erskine, John Witherspoon, John Gillies, John Willison, and Thomas Gillespie, would, together with Whitefield, work to establish a Calvinist consensus in the eighteenth century capable of challenging Anglican Arminianism, deism, and Wesleyan Methodism. If the consensus could not transform England, it could and did define the cultural mainstream of Scotland and America in ways that defied their status as "cultural provinces." The future was bright, and no one, including the twenty-eight-year-old Whitefield, knew where it would end.

9 Women and Marriage

Whitefield was between his triumphant tours of Scotland when he made the quiet announcement that on November 14, 1741, he had married the widow Mrs. Elizabeth James in Abergavenny, South Wales. For one as attuned to making news as Whitefield, the lack of fanfare is surprising. Within two weeks of the marriage, he was back in his usual pattern of preaching, traveling, and preparing for the great revival at Cambuslang, as if nothing had happened. And, in fact, little had. Judging from letters, memoirs, and Whitefield's own writings, Elizabeth Whitefield played no direct role in her husband's travels and ministries. Over the years, what little emotional content there may have been to the relationship diminished in the face of extended absences, infrequent communications, and public preoccupations. To all intents and purposes, Elizabeth Whitefield lived out her marriage as little more than one more treasured but distant ally in Whitefield's public ministry.

To a remarkable extent, Whitefield's nineteenth- and twentieth-century biographers have shared in his silence. One reads their work in vain for any direct attention to Elizabeth James or, for that matter, to the role women played more generally in Whitefield's life. Yet, there is an important story here that reveals both Whitefield's complex relationship to women and the role of women in the evangelical revival generally.

Historians have identified the mid-eighteenth century as the crucial point of transition in which a new culture of romantic love began to replace traditional matrimony determined by community and parental involvement. The same forces of mobility and marketplace anonymity that were transforming religion and creating an unprecedented focus on the self were transforming the family and relations between the sexes. "Falling in love" was becoming to marriage and the family what being "born again" was to religion and the church. In both cases, the experience was intensely subjective and personal, transcending understanding and rationality and appealing to the passions for corroboration and "assurance." Trends begun in the 1750s continued into the nineteenth century, leading to the triumph of Victorian sentimentalism in the family and of highly emotional "great revivals" in Anglo-American evangelical Protestantism. Both were expressions of the same transformations. With the public square increasingly devoid of extended family, community, and national churches, the private self and its experience became the locus of meaning.

Given the parallels between impassioned romantic love and the New Birth, methodists might be expected to have embraced both conversion in religion and romantic love in marriage. But, as in so many social transformations, changes in family and spirituality were uneven and inconsistent. In fact, methodists opposed impassioned love with the same hostility they directed toward the theater, and for many of the same reasons. Each represented an "idol" that competed with the self-contained and exclusive world of the New Birth. Romantic love, like the theater that did so much to promote it, was part of "the world" and, as such, entirely condemned.

To a considerable extent, Whitefield's world was shaped

by methodist demands. His old attraction to the theater had to be redirected in light of the New Birth and the methodist code of behavior. His old attitudes and inclinations toward women and marriage had to be similarly reshaped. Central to the methodist code was the insistence that no passion or emotional commitment be stronger than the "spiritual marriage" to Christ and his church. In practice, this meant that impassioned feelings between the sexes had to be suppressed to prevent the possibility of idolatry. Instead of watching romantic passions carefully to keep them in rein or using them as an analogy for spiritual regeneration, methodists sought to annihilate them altogether. In this system, celibacy was the highest calling. If celibacy was not possible, then marriage was allowed, but only within carefully prescribed emotional and sexual limits. Sex existed primarily for procreation. Passions could not be given full play lest they destroy self-control and Christian discipleship.

Methodists did more to subvert the dawning Victorian morality than simply to renounce sentimental love. At the same time they suppressed human passion, they elevated women to major leadership roles in the movement. Here too, we see the unevenness of historical change. The same all-embracing counterculture that renounced romantic love and targeted attractive women for special criticism affirmed women in ministry. Methodism provided eighteenth-century women with outlets for leadership and influence outside of the home that would not be seen again in mainstream Protestant churches until the twentieth century.

Judging from the Methodist denomination's later rejection of women in ministry, it would appear that the earlier encouragement of female preaching stemmed less from an ongoing theological commitment to inclusive ministry than from the desperation of a "dispossessed" religious movement. It was this, along with the numerical dominance of women in the revivals, that led methodists to grant women a dominant position in the early period; in fact, they exercised power in disproportionate numbers at all levels of organization. Some served as class and band leaders, "callers" on the sick and imprisoned, "exhorters" who prayed and preached in female societies, and, most significantly, as itinerant ministers throughout the English and Welsh countryside. Some of the powerful noblewomen who were drawn to the inclusiveness and spirituality of methodism such as Darcy, Lady Maxwell of Scotland, Lady Margaret, Lady Betty Hastings, Mary, Lady Fitzgerald, and, most importantly, Lady Selena, Countess of Huntington, served as essential supporters — and sometime exhorters — who opened chapels and underwrote many methodist expenses. Most of these methodist women gravitated toward the Wesleyan Arminian camp, but some could also be found among the Calvinist methodist "connexion," especially in Scotland and Wales.

Women preachers encountered opposition and persecution to an even greater extent than the men. As uneducated women speaking publicly, they were doubly offensive. Their crude delivery and manners were an offense to the studied oratory of the pulpit, and their gender was an offense to the implicit "rules" of public address and propriety. Methodist women not only spoke — and, by that act alone, challenged authority — but they often did so in loud, aggressive voices, with dramatic gestures that demonstrated an "unfeminine degree of boldness." Women were supposed to be timid and silent; methodist exhorters were neither.

A case in point was Sarah Crosby, who began an itinerant ministry in the 1760s and whose career paralleled Whitefield's in significant ways. Like Whitefield, she had both stamina and intensity, extending her itinerancies over twenty years and sometimes preaching to as many as four meetings a day. She was known and approved by both Whitefield and the Wesleys, who saw in her a "maternal pastor" who cared for nothing save her public ministry. Like them, she was a gifted extemporaneous speaker who often experienced "great liberty in speaking." In one year Crosby traveled 960 miles, preached 120 sermons, led 600 private band meetings, and composed over 100 letters to associates in the methodist network. As Whitefield grabbed international attention and the Wesleys founded an institution, exhorters like Crosby carried the mission of New Birth inland to the rural heartland of England, speaking in homes, fields, and cottages with great success. Revivals came and went, but the work Crosby and women like her established in homes and neighborhoods provided the enduring base on which the rising Methodist denomination would rest.

In other ways as well, methodist women participated as equals in the new evangelical world. When not actively preaching, they kept journals for circulation among their colleagues. Crosby's journals totaled over one thousand pages. In them appears the same systematic attention to devotion, service, and careful use of time found in the diaries of male methodist leaders. Anything that detracted from the movement or seemed worldly was repudiated. Another diarist, Hester Ann Roe Rogers, described her conversion and ensuing renunciation of such "ensnaring follies" as theater and dance. She also told of cutting her hair short and destroying her fine clothing and caps, limiting her attire to a plain homespun that effectively hid her sexuality.

As "maternal pastors," women preachers suppressed their sexuality and viewed themselves as "sisters" or "mothers" to the church. Most renounced the world, and to some extent this entailed a renunciation of private love and marriage. Insofar as the language of sexuality or love appeared at all, it tended to be as metaphor for the believer's "marriage" to Christ. Female methodists, no less than male, evidenced a loyalty to the cause of revival that was so monolithic as to place all private joys and affections — including the family — in a secondary role.

Not surprisingly, many marriages among early methodist leaders were unhappy and unfulfilled. John Wesley made a notoriously unsuccessful marriage to Grace Murray. Receiving no support from his wife, he often turned to other committed pastors, male and female, such as Hester Ann Roe Rogers, whose chief loyalty as a young methodist centered in the fifty-year-old Wesley. When Elizabeth Ritchie, another Wesley admirer of particular beauty, turned down a proposal of marriage, she explained to Wesley that "to be wholly devoted to God seems to me all that is worth living for. This may be done in a married state, I make no doubt, but I cannot see that I have any call to change." Later Ritchie did change and, with her marriage, confirmed the itinerants' worst fears by leaving the ministry. Sarah Crosby, on the other hand, embarked on her long itinerant career only after her disapproving husband deserted her. With that, however, she discovered a lifelong public calling that took her out of the household and into the front ranks of methodist "disturbers."

In the absence of extensive families or fixed private relationships of their own, most of the traveling male and female itinerants concentrated their social activities within methodist "companies" whose primary function was devotion, prayer, confession, and mutual support. Rarely would male and female itinerants travel together, but wherever they stopped, they held protracted meetings for prayer and mutual encouragement. Powerful bonds developed among them that transcended more conventional attachments to husband, wife, or family.

In Whitefield, we find one who was very much a part of this male and female methodist network. Like the others, he held ambivalent attitudes toward women and marriage that inclined him toward women-in-ministry rather than women-in-love. Privately he renounced romantic passion and determined on a course of celibacy. Failing that, he resolved to marry only on the condition that he would not "preach one sermon or travel one day less, in a married than in a single state." Publicly, he welcomed female preachers as co-pastors and targeted women as his primary support group. While he made it a point never to travel with women, he did meet with them at every stop and relied heavily on their assistance. Throughout his writings, there is not so much as a hint of a theological scruple against women in ministry. Nor did he hesitate to solicit their help in whatever form it appeared. In the pages of his early *Journals,* he described no fewer than fifty women in a variety of roles ranging from matrons to hosts to supplicants and admirers. Many also appeared in his correspondence. In the three-volume set of collected letters preserved in his *Works,* over three hundred are addressed to women. He conveyed in all of them a sense of shared ministry and mutual concern. In fact, from the letters alone, it is often impossible to ascertain whether the correspondent is male or female.

Many women in Whitefield's journals and correspon-dence are reminiscent of his mother — older, spiritual, and liberal with their encouragement and financial support. Early in his career, he happily met with "that elect lady" Betty Hast-ings and gratefully "partook of her ladyship's bounty." Later, when orphan house finances sagged, he was pleased to report a gift for the "society Room": "Mrs. C—— gives it, and I believe, will make it fifty. This gentlewoman has been made instrumen-tal in relieving me of my late distress." Through their gifts and support, maternal women supplied the emotional comfort that would constitute the central theme of Whitefield's message of redeeming grace.

But older women were not the only women in his life. As a young, charismatic itinerant, Whitefield soon discovered that young women — no matter how spiritual and committed — would not assist him in his vows of celibacy. So attractive women who were neither maternal benefactors nor field preachers had to be in spiritual distress before he would grant them his personal attention. And the number of such cases grew steadily. In Philadelphia, for example, he noted, "I was sent for to a young woman, who was carried home from meet-ing, and had continued almost speechless. I prayed with her, and heard afterwards she was in a more comfortable state." These women — and one suspects the numbers increased as they realized his concern — did receive Whitefield's attention, and, coincidentally, weakened his resolve for celibacy. As one who in his youth had evidenced all the normal interests in sex and passion, he simply could not maintain his resolve of celibacy. Marriage became necessary, in part to relieve his own sexual needs and, perhaps equally important, to eliminate the advances of eligible young women and so restore his full attention to the pulpit.

In confronting the necessity of marriage, Whitefield also confronted the passions that raged within. The extent of his attraction to women and sex — and his own fears of both — can be inferred from the virulent condemnations he leveled at attractive women. Where Jonathan Edwards concentrated his greatest attacks on the merchant "river gods" who threatened his Northampton pulpit, with their characteristic sins of male pride, covetousness, and greed, Whitefield focused his attacks on attractive women and the accompanying sins of "lust," "worldliness," and "idolatry." In Boston he praised the piety of the male ministers but complained of "much of the pride of life to be seen in their assemblies. Jewels, patches, and gay apparel are commonly worn by the female sex." At Newport, he observed "some foolish virgins" at church, "covered all over with the pride of life." Later he complained that "nothing gives me more offence than to see clergymen's wives dressed out in the pride of life. . . . From such a wife, good Lord, of thy Infinite mercy, deliver me!" If women-in-service gained high marks of praise, other women — particularly attractive women — received the harshest censure. Rarely did he level similar charges against young men.

Given the methodist code and his own sense of destiny, Whitefield somehow had to marry without sacrificing his passion for ministry. In his own mind, this meant that feelings of attraction and sexuality had to be ruthlessly suppressed, even as he searched for a compatible wife. The search occupied him for two years, through 1740 and 1741, and involved two proposals. His first proposal culminated an unacknowledged affair of the heart that virtually destroyed itself; the second, successful proposal was a product of sheer calculation.

Whitefield first proposed marriage to a young and attractive convert named Elizabeth Delamotte. He had first met her through her brother Charles, who had traveled to Georgia with the Wesleys and stayed on through Whitefield's first visit. Through Charles, Whitefield gained entry into the well-to-do Delamotte home and preached there often. In the course of meeting with the family, he came to fall in love with "Betsy" — a fact that was never recognized for what it was. His diary entries simply note a newfound source of enthusiasm and vigor. While staying with the Delamottes, he rejoiced in his *Journal*, "Oh, the comforts of being all of one mind in a house! It begins our heaven upon earth." Later, after preaching at the Delamotte estate, an ebullient Whitefield proclaimed that "my mouth was ever filled with the Divine praise!" But he never specifically identified these enraptured feelings with Elizabeth.

Whitefield was clearly falling passionately in love but was unable to admit it to Delamotte or himself. Such feelings had no place in the heart of a famous itinerant bound for a New World ministry. At the very time he departed for his second great tour of the American colonies, he was in a romantic crisis. Yet at some level he neither articulated nor understood, the passions that created such conflicts within him also helped fire preaching performances unrivaled by any he had yet delivered in America. Whitefield's diary entries for this period are revealing. In between accounts of stunning triumphs, he makes frequent but unspecified references to "inward trials" that turned on his uncertain love. Also conspicuous in the diary entries is guilt — "a deeper sense of my own vileness, than I have felt for some time." Clearly, he was both obsessed with Delamotte and hating himself for the "vile" passions and potential ruin such love might bring to his public career. There was no middle ground. He could not think of a woman in sensuous terms as anything but a rival of Christ, a threat siphoning off passions that ought to be reserved exclusively for ministry.

The more Whitefield poured his frustrated love and

loneliness into his preaching, the more spectacular were the results. But at the same time, he could not rid his mind of Delamotte. Finally, in desperation, he wrote Delamotte's brother William a letter obviously intended for her to read. In it, William became the surrogate for Whitefield's fears for Betty and himself. The letter warned William to be "kept from idolatry" and not to "be led into temptation." Such sentiments hardly seem appropriate with respect to William, but as a warning to Elizabeth and George they make perfect sense. Whitefield feared he was losing the battle against the idolatry of love, and if he lost that, his whole ministry could be lost with it. Understandably, he was in desperate straits. The letter does not reveal where Elizabeth stood in all of this, though she must have given strong encouragement at some point along the way. Ever the brave actor, Whitefield closed on a note of bravado that belied the rest of the letter: "my heart is quite free. . . . I endeavour to resign myself wholly to God."

In fact, Whitefield's heart was not free. The "inward trials" simply grew more trying, and at length he realized he must write Delamotte directly. On April 4, 1740, after "strong cryings" and "unspeakable troubles with my own heart," he penned her a letter that expressed his inner turmoils perfectly. The main tone of his letter to her, like the earlier letter to William, was one of dire warning. This love business was not at all enrapturing for a good methodist itinerant; it was terrifying. And so, to begin, Whitefield assumed a pastoral tone and admonished Delamotte to give all attention and passion to Christ, for "nothing else can preserve you from idols." That it was for *himself* that Whitefield feared idolatry, however, becomes apparent in the next sentence, where he confesses, "There is nothing I dread more than having my heart drawn away by earthly objects." The language here, though indirect, is unambiguous. As ministers, women might be "Mothers in Israel," but as lovers they were "objects" that represented "idols" like the golden calves of old. Nowhere did Whitefield acknowledge that a "sex object" might be solely in the eye of the beholder.

As the letter progressed, Whitefield abandoned direct address to Delamotte and focused on himself. In place of the superior pastoral tone came the impassioned self: "My blood runs cold," he exclaimed, at the thought of "a rival" taking Christ's place at the center of his heart. By this point, he was allowing Delamotte, as it were, a glimpse at the debate he had played out so often in his heart. Even as he felt overcome by a powerful love for Delamotte, his methodist-formed conscience told him that this was idolatry.

By the close of the letter, Whitefield was utterly caught up in himself, while reference to Delamotte appeared merely in the form of a third-person prayer. Only in closing did he allow his guard to slip, when, in a revealing juxtaposition to his prayer, he burst out: "My heart is now full. Writing [to you] quickens me. I could almost drop a tear, and wish myself, for a moment or two, in *England*. But hush nature: God here pours down His blessings on Your sincere Friend and servant in Christ, G. W."

If Whitefield thought the letter would purge his inner turmoils, he was wrong. The feelings persisted, and in desperation he turned 180 degrees and proposed marriage. On April 5, 1740, on the eve of his triumphant return to Philadelphia, he penned separate letters to Delamotte and her father proposing marriage. The letters were so devoid of love or affection that they seemed, consciously or not, virtually guaranteed to elicit a rejection. The impassioned man in him had to propose; the public minister had to do so in a manner utterly without feeling so that all his passion could be reserved for preaching. By proposing marriage without any confession of love, the tortured Whitefield believed he could both find a wife and remain true to his first love. Again he was wrong.

Whitefield opened his letter to Charles Delamotte with a dark description of the conditions Elizabeth could expect to encounter as matron of the Georgia orphan house. The climate was harsh and the heat oppressive. Only recently, he noted, several deaths had been brought on by the sweltering heat and difficult conditions. In addition, life was constantly threatened by the Spanish troops on Georgia's border. At any moment war could destroy all. From there, Whitefield went on to describe his intentions, which, by methodist standards, were entirely honorable. He assured Delamotte that his interest in marriage did not stem from any base love, but from the "absolute necessity" of securing a wife for his "increasing family" of orphans and hapless debtors. As for romance, Mr. Delamotte could be assured that Whitefield felt nothing but love for Christ: "you need not be afraid of sending me a refusal. For, I bless God, if I know anything of my own heart, I am free from that foolish passion which the world calls *Love*."

Amazingly, Whitefield assumed the same diffident pose in his accompanying proposal to Betsy. In this letter there were no slips in the affections or unwanted teardrops. The tone was cold and businesslike. Elizabeth could be sure that marriage to him would bring "fatigue," uprooting from home, the care of a "family" of one hundred, and all in an oppressively hot "foreign climate." Worse, she could count on no ongoing residential relationship with him. His duty to God would often compel him "to leave you behind." Lest there be any doubt about the earthiness of his proposal, he went on to assure her that his proposal was "not for lust." For one whose forte was passion in the pulpit (and in correspondence with adversaries), Whitefield penned a remarkably bland and passionless proposal. It closed, "the passionate expressions which carnal courtiers use, I think, ought to be avoided by those that would marry in the Lord. . . . I trust, I love you only for God, and desire to be joined to you only by His command and for His Sake."

Whether or not Whitefield got the response he wanted, he certainly got the response he deserved. The proposal was rejected, and he was back where he began. He still needed a wife. But never again would he go through the "inward trials" his love for Delamotte had elicited. He would select a wife who could be a Mother-in-Israel to his Bethesda children and who would not divert his inner passions. And his search would be a matter of cold, dispassionate public record.

Interestingly, through all of his letters and ruminations, Whitefield never evidenced a sense that he was making himself an object of desire, idolized by adoring crowds of females less for the gospel he proclaimed than for the embodied manner of his pulpit delivery. Throughout, his fears were one-way. If women fell in love with him, it was not he who had made himself the object, but they who had misperceived him.

At every stop on his American tour and into 1741, Whitefield was privately taken up with "secret prayer" to God that he might be directed to a wife. From New England Whitefield wrote William Seward, "I want a gracious woman that is dead to everything but Jesus." Despite the large number of women interested in him, Whitefield went on to assure Seward that God "will not permit me to fall by the hands of a woman." At this same time, while visiting the Edwardses, he observed their marriage closely: "a sweeter couple I have not yet seen." Sarah's ascetic communion with God together with her pious manner in the household epitomized what he sought in a wife:

> Mrs. Edwards is adorned with a meek and quiet spirit; she talked solidly of the things of God, and seemed to be such a helpmeet for her husband, that she caused me to renew those prayers, which, for some months, I have put to God, that he would be pleased to send me a daughter of Abraham to be my wife.

Upon his return to England, Whitefield took stock of his needs and situation and considered "several tokens" — that is, women (again note the language of objects) — whom he discarded for one reason or another. At the same time he was clearly becoming distracted over the issue and disingenuously confessed to a friend, "I know not when my heart was more disengaged from earthly thoughts than now." Soon he publicized his needs. In February he confided to Ralph Erskine (whom he had not yet met) that "I believe it my duty to marry.

You see, dear sir, how freely I open my heart to you, though I have never seen you face to face." So cavalierly did Whitefield dispense with his private life that he did not hesitate to make his most intimate needs known to strangers in the faith.

At the conclusion of his Scottish tour, Whitefield found Elizabeth James, or rather had her found for him by his close friend Howell Harris. In effect, Harris acted as Whitefield's agent, playing John Alden to Whitefield's Miles Standish. This time, however, love would not win out. Despite the fact that James felt drawn to Harris and felt nothing for Whitefield, Harris persuaded her to marry Whitefield. To Whitefield's mind, it was the perfect match. A widow and ten years his senior, James was neither attractive nor emotionally attracted to him. Yet she was a good methodist. She would not engender passionate feelings in Whitefield, nor would she grieve for unrequited love. In four brief days, Whitefield's courtship and proposal were completed. James confessed she loved Harris and "could not help it." Harris, feeling the same fear of passion as Whitefield, felt he could not marry her and instead urged her to marry Whitefield. Whitefield, completing the triangle, reiterated his desire to marry and assured James that "he would not love her the less or be jealous" of her love for Harris. He wanted a wife who could look after his household and support the Bethesda orphan house. He neither needed nor desired romantic love.

James was a better — or older — methodist than Elizabeth Delamotte and at length agreed to the terms. With that the negotiations were settled and, at a private and inconspicuous ceremony, Harris gave the bride away and wished the couple well. Immediately Whitefield and Harris resumed their friendship and travels as if nothing had changed. And in fact, little had.

Whitefield announced his marriage publicly with hardly a shred of passion. In a letter to Gilbert Tennent he rejoiced over the revivals in Scotland, which were "greater than at New-England." Then, as an aside, he announced that: "About eleven weeks ago I married, in the fear of God, one who was a widow, of about thirty-six years of age, and has been a housekeeper for many years; neither rich in fortune, nor beautiful as to her person, but, I believe, a true child of God." Most importantly, Whitefield concluded, she "would not, I think, attempt to hinder me in his [God's] work for the world." A more desirable or attractive woman might have distracted Whitefield, but James — neither beautiful nor in love with him — was no threat.

Immediately following the marriage, Whitefield announced in the press that he had "left her" for three weeks to preach in Wales, commenting at the time: "I hope God will never suffer me to say, 'I have married a wife, and therefore I cannot Come.'" Readers of the *Weekly History* were informed of his marriage through a printed letter "from a gentleman at Edinburgh to his friend in London," which read as though it could have been written by Whitefield himself: "I am glad to hear our dear friend Mr. Whitefield is married, I hope she is such an one as will not interrupt him, but rather forward and encourage him, to go on in the good Work he has been now for some years so happily imployed in."

The gentleman's wish came true. In time, Whitefield developed a respect for his wife's courage and an admiration for her faith, but he showed no signs of passion or camaraderie. The couple had one child, John, two years after their marriage. At the time, Whitefield dared believe the boy would be blessed with a great ministry. He hoped to pass on the same destiny to his son that his mother had passed on to him. But then the child died at age four months. Whitefield blamed himself, fearing he had made an "idol" of his son. Ever the preacher, however, he delivered John's funeral oration and returned immediately thereafter to full-time preaching. As always, private failures, frustrations, and illness were best cured in the pulpit. In a letter to a friend he referred to John's death in the context of his favorite sermon: "Last night I was called to sacrifice my *Isaac;* I mean to bury my only child and son about four months old."

While never impassioned, Whitefield's marriage continued to be consummated. In all, Elizabeth suffered four miscarriages, leaving the couple childless. Whitefield compensated with his Bethesda "family." But Elizabeth never really felt connected to the orphan house and, in classic fashion, interpreted her emptiness as a personal failing. To a friend she confessed, "I have been nothing but a load and burden to him yet and pray that all our trials may be sanctified."

After her near death from a miscarriage in 1746, the forty-two-year-old Elizabeth was left permanently weakened and unable to accompany Whitefield on his extended tours. From February 1747 to June 1749 she remained in America without him. After returning to London that June, she remained there for the rest of her life. She was often separated from Whitefield for months at a time. While away he wrote to her infrequently, and in matter-of-fact terms. His tone was concerned but never impassioned or deeply affectionate. In correspondence with others, he rarely mentioned her name. When he did, he would refer to her as his "yoke-fellow" — a term that perfectly expressed the businesslike nature of their relationship.

Cornelius Winter lived with the couple in their last years and probably understood their relationship as well as anyone. He later described the marriage in sterile terms:

> He was not happy in his wife, but I fear some, who had not all the religion they professed, contributed to his infelicity. He did not intentionally make his wife unhappy. He always preserved great decency and decorum in his conduct towards her. Her death set his mind much at liberty. She certainly did not behave in all respects as she ought. She could be under no temptation from his conduct towards the sex, for he was a very pure man, a strict example of the chastity he inculcated upon others.

That about summed it up. Always courteous, always faithful, always proper, but never impassioned. Winter's point that she did "not behave in all respects as she ought" suggests

some tension over the attention other women paid to Whitefield, but not so much that it changed his course of action.
Through the rest of his life, women would continue to figure
prominently in his life, though passion and love would not.

Over the course of his life, Whitefield's closest relationship with a female would not be with Elizabeth but with the
methodist noblewoman Lady Selina, Countess of Huntington.
Like Elizabeth, Selina was somewhat older than Whitefield,
and utterly taken up with the methodist cause. In other circumstances she might have been the wife he never had: wealthy,
committed to Christ, and eager to share in his ministry. But the
timing was bad. When he first met her in the London revivals
of 1739, she was married. Her husband died in 1748, leaving
her free to dedicate herself and her fortune to the Calvinist
methodist cause. But by then Whitefield was married. Beyond
that it seems likely his servitor status would never really have
fit with her nobility.

Instead of a romantic relationship, the two engaged in a
lifelong working partnership of mutual support and edifica-
tion. In 1747, Huntington named Whitefield her chaplain, and
from that point on he would proudly add to his title "A.B.,"
that of "Chaplain to the Countess of Huntington." In 1748 he
began a preaching mission to the wealthy in her home. He also
began to write her weekly letters that for frequency and passion
exceeded any to his absent wife, who would not return to
England until the summer of 1749.

In all, ninety-three letters to Huntington survive in the
collected *Works* — a total far outdistancing those to any other
correspondent, male or female. In most of them Whitefield is
both extremely deferential, befitting the old servitor, and
deeply concerned. After receiving two letters from Huntington
sharing an unspecified "concern" in 1750, for example, Whitefield wrote back,

> [the letters] both led me nearer to, and laid me lower
> before Him, at whose throne I am daily pleading for the

welfare of your Ladyship, both in temporals and spirituals. . . . I have confidence with you that your ladyship shall have all the deliverance you long for. By divine grace, I will let the Lord have no rest, till he fulfills all your desires. I quite forget myself, when I think of your Ladyship. Ever honoured Madam, the Lord as yet hath but begun to bless you; you shall, you shall, you will be made a greater blessing indeed.

The subject matter of this, as of the other letters, is utterly taken up with the methodist cause and the Lord's work. Neither in this letter nor anywhere else is there the slightest hint of an impropriety. Nevertheless, in tone, if not in substance, the feeling expressed in the letter comes much closer to Whitefield's earlier letters to Elizabeth Delamotte than to his wife Elizabeth.

Did Whitefield feel any romantic passion for Huntington? If he did, he probably would not have recognized it or admitted it even to himself. After his experience with Delamotte, Whitefield's private feelings were undoubtedly suppressed and never again recognized as anything other than Christian zeal and mutual encouragement. The same methodist culture that opened Whitefield up to personal experience in religion closed his eyes to it in human love and marriage. The very passion that brought stunning successes in public remained closed off and unexpressed in private. In this he proved himself a true methodist.

10 Growing Up

In a remarkably short period of time Whitefield had become the evangelical "wonder of the age." While still in his twenties, he was more widely known across two continents than any save royalty. His radical innovations and unique style had won him international acclaim. The resiliency of youth had carried him through rigorous travels despite a callous disregard for his own health. As a young outsider he had cajoled, inspired, and berated without fear of social or ecclesiastical reprisals. Success had come easy — too easy, as it turned out.

In 1745 Whitefield at last had to face the results of his meteoric rise to celebrity. Words spoken in the impetuosity of youth reaped unanticipated consequences. Popularity had also bred a nasty competitiveness among rivals. In fact, Whitefield was discovering what all celebrities eventually discover — that unprecedented popularity brings unprecedented conflict and confrontation. The orphan house, the Tabernacle, and his own life were threatened, and the future of the Calvinist and Wesleyan Methodist movement came into doubt. Finally, his health did not hold up to the demands he placed on it. Now in his thirties, Whitefield discovered that creating a name and a reputation was far easier than preserving it. Circumstances from without and within now compelled the boy preacher to grow up.

Hostility and obstructionism from the Anglican bishops, for one thing, continued unabated. Both sides now had their parts down pat and routinely hurled charges back and forth. Whitefield still insisted that many of the bishops were unconverted and therefore opposed to his evangelistic messages. The bishops still viewed Whitefield as an alien presence who did not complement their ministry but actively competed with it and drew followers (and offerings) away from the church and into the fields. Throughout the controversy neither side had shown any desire to mute its censure. But in Whitefield's view, things took an ominous turn for the worse when bishops began tolerating or, worse yet, actually inciting mob violence.

In the 1730s, field preaching had still been both novel and impermanent enough that other marketplace entrepreneurs did not recognize it for the competitive threat that it was. Whether Whitefield would be a permanent fixture in the marketplace or a passing fad had been unclear. By the 1740s, any lingering uncertainties were gone. Vendors, peddlers, spirit sellers, and strolling actors now recognized in Whitefield, and to a lesser extent other methodist exhorters, a competitor draining away valued customers and cash. Methodist itinerants, led by Whitefield, had served notice to the new entrepreneurs of the marketplace that "worldly" activities would no longer enjoy a monopoly in their venues of trade. Religion would take its place alongside them and compete for the loyalties — and royalties — of the people. In response, the threatened parties gradually began to join forces with the bishops in opposition to Whitefield and his associates.

When he committed himself to an outdoor ministry, Whitefield had understood that he entered a no-man's-land of opportunities and dangers beyond the protected walls of

175

churches and meetinghouses. The rules of the marketplace were fuzzy, and the enforcers few. Fluid social boundaries meant that the restraints of class, neighborhood, and personal familiarity generally did not prevail. The swirls of humanity that gathered for market day or holiday could become ungovernable and dangerous. Preachers entered at their own risk.

Instances of mob violence against Whitefield and his methodist allies grew increasingly serious as the movement grew increasingly popular. Upon returning from America, Whitefield learned the tragic news that William Seward was killed by an unruly mob in October 1740. Whitefield's Tabernacle associate John Cennick told the chilling tale of an armed mob in Wiltshire, where Whitefield was preaching with Howell Harris. The mob fell upon the assembly and fired guns "over our heads, holding the muzzles so near to our faces that Howell Harris and myself were both made as black as tinkers with the powder." The assailants continued by dousing the speakers with fire pumps "filled out of the stinking ditches." When Harris and Cennick sought refuge in the house of a friend, the mob "broke all of his windows with stones, cut and wounded four of his family, and knocked down one of his daughters."

Sometimes the mob would target the speakers; other times they would wade into the crowd and simply assault without regard to gender or age. Three months after the Wiltshire incident, Cennick was preaching in Swindon when he was again assaulted by a mob bent on general mayhem: "they knocked down all who stood in their way, so that some had blood streaming down their faces, and others were taken up almost beaten and trampled to death. Many of our dear friends were cut and bruised sadly; and I got many severe blows myself." Many of the victims were women. Charles Wesley reported an assault at St. Ives, where the mob moved from Wesley to his female supporters: "they beat and dragged the women about, particularly one of great age." At Essex the violence was explicitly sexual. Rioters forced their way into the meetinghouse, and then proceeded to assault the preacher and abuse the women:

176

Some were stripped quite naked. Others, notwithstanding their most piercing cries . . . were forcibly held by some ruffians, while others turned their petticoats over their heads and forced them to remain in that condition. . . . One of the mob forced a woman up into the gallery, and attempted other outrages three different times. After many struggles she freed herself, leapt over the gallery and made her escape.

Inevitably the violence reached Whitefield. The more he condemned peddlers, entertainers, dancers, jugglers, and actors, the more they, along with their usual customers, responded with disturbances and violence aimed at forcing him back indoors where religion belonged. Often his preaching would draw crowds away from vendors and entertainers, for which, as he reported, "I was honored with having a few stones, dirt, rotten eggs and pieces of dead cats thrown at me." At Moorfields, he was routinely interrupted by hecklers and rioters bent on outshouting him and frightening his listeners. "Drummers, trumpeters, merry andrews" all ready "not for the Redeemer's but Beelzebub's harvest" would raise a din that even his voice could not overcome. Sometimes it got worse. At Mary Le Bon Fields, a "young rake" tried to stab Whitefield but was prevented by Whitefield's inner circle of supporters, who themselves made an uncharacteristic show of violence and had to be restrained by Whitefield from assaulting the would-be assassin.

When Whitefield was most successful, the mob was most determined to silence him. They beat drums, shouted, and mimicked him in ways designed to expose and disrupt his own dramatic style. On several occasions, rioters climbed into trees behind his pulpit to "shamefully expose" themselves or urinate in his direction. Yet Whitefield rarely ceased preaching under these pressures. Instead he would patiently wait the rioters out, sometimes singing, sometimes praying, until they grew bored or tired, and then he would pick up where he left off. Eventually, he reduced his tactics to a science. Sometimes he preached over the disturbance with his powerful voice. Sometimes he led his listeners in songs so loud they drowned out the opposition. In the process, he sent the message to the marketplaces and open fields that public religion in its highly experiential, evangelical form had come to stay. Services might last three hours while they rode out disturbances, but they were invariably completed.

Persecution simply fueled Whitefield's determination to continue. The pulpit had always been the place where he discovered his courage, and now he put it to the test. Along with his magazine readers, Whitefield took comfort from such accounts as Howell Harris's heroic report that while he was being beaten, his "voice [was] lifted up, and though by the power going with the words my head almost went to pieces, such was my zeal that I cried, 'I'll preach of Christ till to pieces I fall.'" In this and other similar accounts, readers found the words that gave them the strength and resolve to surmount all opposition.

Yet, the anger and fear Whitefield and his associates felt at the hands of the mob paled beside their fury at the thought that outdoor disturbances were legitimated — and even instigated — by nefarious churchmen who were pleased to let the mob do their dirty work for them. Conspiratorial thinking was at this time common throughout Britain and the colonies. It grew directly out of a highly personalized sense of history as a contest between good and evil and permeated all sides on any given issue. As Whitefield was certain that a plot against his ministry was being conceived by the bishops and executed by the mob, so the clerics were certain that Whitefield was plotting a secret "party" to deprive them of their livings. How else to explain the evil and immorality in the world?

Plots or no, violence *was* increasing, and the church showed little initiative in stopping it. If there was exaggeration in methodist accounts of violence, there was also substance. Following Cennick's mugging in Wiltshire, Whitefield appealed to the bishop to rebuke his clergy for not condemning the mob's violence. In an open letter to the Bishop of London,

Whitefield pleaded for help in stopping the violence. This could be done, he asserted, if the priests were discouraged from collusion with the mob. In addition, the bishop could speak out: "I should be glad if you could mention the cruelty of the ministers . . . to their Bishop of Sarum. Indeed, their doings are inhuman." Whitefield had little hope that his letters would persuade the bishop, but he was astute enough politically to print them widely, along with firsthand accounts of mob violence, so that others might learn of the methodists' plight and act against it.

In addition to printing letters, Whitefield invoked the power of the courts and the press to justify the methodists' right to exist and to condemn their attackers. A particularly nasty incident at Hampton furnished him with the materials he needed to take his case to the courts. In July 1743, a mob "one hundred strong" stormed a methodist meeting and threw the minister Thomas Adams into a lime pit, "wounding him severely." Whitefield hurried to Hampton to support Adams and preach in his place. The results were predictable: "no sooner had I entered the town than I heard the signals, such as the blowing of horns and the ringing of bells, for gathering the mob." Though frightened badly, Whitefield began preaching and was soon invaded by the mob. On no side did help appear, and a terrified Whitefield made his escape by leaping down a set of stairs. A female follower was not so fortunate and had her arm broken in two places.

Now outraged, Whitefield acquired the names of the chief rioters and took them to court. Much hung on the outcome. Methodists were literally fighting for their survival. Without the support of the courts and due process, their prospects would indeed be bleak. After heated testimony in the courtroom, where Whitefield identified his attackers, the courts found them guilty of a breach of the peace. The decision was widely noted. Until then, rioters had lived with the illusion (perhaps fostered by some clergy) that they could attack with impunity. The courts now taught them otherwise. Having made his point, a conciliatory Whitefield dropped the charges against the rioters and — very much in character — invited them to attend his meetings.

Besides using the courts, Whitefield worked through the press to uphold the embattled methodists. No one on either side of the controversy recognized the value of publicity as did Whitefield. Between 1741 and 1745 he issued a barrage of pamphlets defending the methodists and his own preaching on both religious and political grounds. The political defense was increasingly important, because the national loyalties of methodists were being called into question. Both a looming war with France and rumors that Prince Charles Stuart, the "young Pretender," was planning to invade England fed xenophobic fears that targeted methodists for charges of disloyalty to their country. If left unanswered, such accusations could feed a legal and political witch-hunt.

One especially pejorative charge demanded an instant response. A pamphlet entitled "Observations upon the Conduct and Behaviour of a Certain Sect, Usually Distinguished by the Name of Methodists" was published anonymously in 1744 (it was thought to come from an Anglican bishop). It accused Whitefield personally of disloyalty and said that he had "set the government at defiance" like the hated seventeenth-century radicals who had beheaded Charles I. It further charged that Whitefield "worked the body of the people into a national madness and frenzy in matters of religion." Unless suppressed, this frenzy would soon spill over into politics and threaten a violent overthrow of government.

Until then Whitefield had been largely silent on the subject of politics. His concern had been exclusively with the New Birth. He knew himself to be extremely loyal and deferential to government dignitaries and assumed that his refusal to criticize government would leave his loyalty unquestioned. But now, in the particularly paranoid atmosphere of war and invasion, the charges could no longer go unanswered. He would have to declare his political loyalties. In the process, he would learn that public figures — and movements — were inevitably political. Either they spoke up for the government and its authority or they were its enemies.

In fact, Whitefield had no problem with strong assertions of political loyalty. He had never been a social or a political radical bent on overturning an existing order. Neither was he a seventeenth-century Puritan eager to reform the nation. In his widely circulated "Answer to the First Part of an Anonymous Pamphlet," he pointed this out. Indeed, far from being a threat, he argued, his revivals were actually a public service. Anyone who had ever attended knew this; and if people thought otherwise, it was owing to the subterfuge of the church's bishops, who, he darkly hinted, had probably authored the anonymous libel sheet in the first place. For all their differences, methodists "all agree" on one point: to "Love and honour the king." As for himself, "I profess myself a zealous Friend to his present Majesty King *George*. . . . May the Crown long flourish on his Royal Head, and a *Popish Pretender* never be permitted to sit upon the *English* throne!"

This more mature Whitefield had discovered that his words — or silences — had national consequences. He could sidestep denominational differences in his preaching, but he could no longer ignore politics. Henceforth he would step up his pronouncements of loyalty to the crown and lend his voice to the success of military engagements.

While he was defending his loyalty, Whitefield also defended the right of nonseditious speakers to preach out-of-doors. Many churchmen were unwilling to grant preaching a market status, declaring that such a practice opposed both state and canon law. This too required an immediate response. Field preaching, Whitefield wrote, was not illegal or anarchical per se. It was perfectly allowable by civil and canon law, the only exception being "seditious conventicles" that sought to "contrive Insurrection." Such was hardly the case with his orderly services. Whenever preaching out-of-doors, he wrote, "I think it my Duty to pray for and preach up Obedience to [the crown]." And, in regard to the church, he was no separatist: "neither would I persuade the Methodists to leave their own parish churches when the sacrament is administered there." For this reason, Whitefield concluded, he always scheduled outdoor meetings before or after regular worship hours and urged his listeners to support their local churches. In fact, a youthful Whitefield had not always urged support of local churches as urgently as he now claimed, and there was a fine line between damning bishops and praising their services of worship. But for the rest of his career he would increasingly distance himself from separations and schism in Scotland, England, and America.

During all the controversy and mayhem in London, Whitefield longed to return to America. He planned to leave in 1744, but before he could do so there was one more great and unpleasant surprise. In June he traveled to Plymouth, there to await a naval escort to America. While working in his quarters late one night, Whitefield was visited by a naval officer posing as a religious seeker. Upon entering Whitefield's room, the officer soon fell into a murderous rage and "beat me most unmercifully with his gold-headed cane." Soon a second attacker appeared with clear intent to kill. Only Whitefield's voice saved him as he screamed "murder!" It reverberated throughout the neighborhood and frightened the would-be assassins away, but not before they had left the preacher badly wounded.

This savage farewell was the first real physical persecution Whitefield had personally experienced. He never ascertained a motive for the assault, nor were the assailants ever caught. But the incident reminded him of the reality of persecution and the danger of methodist itinerancy. It also left him badly weakened for his return to America, at a time when he needed all his strength.

It took six weeks for Whitefield to recover from his injuries to the point where he could travel. Finally, in October 1744, an exhausted and still convalescent Whitefield arrived in York,

Maine, hoping to pick up where he had left off on his previous visit. Instead, he encountered unprecedented controversy and contention. Once again, the height of his popularity was associated with the height of his offenses, and there was a predictably harsh backlash. Never in New England's century-old history had clergy and laity been so badly divided as they were in 1744. Many, including Whitefield's friends, were asking whether his new revivals had not caused more harm than good.

In America, it is true, there would be no mob. The conditions that encouraged urban disturbances, with all the sharp edges they manifested in England, did not exist in the colonies. There was no national church to suppress Whitefield from above, nor the bitter extremes of inequality in this "Best Poor Man's Country" to create havoc in the common citizenry. And Whitefield's greatest competitors in England — theaters, dance halls, pugilists, strolling actors, and Sunday entertainments — were illegal in most of Calvinist America. But conflict and bitter acrimony followed him nevertheless, and this from *within* the supposedly friendly and Calvinist Congregational and Presbyterian churches. The evangelical movement was, to put it bluntly, in a shambles.

All of the bright spots of 1740 were tarnished. Gilbert Tennent made one trip to New England in the winter of 1741 and went home with a bad ear and permanent disability, never to return. However, his sermon "The Danger of an Unconverted Ministry" continued to be read widely and encouraged separations. Even though Tennent later repudiated the divisive tone of his pamphlet, others picked it up. Once unleashed, the rhetoric of an unconverted ministry would not disappear and came to be directed at one-time friends of the revivals. Radical separates such as New England's Andrew Croswell and the Long Island Dutch pietist John Henry Goetschius modeled their preaching on this rhetoric, which had first been sounded on Whitefield's earlier tour.

The most infamous disturbance centered on Whitefield's youthful colleague and native imitator James Davenport. In

1741 and 1742, Davenport traveled widely throughout New England, reporting conversions in numbers that exceeded those of Whitefield or Tennent. His center of operations was New London, Connecticut, where a separatist group of admirers had broken away from the Congregational church and announced the creation of a new congregation as well as a new home-grown college called the "Shepherd's Tent." From New London, Davenport traveled widely throughout Connecticut and Massachusetts, urging separations and labeling local ministers "unconverted" sight unseen. Twice he was arrested and dismissed for being *non compos mentis*. But by 1743 his campaign had exceeded all restraints.

With great fanfare and innumerable witnesses, Davenport's ministry burned itself out in New London, where it had begun, when his followers built a bonfire and cast into it items representing "the world." Included among these items were books by the respected Boston ministers Increase Mather and Benjamin Colman, and eventually Davenport's "britches." Immediately a ministerial council led by Jonathan Edwards and Eleazar Wheelock (later the founder of Dartmouth College) condemned the whole affair and brought Davenport to a church trial. Davenport was ashamed and issued a public retraction, but the damage was done. Opponents of the revivals such as Boston's Charles Chauncy were delighted by it all, for it "proved" that mass revivals were inevitably schismatic, disorderly, and ultimately insane. Supporters were embarrassed and confused.

The "New London affair" cast the whole transatlantic revival into question and raised fears on the part of clerical proponents as well their detractors. While Whitefield was preaching in Scotland and London, many Americans, including his friends, wondered if the opponents were right and Whitefield really was the source of the present disorders. Most conceded that the rhetoric of an unconverted ministry had begun with him. His friendship with Tennent and Davenport was well known, and word of his break with the Scottish

Seceders had not yet reached American revivalists. Upon his arrival, the tide began to shift ominously. In the face of the separatist threat, former sympathizers became less worried about reviving their churches than about simply keeping the churches together. Again Whitefield had to face the consequences of his youthful indiscretions.

Before Whitefield could resume his New World mission, he first had to restore these broken or at best badly eroded relationships. In the wake of his previous tour, he had heard rumors of disturbances and excesses that were dividing churches in New England, but he had not realized the extent and virulence of the rift. Many ministers who had initially been curious or supportive of Whitefield now turned against him and organized petitions to exclude him from their pulpits. In this they were supported by the colleges in Cambridge and New Haven and by some of the newspapers. The faculty of Harvard College was particularly hostile, having never forgiven the brash evangelist for intimating that their *lux* had become darkness. In retaliation they issued a "testimony" against Whitefield's censorious preaching that was widely reprinted and circulated throughout New England. Every week, the presses of Boston's Thomas Fleet cranked out pamphlets by Congregational clerics who denounced Whitefield's intrusive ministry and warned the people that he was a "dangerous man," conducting his ministry "under the Frowns of the Church of England." His preaching, the Reverend Nathanael Henchman exclaimed, was an example of "insufferable pride and vanity" that had instigated the "strolling *Itinerants,* and swarms of mean Animals called Exhorters" who threatened to overturn the established churches and all social order.

The leading intellect behind the ministerial campaign against Whitefield was Boston's young and aggressive Charles Chauncy, who matched Whitefield's energy and traveled nearly as widely throughout New England cataloguing errors in doctrine and emotional excesses. Already in 1743 he had penned a massive critique of the revivals entitled *Seasonable*

Thoughts on the State of Religion in New England that was directed largely at Whitefield's *Journal* and Edwards's supportive *Thoughts concerning the Revival of Religion in New England.* Chauncy cited excesses and aberrations gathered from his exhaustive tour of colonial churches and went on to argue that the revivals were not a work of God but of the Old Deluder, Satan. Edwards's defense of revivalism, he charged, was a mistaken concession to "enthusiasm" — literally, a disease of uncontrollable passions. Unless duly checked and reined in by reason and by clergy of superior intellect, the movement would upset all order in churches and society.

Historians have generally considered Chauncy the loser in this debate, and so he was, at least as far as Edwards was concerned. By carefully distinguishing intellectually informed "affections" from base "passions," Edwards could draw on the rich intellectual heritage of "voluntarist" philosophy epitomized by the Third Earl of Shaftesbury and the new Lockean psychology to defuse Chauncy's critique and even make it seem old-fashioned. For Edwards, the New Birth was essentially a supernaturally infused "new sense" that bypassed both the natural understanding and the passions. Everything hung on precise definition and scholarly discrimination. By properly distinguishing supernaturally infused affections from the natural passions, Edwards could defend emotional preaching without defending the passions.

But Whitefield would not find it so easy to escape Chauncy's grasp. Whitefield had no interest in aesthetics or divine epistemology, nor did he have much interest in Edwards beyond the account of the Northampton revival. By "affections" he meant passions — feelings in the ordinary sense of the term. His whole ministry depended on his capacity to enlist body and pathos in the cause of passion. He preached exactly as Chauncy accused the revivalists generally of preaching: from the passions up.

If Edwards was something of an enigma to Chauncy, Whitefield was not, and it was Whitefield he targeted in the next round. In January 1745, Chauncy greeted Whitefield's return to America with a pamphlet printed in the form of a public letter urging him to go back where he came from. The churches, Chauncy asserted, had been in much better shape before Whitefield arrived; his impassioned preaching had encouraged scores of enthusiastic "ranters" of whom Davenport was merely the most notorious. In tone and vituperation, Chauncy's letter fell considerably short of the character assassination Whitefield had encountered in London, but it still exceeded anything he had seen in America. If anything, the more reasonable style carried greater weight. According to Chauncy, Whitefield's unsubstantiated accusations of an "unconverted ministry" throughout New England, his censure of Harvard and Yale, and his encouragement of itinerant exhorters had all worked "great injury to the *Church of God.*" In addition, his highly impassioned oratory had infected New England with the disease of "enthusiasm," which, among other things, encouraged people to desist from their daily labors and separate from their local, established churches. In America, where there was little leisure time or unemployment, the threat to labor was a more common complaint.

Chauncy's charges were reinforced in the pages of Fleet's *Boston Evening Post*. More than any other New England newspaper, the *Post* sought to emulate English periodicals and aimed its essays at Boston's "polite" readership. Edwards, with his theological rigor and philosophical acumen, did not present much of a target, but Whitefield was a different story. Not only was he impassioned, but he was English, and well known to London society. Where Chauncy focused on theology and the primacy of reason, the *Post* targeted Whitefield's clownish manner and ridiculed the "Methodist" characters who were caught up in his madness. Most ridiculous, charged the *Post*, were the women. In a satiric letter "from a gentleman" reprinted from the London *Spectator*, the *Post* described the response any aspiring gentleman should have to the news that his wife was caught up in the revivals:

I am one of those unhappy men that are plagued with a gospel-gossip. Lectures in the morning, church-meetings at Noon, and Preparation-Sermons at Night, take up so much of her time, tis very rare she knows what we have for Dinner, unless when the Preacher is to be at it. With him comes a Tribe, all Brothers and Sisters, it seems. . . . If any time I have her company alone, she is a meer sermon pop-gun, repeating and discharging Texts, Proofs, and Applications so perpetually that however weary I may go to bed, the Noise in my Head will not let me sleep.

Behind the theological critiques and bitter social parodies were real social fears. The colonists' distance from the center of power made them even more susceptible to fears of conspiracy than the English. Many voiced the suspicion that Whitefield was not what he appeared. In fact, they suspected, his religious crusade and apparent lack of interest in denomination covered up a deeper conspiracy to create a "party" — a self-serving clique of corrupting evil forces. This conspiracy would be no small local affair, but a vast transatlantic campaign carefully orchestrated to abolish traditional authority, both social and ecclesiastical. A "Letter to a Gentleman" printed in the *Post* expressed the fear that, while Whitefield "put on a shew of meekness," he hid underneath it a plot to found a faction: "In some places he has been bold, if not insolent, in thrusting himself in to preach, contrary to the endless Remonstrances of the People. . . . These proceedings convince me more and more, that he has a Design to divide, and utterly to subvert the churches in the land." Unless due care was taken and pulpits resolutely closed, Whitefield would emerge as the "Head of a Religious Party," and should that happen, "the Destruction of all our Churches is the certain consequence."

The hysterical language of anti-Whitefield tracts and polemics is revealing. This was not mere rhetoric or hyperbole. The very urgency of the language confirms how, in the minds of Whitefield's critics, a real plot was afoot to destroy New

England's glorious tradition and, with it, its glorious destiny. This same mentality would surface twenty years later when New England "patriots" became convinced of a British plot to destroy their liberties. In both cases the inflated language of conspiracy was neither calculated upper-class propaganda nor irrational paranoia but rather an inherited rhetoric that seemed to make sense of rapid changes taking place in church and society.

Although weakened by his still-healing wounds and high fevers, Whitefield well understood the pressing dangers that the language of "plot," "Party," and "subversion" posed to his ministry. Having just defended himself against charges of faction in England, he recognized that if he did not respond immediately, his entire New World mission would be jeopardized. In the early days of 1745, this meant acting simultaneously on all fronts to restore his tarnished reputation and counter the charges that were gaining a dangerous momentum. Few in America knew of his conflict with the Scottish Seceders or his own increased suspicions of separatism. But they soon learned of the latter, for Whitefield wasted no time in lining up solidly on the side of hierarchy and order in the American churches. With that, his brief flirtation with separatism came to an end once and for all. As in Scotland, this stance would play a major role in limiting the growth of hyper-Calvinist dissent.

Before defending himself before his critics, however, Whitefield first had to reestablish connections with his clerical allies, who had been left badly shaken by popular defections and the prospect of a Separatist takeover. They needed to know where Whitefield stood. On November 27, a still-ailing Whitefield met in Boston with his core supporters, Joseph Sewall, Ebenezer Pemberton, Thomas Prince, Thomas Foxcroft, and, most importantly, the patriarchal Benjamin Colman. While still in England, Whitefield had written Colman a letter bemoaning the Davenport affair and regretting that "wild fire will necessarily blend itself with the pure fire that comes from God's alter." Now he repeated those regrets publicly. Again he repudiated separations and told all he was "sorry if anything I wrote had been a means of promoting separations, for I was of no separating principles." He was not competing with churches, he declared, but with "worldliness," and his loyalties would forever remain with all established clergy who welcomed his ministry and mission.

Satisfied by his account, the Boston allies reaffirmed their support for him and opened their pulpits to his ministry. Following the meeting, Whitefield immediately released an announcement for the press that "Dr. Colman invited me to preach the next day at his Meeting house." John Webb soon followed suit with an invitation to preach at the New North meetinghouse, and so the near-breach was healed. With at least some pulpits open to him, Whitefield had the entrée he needed to ensure that his preaching tour would go on despite continued opposition. He would deliver his impassioned presentation of the New Birth as always, but with it he would now invariably promote the cause of established churches as well.

Having solidified his clerical supporters, Whitefield turned to his critics. If, as he suspected, he could never convince them to endorse his impassioned preaching of the New Birth, he could at least allay their social fears — and for many, the social fears were primary. He proceeded to make repeated and unabashed apologies for the indiscretions and rash censures of his younger ministry. In a widely printed letter, he confessed,

> Being fond of Scripture Language, I have often us'd a stile too Apostolical, and at the same Time I have been too bitter in my zeal. . . . I have likewise too much made Impressions my Rule of acting, and too soon and too explicitly published what had better been kept in longer, or left to be told after my Death.

Here, and elsewhere, readers and witnesses were presented with a more mature, socially responsible Whitefield, who,

190

given the choice of radical or mainstream, unhesitatingly preferred the latter. His goal was the largest possible audience.

Opponents were expecting the George Whitefield of 1740. Instead they met a chastened Whitefield who owned up to his excesses and condemned separations. Whenever confronted with blame for earlier separations, he apologized profusely, thus establishing his credibility in the rhetorically persuasive and self-deprecating code of Puritan discourse. In place of the familiar combatant, a tempered, more mature Whitefield appeared ready to withdraw some of his more aggressive statements.

Much had happened between his second and third visits to America, both in Whitefield's own development and in the churches. The egocentrism that had dominated his early journals he now saw for what it was — the inflated prose of a young preacher whose heart had all along been in the right place but whose immaturity had encouraged regrettable pretensions to inspiration and discernment. He was now convinced by the more extreme actions of the Seceders in Scotland, the Moravians and Methodists in England, and the Separatists in America that pious reform had gone too far in contesting all order and authority. And he recognized that his rash censure of ministers was reaping a tragic whirlwind in which, as Chauncy claimed, many good and godly men were abused simply because they lacked charisma or a willingness to preach nothing but the New Birth week after week.

From general apologies, Whitefield turned to particular antagonists. First on his list was Harvard College. On January 23, 1745, he penned a public letter of apology to the faculty of the college. His former condemnation, he now saw, had been unfounded but unfortunately effective in encouraging defections. Again he repeated his denunciation of separatist principles and, in the strongest possible terms, disassociated himself from any attempt to found a clique: "I have no intention of setting up a party for myself, or to stir up people against their pastors." Nor, he added, did he wish to upset the rich

191

legacy of the college: "I profess my self a *Calvinist* as to Principle, and preach no other Doctrines than those which your pious Ancestors and the Founders of Harvard College preached long before I was born."

Whitefield's apology was widely printed and encouraged other ministers and newspapers to come out in support of his itinerant ministry. Once assured that he would not lead a Separatist uprising, Whitefield's friends returned to the fold and hastened into print to counter the testimonies prepared against him. In retrospect, what was most remarkable about the American phase of his 1745 "paper war" was not the virulence of the opposition but the wave of support from the press and from the established Presbyterian and Congregational clergy. For every testimony against him, there was another for him that endorsed his ministry and claimed his revivals as a work of God.

In Boston, where genteel opponents were centered, pro-Whitefield clerics won outright control of three churches and shared control in three others, including the venerable Old South and North churches and the wealthy Brattle Street Church. When Boston's opposing clergy garnered thirty-eight signatures against Whitefield and other revivalists, supporters countered with sixty-eight signatures endorsing his ministry. Opposing clergy could complain about Whitefield's tactics and character, but, unlike their Anglican counterparts, they could not mount a united front. Whitefield had simply become too close to the American soul to be dislodged.

Not surprisingly, additional support for Whitefield's ministry came from the press. Since 1743, Thomas Prince, Jr., son of the eminent Old South pastor and historian, had been printing a religious news magazine called *The Christian History*, modeled exactly on Whitefield's *Weekly History*. Like its English parent, *The Christian History* gave ordinary people a sense that they were making "news" through their participation in the religious revivals. These revivals, moreover, were not merely local but international in scope, bringing together Calvinist evangelicals from Scotland, England, Wales, and the American colonies. American readers learned of the Cambuslang revivals, where, as in America, the central characters in the drama had been ordinary people. More importantly, readers learned of the central role that Whitefield had played.

Letters from Edinburgh and Glasgow affirmed his character. As one correspondent put it, Whitefield "is really the most assiduous fervent Preacher of the Gospel I ever knew, and has something extremely uncommon about him." Another writer, the Reverend James Ogilvie of Aberdeen, reassured American readers that "his attachment to no *Party* but to *Christ* and *true Grace* alone, has long appeared to me a peculiar Excellency in him."

Soon other newspapers carried letters and essays endorsing Whitefield's character and defending his nondenominational evangelical intentions. In a widely circulated letter, William Hobby of Reading, Massachusetts, pointed out that instead of pocketing money from his New England collections, Whitefield had taken out only £35 for personal expenses at a time when pastors of *small* parishes could count on at least £100 per annum. Throughout the winter of 1745, Rogers and Fowle published a steady stream of pro-Whitefield letters from ministerial associations and clergy outside Boston, all echoing the support of the Boston clergy. Equally prolific was Samuel Kneeland and Thomas Green's *Boston Gazette,* which, during Whitefield's time in New England, became virtually a religious magazine. Throughout the colonial era the *Gazette* was clearly attached to the cause of "the people," and in 1745 that meant the cause of revival. Without fail the paper printed the schedule of Whitefield's travels, together with character endorsements that denied such charges against Whitefield as the embezzlement of funds and the founding of a party.

Whitefield's alignment with the established churches over against the Separatists did nothing to dampen his popularity. In fact, the established clergy had regained much of their losses and so had stemmed the tide of separations. Whitefield accelerated that trend. Wherever he preached, he attracted mass audiences and moved many to tears and conversion. Unlike his first tour, however, there was no rhetoric of an unconverted ministry, censure of the colleges, or suggestion that spiritually starved souls might leave their parishes in search of greener pastures.

In his spring tour outside Boston, the symbolic moment of truth came when Whitefield spoke from Benjamin Adams's New London pulpit. Two years earlier, Davenport had branded Adams "unconverted" and urged good Christians to leave his church and found their own separate congregation. Now Whitefield preached a conciliatory sermon on the New Birth and at the same time condemned the earlier separation and all other defections from established churches. The *Gazette*, in its coverage of the event, noted that Whitefield preached three sermons to overflow audiences at New London praising the beauty of union and love of godly ministers. Throughout his sermons, the *Gazette* noted, he was "very explicit against the separations and some erroneous wild notions which were propagating in those parts."

Once again, Whitefield's timing was perfect. His conciliatory sermons fit with a broader pattern of clerical rapprochement that sought to put party divisions behind and to move ahead despite differences in style and emphasis. Matters that had once been choices between truth or heresy came instead to be seen as matters of personal preference and taste. In fact, all Congregational ministers proclaimed the New Birth, though not all in the same style or with the same regularity. Asserting that common foundation, Whitefield could, and did, reach out to audiences inclusively without raising the specter of defection or separation.

Following the New London sermons, criticism continued to sound against Whitefield, but without the bite and conviction of earlier disputes. In no sense did the criticism approach the bitter invective of London journalists and bishops. Nor did Whitefield give back in his customarily aggressive London style. With Whitefield himself conceding the errors his earlier ministry had propagated, the opposition lost its advantage. The Grand Itinerant had apologized, and that was that. In a letter to a friend in England, Whitefield described the harsh criticism he had first received but then went on to note a wave of clerical and popular sympathy: "amidst all, the word runs and is glorified and many are so enraged at the treatment I meet with, that they come to me lately, assuring me, that if I'll consent, they will erect in a few weeks time, the outside of the largest place of worship that was ever seen in *America:* but you know ceiled houses were never my aim."

Whatever doubts New England leaders may still have harbored concerning Whitefield were finally and conclusively resolved when, toward the end of his New England tour, he agreed to support publicly the all-colonial military expedition to Louisbourg, the French-built fortress in Nova Scotia. Whitefield had recently learned the value and necessity of political commentary, and, after a brief hesitation, agreed to the American commander George Pepperell's request to preach an enlistment sermon. The commander convinced him that "if I did not encourage it, many of the serious people would not inlist." Never one to act half-heartedly, Whitefield threw himself into the task of recruitment and by February 1745 could point with pride to the role he had played in raising the largest expeditionary force ever assembled in North America. On the eve of embarkation, he supplied the apprehensive troops with their motto, *Nil desperandum Christo duce* (If Christ leads, never fear), and preached a sermon promising that, if Christ was truly king, "we should receive good news from Cape Breton."

On June 16, the unthinkable happened. The "Gibraltar of America" fell to the invading colonial forces, sparking celebrations throughout the colonies and in England. In New England, General Pepperell (now dubbed baronet) and Whitefield enjoyed universal praise and adulation. From that point on, through subsequent wars with France and England, Whitefield was associated with American military success. Soldiers through the Revolution would take his motto to heart, believing also that if *Whitefield* was for them, they need never fear.

War had always been a unifying force in New England's history, and on this occasion it completed a unification as former clerical antagonists commonly dwelt on the joys of victory. While Chauncy delivered a thanksgiving sermon in Boston and Edwards in Northampton, Whitefield added his voice with a thanksgiving oration on the traditional Puritan thanksgiving text: "By this I know that thou favourest me, since thou hast not permitted mine enemies to triumph over me." In oratory, if not on the battlefield, Whitefield "played the man" for his American hearers and enacted for them the brave and pious sentiments that would render the colonial militia unconquerable.

Following the expedition, Whitefield traveled south and realized the same conciliatory successes he had won in New England. Along with clerical endorsements and invitations came unanimous journalistic support from the Bradfords' *American Weekly* and Franklin's *Pennsylvania Gazette,* both in Philadelphia. Of the two, Franklin's was more important. His glowing endorsement of Whitefield's character and integrity was particularly persuasive, coming as it did from such an avowed skeptic and critic of established denominations. Franklin had no reason to applaud Whitefield's character unless he sincerely believed it.

In Philadelphia, Whitefield received a hero's welcome at the "New Building" constructed especially for his mass ministry. As always, women and blacks remained conspicuous among his most vocal supporters. Female adherents found a cause through Whitefield's ministry that could take them out of their homes and into a new religious freedom. In a letter to the *Boston Evening Post* (printed, ironically, in an attempt to discredit Whitefield's ministry), Deborah Sherman raised the banner of female support, noting:

> Fair would they discourage the women, who you know
> are your best friends, if they fall off all is gone, by telling

them that St. Paul would have all the women . . . to keep at home and mind their families. But I am sure St. Paul did not mean this when dear Mr. Whitefield preached. But if he did — Ay, ay, let the hard hearted wretches say what they will, we will go to hear you preach, we will follow you, we will come to all your lectures, have as many as you will, the more the better; and for my own part, I would go with you with all my Heart to Georgia, and I know a great many more would do so too.

Blacks too found in Whitefield's open sympathy and attention the beginnings of an evangelical Christianity that they would, in time, take over for themselves. Wherever slaves attended, Whitefield addressed them particularly and often met with them in private. When preaching at Raynham, he noted that "after sermon, five or six Negroes desired to speak to me. One seemed to be filled with love of God, two had been Backsliders, and the other was slightly wounded. I was much helped in discoursing with them." Through his highly publicized attention to blacks, Whitefield both supplied them with an evangelical vocabulary they later adapted to their own purposes and he served notice to white Americans that the souls of their slaves could be ignored only at the cost of divine wrath.

Whitefield's love for the slaves was genuine and invariably reciprocated. Once when gravely ill, he reported, "a poor Negro woman" visited him and "sat down upon the ground, looking earnestly in my face, and said 'Master, you just go to heaven's gate; but Jesus Christ said, Get you down, get you down; you must not come here yet. Go first, and call more poor Negroes.'"

From the middle colonies, Whitefield continued south and realized greater gains there than ever before. In Hampton County, Virginia, he planted the seeds of evangelical revival that eventually led to a "Great Awakening" there. For the first time, he added Maryland to his circuit and, as in Boston and Philadelphia earlier, he received the offer of "a large living" amounting to hundreds of pounds and requiring residence for only six months out of the year. He turned this offer down as he had turned them all down, though not without letting readers know of his sacrifice in the cause of itinerant ministry.

Throughout the winter and spring of 1747, he traveled by horse and canoe a circuit of four hundred miles, addressing "thousands and thousands . . . who . . . are ready to hear the gospel from my mouth." Even the tidewater aristocracy conceded honors to the famed itinerant. From Charleston, Josiah Smith wrote in the *Boston Gazette* that

> Whitefield shows so much of the Orator in the Pulpit, and so happily unites the gentleman and the Christian in his polite, prudent and serious conversation, that he has triumph'd over a thousand Prejudices, and become the Admiration of several who had before conceived the worst Idea of him imaginable . . . as a further expression of our great esteem, [his admirers] have subscribed and given him much above Two hundred pounds sterling.

To this, Smith added the ominous note that the offerings would be used "to purchase and improve with Negroes a very good plantation."

Smith's reference to the slaves confirms the limits of evangelical "liberation" in eighteenth-century America. In fact, Whitefield spent much of his time in the South actively promoting the legalization of slavery in Georgia. In a revealing but seldom-cited letter to the trustees in 1748, he enumerated the expenses of the orphan house and its precarious existence. Then he pointed to the solution: "Had a negroe been allowed, I should now have had a sufficiency to support a great many orphans, without expending above half the sum which hath been laid out." From there he went on to actually threaten the trustees if they did not admit slavery:

> Georgia never can or will be a flourishing province without negroes are allowed. . . . I am as willing as ever to do all I can for *Georgia* and the Orphan-house, if either a limited use of negroes is approved of, or some more

198

indented servants sent over. If not, I cannot promise to keep any large family, or cultivate the plantation in any considerable manner.

Recognizing that the legalization of slavery in Georgia might require years, Whitefield pursued other alternatives. With his friend James Habersham retiring from the orphan house to pursue a career in private business, Whitefield looked increasingly to slaves in South Carolina as his salvation. With financial backing from Habersham and Hugh Bryan, White-field purchased a plantation and rejoiced that immediately "one Negroe has been given me" to begin working the 840-acre plantation and "support Bethesda."

The same Whitefield who brashly had censured all slave owners in his youth had now joined their ranks. This too was a mark of his maturity, though one that later biographers have preferred to ignore. Tragically, the very eighteenth-century evangelicalism that had opened his eyes to the spiritual needs of the slaves also blinded him to their inhuman temporal and cultural conditions. His new popularity among the southern gentry was, in fact, directly proportional to his endorsement of slavery. And like those planters who would lead America's campaign for independence, he was incapable of seeing the contradictions between a rhetoric of freedom and the reality of slavery.

In June 1747, Whitefield's years of nonstop preaching and controversy caught up with him. The heat that summer was especially punishing, and in June he collapsed with high fevers and recurrent convulsions. Many, including himself, thought he would soon die. The prospect did not terrify him. Indeed, he seemed almost to relish it as his last triumphant act, confiding to one, "I hope yet to die in the pulpit, or soon after I come out of it. Dying is exceeding pleasant to me; for though my body is so weak, the Lord causes my soul to rejoice exceedingly."

Whitefield did not realize his wish — yet. Instead, he re-covered sufficiently to return to Philadelphia and Boston once more before a recuperative visit to the Bermuda colony. The return visits were satisfying in all regards. In contrast to the bitter controversy that had greeted him in 1745, he could now point to renewed public enthusiasm that was "near the same as when the work began seven years ago." In Philadelphia, Franklin observed that "he was never so generally well esteemed by persons of all ranks among us; nor did he ever leave us attended with so many ardent wishes for his happy journey and a safe return to this place."

By the time of his departure for Bermuda, Whitefield had turned the tide of opposition and become once more a colonial hero — indeed, America's first intercolonial hero. And he would also be America's last universally recognized religious hero. The years of controversy were passed. Never again would he encounter the sort of resistance in America that would plague him to his dying days in England. Scotland and America would remain his home of preference as well as the nerve centers for "revivals" that only he could replicate in every community on every tour.

11 Revivals in a New Key

When Whitefield returned from his Bermuda convalescence in July 1748, he had no more worlds to conquer. He was thirty years old, grown up, and married. It was time to start thinking about settling down. This meant it was time to decide whether he would settle in England. His London Tabernacle clearly needed his presence if it was to flourish. In his absence, many, including his two chief assistants, John Cennick and John Syms, had converted to the Moravian camp. Others had left to follow the Wesleys. But for Whitefield, permanence seemed to require institutional identification either with Anglicans, Methodists, or perhaps a movement of his own making. Was that the destiny awaiting him?

It was not. When offered a role within the Wesleyan Methodist fellowship, he declined, noting that despite his ongoing friendship with the Wesleys, "we differ in principles more than I thought." Whitefield could not tolerate John Wesley's widely publicized Arminianism. Besides that, both were dominant personalities. Even with a common theology, it was unlikely that either could have submitted to the other's dominance.

Another option for Whitefield was to start a new, rival Calvinist-Methodist denomination. But he dismissed that idea with equal finality. In fact, at the same time he turned down the Wesleys' offer, he assured them that he had no intention of founding a movement of his own. His official excuse was the Georgia orphan house: "My attachment to America will not permit me to abide very long in England; consequently I should weave a Penelope's web if I formed Societies; and if I should form them I have not proper assistants to take care of them."

Certainly the orphan house mission was a valid reason not to settle permanently in England. But Whitefield's decision depended on far more than that well-established work. Other considerations had to do with more personal factors, including his Anglican upbringing, his own dramatic personality, and, perhaps most importantly, his novel vision of a religious culture in which denominations were subordinated to larger unities.

Though he seldom admitted it in a loud voice, Whitefield was a loyal Anglican. This was the church of his youth and family heritage, the church that had reclaimed his family's lost status. It was his spiritual home as well. He genuinely valued the church's liturgy and sacramental piety, finding in it a familiar source of comfort and solace. Historical accounts of his ministry focus on his activities in the fields and nonconformist meetinghouses, but such records fail to appreciate the amount of time Whitefield spent in Anglican services. The very pomp and ritual that dissenters found so offensive and "papist" were to Whitefield, in light of both childhood experience and a theatrical eye, consistent with the gospel he proclaimed. He had seen enough Roman Catholic ritual to know the difference and did not hesitate to praise the Anglican liturgy as a true expression of Reformation doctrine. In a letter written later in life to the Bishop of Bristol, he declared his loyalties:

For near these twenty years last past, I have conscientious-

ly defended her homilies and articles, and upon all occasions spoken well of her liturgy. Either of these,
together with her discipline, I am so far from renouncing,
much less from throwing aside all regard to, that I earnestly pray for the due restoration of the one, and daily lament
the wanton departure of too, too many from the other.

The same dramatic personality that remained drawn to
Anglican ritual and ceremony, however, also fed an actor's
desire to attract the largest possible audience. All great figures
seek out a destiny and fame. But most eighteenth-century religious luminaries, such as Edwards, Bishop George Berkeley,
and the Wesleys, found this fame in traditional outlets of theology or church leadership. Whitefield's achievement lay in
neither theology nor polity but in novel proclamation to heterogeneous audiences. He was an actor-preacher, and like all
actors he desired a standing-room-only audience. This meant
he could align himself with no single movement so exclusively
that others would turn away in rejection. It meant as well that
he could give no enduring commitment to one place or one
audience.

Alongside Whitefield's Anglican loyalties and his need
for a broad-based appeal, he also had an anti-institutional bias
that redefined his deepest understanding of the nature and
meaning of religious assembly. Negatively, he expressed his
bias as often-repeated contempt for the tiny ambitions of clerics
and nonconformists who had no greater object in mind than
their self-perpetuation: "But what is Calvin, or what is Luther?
Let us look above the names and parties; let Jesus be our all in
all. . . . I care not who is uppermost. I know my place . . . even
to be the servant of all. I want not to have a people called after
my name."

Positively, Whitefield had in mind an alternative religious
vision that drove his ministry from the start and gained in
clarity as time went on. His itinerant ministry taught him the
invaluable lesson that rival churches with visions of national
hegemony could be a thing of the past: they could be made old

history — the history of a traditional, localistic, and coercive culture. A new history would be transdenominational and revival-centered. In such a system, existing churches would not be supplanted so much as sidestepped in the interest of creating larger, translocal associations. These associations would be purely voluntary and would allow people to remain in their favorite denomination even as they bound themselves to larger association with international significance. The new forms would succeed or fail in direct relation to their ability to attract religious consumers.

Whitefield's vision was profound not in its theological depth but in its very popularity. His revivals were not really a church, nor were they connected to local communities and congregations. The appearance of Whitefield's audiences as religious congregations defied the traditional sense of the term. The audiences changed with every meeting, evidencing no permanent structure or leadership aside from Whitefield's own charismatic ministry. In addition, they were routinely enjoined to support their local congregations and parishes, even as they were assured of bigger things afoot. In reality, Whitefield's audiences and loyal supporters represented powerful new "parachurches" — voluntary religious associations based on a marketplace organization and destined to characterize pan-Protestant "evangelical" organizations in the nineteenth and twentieth centuries.

In an ironic process that Whitefield could not have foreseen and may not have realized, his revivals had become, in effect, an institution. He brought new meaning to the term *revival* and, in so doing, achieved an unanticipated social respectability.

As institutions, revivals could be staged at will and enlisted as engines of enormously powerful social and religious organization. Sometimes, as in the case of the Wesleys, Moravians, and a host of nineteenth-century "Christian" movements, they were instrumental in the formation of new denominations. At other times they remained centered in the charismatic min-

istries of transdenominational revivalists and so stayed autonomous. In either case, they represented a force entirely new
and "evangelical" — a force that defined the future for much
of modern Protestantism in England and America.

In one sense, Whitefield's vision of a revival-driven
transatlantic parachurch committed to the individual experience of the New Birth was nontheological. By not calling the
participants in his revivals a denomination, he got away from
having to craft creedal statements of faith or establish doctrinal requirements for membership that would set one group
of Christians off from another. Yet in another sense, Whitefield's conception was profoundly theological. He avoided
creeds and denominations in the revivals, but at the same time
presented a new theological perspective contained less in his
own Calvinist convictions than in the radical new significance
ascribed to religious experience and spiritual legitimacy. In
answer to the question of what makes for membership in the
true Church of Christ, Whitefield implicitly set forth an alternative model that fit with the modern circumstances of his
revivals.

In the evangelical parachurch, individual experience became the ultimate arbiter of authentic religious faith. Experience — or, in the terms of John Locke, "sensation" — came to
be the legitimating mark of religion over and against family,
communal covenants, traditional memberships, baptisms, or
sacraments. As sensation represented the only avenue for natural knowledge in Lockean epistemology, so the supernatural
experience of the New Birth became the sole authentic means
to spiritual knowledge in the evangelical revivals. Both were
of a piece with the eighteenth-century world in which they
emerged.

The parachurch was not a school for communal nurture
and theological indoctrination so much as it was a context for
individual experience. In it the conversion experience engulfed
all else. Revivalists might argue about the means of the New
Birth and the respective roles of human will and supernatural

205

grace in regeneration, but the experience itself ruled supreme. If there was no new denomination with a capital letter reflecting its establishment, the New Birth itself assumed capital letters as the institutional and theological embodiment of a new religious movement.

Experience. It all came back, in every revival, to this. Seventeenth-century dissenters had spoken often of regeneration and the New Birth, but always in the context of local congregations and weekly education in the sermon. When pressed, they had denied that true conversion could be experienced by those who were ignorant of the theological terms on which it rested. This meant that the teaching function of the church had always received primary emphasis. In a subtle but profound way, Whitefield reversed this emphasis. Instead of theological indoctrination being the foundation of spiritual experience, individual experience became the ground for a shared theology of revival. As long as the foundation was individual experience and the sensation of grace, whatever — or whoever — created it received theological legitimacy at once. Whitefield's stated theological preferences were, of course, Calvinistic and predestinarian. But other revivalists could, and did, build quite different theological frameworks that enjoyed the same experiential legitimation. In the end the revivals were simply not about theology but about experience. Calvinists, Moravians, Methodists, Whitefield — and their evangelical heirs in later generations — would all discover legitimation in the experiences they produced. All would ask the same question: Would God bless a counterfeit movement with true saving grace? The answer would always be No. By their experiential fruits they would be known.

Clearly Whitefield's vision was audacious and far outranged that of his London audiences. But while at home in London, he had no intention of losing those audiences that had first brought him international attention. If he would not found a denomination, he would continue to preach at the Tabernacle and rebuild the crowds that had been badly weakened by de-

206

fections. And in fact Whitefield soon did restore the Tabernacle ministry, with a regimen of daily preaching and three sermons on Sunday. By the end of the summer of 1748, he looked out with satisfaction on audiences that equaled his predeparture crowds and exceeded any others in England, including those of the Wesleys. With this ministry as the hub, he continued his mission of revival in England.

From the Tabernacle Whitefield traveled throughout all the old familiar spots in Bristol, Gloucester, and surrounding towns. Everywhere people flocked to hear him preach, and everywhere appeared the same unmistakable signs of revival that had first marked his previous itinerant tours. After a particularly successful stint of sermons around London, he commented, "I have not known a more considerable awakening for a long time. The Lord comes down as in the days of old, and the shout of a king is amongst us." With London again secured, he was ready to plan for the provinces.

By now Whitefield had reduced his revival schedule to a science. Spring or fall he would devote to tours of Scotland and, on occasion, Ireland or Wales that lasted five or six weeks each. Winter and summer he would spend in and around London. Whenever possible, he would undertake additional voyages to America. When he was not in America, he left the management of orphan-house affairs to assistants, overseeing them through a steady stream of correspondence.

Whitefield's letters through these travels read much like accounts of his earlier experiences. Audiences in Scotland continued to grow in their love of him as time went on. Next to America, Scotland was his favorite stop, the place to which he returned most often. And, as always, Whitefield's health and spirits improved while on tour, soaring with the response of every enthusiastic audience. Each new visit was a new challenge that, once successfully confronted, rejuvenated and inspired.

Invariably, Whitefield's audiences received him with enthusiasm. He had no peer in the pulpit, and he was careful never to overstay his welcome. Whether from the familiar perch by the Orphan Hospital Park in Edinburgh, the court-yards in Glasgow, or the open fields in Cambuslang, the results were the same. In a letter penned from Edinburgh in July 1751, he rejoiced that "the congregations morning and evening amount to many thousands. People flock more than ever, and are desirous of my longer stay."

For the most part, Whitefield's Scottish itinerations now took place without incident. During his 1748 visit, when one presbyter tried to prohibit Whitefield from preaching in the synod of Glasgow because he was not Presbyterian, White-field's friends and supporters easily overcame the objection. All who knew him, they explained, knew that Whitefield had no interest in denominations. His objectives were larger. As Whitefield later reported, "two synods and one Presbytery brought me upon the carpet; but all has worked for good."

After 1748 there was no sustained or organized opposition to his ministry in Scotland. As in America, no anti-Whitefield mobs gathered. At Glasgow he was reconciled with Ralph Erskine and cemented an enduring friendship with John Gillies. Following one especially powerful sermon on Peter's denial of Christ, Gillies marveled how "the whole multitude stood fixed, and hung upon his lips." Crowds grew steadily "larger than ever." Indeed, Whitefield had the run of the Scottish lowlands and the cities. In a letter to his partner in the faith and supporter Lady Huntington, he exulted,

> Oh Edinburgh! Edinburgh! Surely thou must never be forgotten by me! The longer I stayed, the more eagerly both rich and poor attended on the word preached. Perhaps for near twenty-eight days together in *Glasgow* and *Edinburgh*, I preached to near ten thousand souls every day. It would have melted your Ladyship's heart to have seen us part. Ninety four pounds were collected for the *Edinburgh* orphans.

The same could not be said for Ireland. Of all his speaking

tours, the only prominent exception to his enthusiastic receptions was Ireland, and even there the opposition was episodic, with some enthusiastic audiences mixed in. Whitefield's well-known blasts against "pretenders" and "papists" were not likely to win the friends in Ireland that it had in Scotland and America. Earlier the Wesleys had paid dearly at the hands of Irish mobs for their attempts to revive Ireland. In the spring of 1751, Whitefield attempted the same. All went well in Dublin, where Whitefield addressed audiences he estimated in the range of ten thousand. But in Cork, where the Roman Catholic presence loomed great, support was more restrained. Still, he attracted audiences estimated at three thousand and hoped there had "been a stirring among the dry bones."

On a subsequent visit, however, Whitefield felt the wrath of the Irish mob at the hands of the "Ormond Boys." This gang of youths favored the Catholic Prince Charles whom Whitefield had so stridently attacked. While preaching at Oxmanton Green, Whitefield became separated from his friends. Soon he was victimized by an assault of "perfect cruelty":

> Vollies of hard stones came from all quarters, and every step I took, a few stones struck, and made me reel backwards and forwards, till I was almost breathless, and was covered all over with blood. . . . Providentially, a minister's house stood next to the Green. With great difficulty I staggered to the door, which was kindly opened to, and shut upon me. Some of the mob, in the meantime, broke part of the boards of the pulpit into splinters, and beat and wounded my servant grievously in his head and arms.

Whitefield would carry a deep scar on his forehead as a permanent reminder of this event, and he never again returned to Ireland. Although he was willing to absorb punishment in the cause of revival, unlike Harris or Seward, he did not seek it out. Martyrdom for Whitefield was more a figure of speech than a crown to be actively pursued at the hands of the mobs.

But Whitefield would always pursue revival. Besides his work in London and Scotland, he continued to visit America. By 1751 he was back in the New World, picking up where he had left off on his earlier tours. As in Scotland, he was welcomed with the enthusiasm usually reserved for royalty or high dignitaries. The *Boston Evening Post* offered token resistance to Whitefield's "shocking" and backward Calvinist belief that "man by nature is half brute, and half devil," but in colonial America, attacking Calvinism was tilting at windmills. Americans of all stripes now welcomed Whitefield and flocked to hear him preach.

From Whitefield's perspective, nothing had changed from the first dramatic itinerations in 1740. In his written reports covering the years 1748-1751 there are few evident differences in the visits. Such phrases as "a more considerable awakening," "stirring among dry bones," and "great work" show up again and again, together with audience estimates invariably numbering "many thousands" and "larger than ever." To read Whitefield, it would appear that the awakening was still in full flush, with all the promise of transformation contained in the first revivals. Everything remained the same.

Well, almost everything. Conspicuous by their absence were the great conflicts and battles that had marked Whitefield's first tours of the colonies. Expecting "persecution" everywhere, he now encountered only praise and adulation. With much of the old antagonism gone, much of the *fear* that he had once engendered was gone as well.

In the absence of conflict and controversy there emerged confirmation of a remarkable transformation in the meaning of the word *revival*. What had initially been a convulsive and mysterious force upsetting ordinary life and catching participants by surprise had become something different — a familiar event that could be planned in advance, executed flawlessly, and then repeated at the next stop. Gone was the sense of religious crisis that had earlier generated inflated hopes and fears on the parts of friends and enemies.

The full implications of Whitefield's radical redefinition of revival were never clear to him. He was a visionary, not a thinker, and he acted in an intuitive manner. He could not see beyond the numbers and the enthusiasm he attracted, could not see the great changes taking place around him after a decade of itinerant ministry. And even as he had changed the meaning of revival, so the revivals were changing him from social firebrand to culture hero.

Culture heroes always emerge after the crisis has passed and the transformation is successfully completed. By 1750, the interests of most Americans were moving away from religion to concerns of war and politics. While "religion" was as thriving a concern as ever in audience size and emotional response, the fire was gone, or rather redirected to other more pressing concerns. "Revival" had disappeared in the awakening sense of an all-encompassing phenomenon dominating communal consciousness and erasing all other conversations. In fact, the "Great Awakening" had moved throughout most of the colonies and, with the exception of southern revivals in the 1760s and similar activity in Nova Scotia in the 1770s, they did not reappear widely again until after the American Revolution.

Yet to read Whitefield, nothing had changed. And for him, nothing had. Crowds remained robust, audiences wept, offerings were bountiful, and conversions palpable — all of which confirmed in his mind a continuous and ongoing revival. For him, revivals were as regular and recurrent as the seasons of the year. This could have been the case only insofar as the new revivals he spawned had evolved from outsider events to acceptable — and unexceptionable — additions to the marketplace. Defined by the traditional criteria of communal awakening, mass enthusiasm, obsession with religion in public discussions, and heated controversy, the revivals had died. But defined more functionally as a mass event in an open setting orchestrated by a skilled performer and geared to raising individual experience and passion, "revivals" persisted as strongly as ever. Whitefield came to associate the latter meaning with the term.

211

His own sincerity and spiritual commitment remained constant throughout. Yet his revivals had become, in effect, a form of entertainment. As one could leave a theater profoundly moved by the passions evoked, so one could leave a Whitefield revival transformed by the New Birth. While the New Birth was undoubtedly meaningful in a personal, devotional sense, the social consequences were minimal. In his fateful decision to side against the separatists in Scotland and America, Whitefield had also determined that his revivals would *not* become social threats.

Entertainment, of course, was not Whitefield's intent. His intent was the salvation of lost souls. But inadvertently he had helped to push revivals in the direction of entertainment. In this sense, he was undone by his very success. Deprived of the corrective tonic of failure and social confrontation, "revival" had become a predictable, known quantity of little threat or consequence. The only real surprise for Whitefield now would have come had he gone out to preach and found no one there to listen. This never happened.

In fact, Whitefield's moment of creative and critical innovation had passed with his youth. With no denomination bearing his name, he had become less a fixed planet in a revived universe than a meteor — a metaphor he frequently favored in describing itinerant preachers — that flashed across the sky, dazzled all with its brilliance, and then receded from view. Though brilliant, the "gospel meteors" were apt to be ephemeral. The passions they released were real and the lessons unforgettable, but other movements and events would capture the momentum released by Whitefield's innovations and push it in new directions.

As Whitefield's revivals became routine, they — and he — became less threatening. His gifts *were* extraordinary. But without the fear they had formerly engendered, they were as apt to entertain and edify the gentle as the disinherited. Even in England many of the old fears had receded. By 1747 a socially respectable Whitefield was even ready to play to the English aristocracy. John Wesley seldom appealed to the wealthy and insisted that "the poor are the Christians. I am quite out of conceit with almost all those who have this world's goods." But Whitefield felt no such constraints. If he would not discriminate against denominations, neither would he discriminate against classes. His own climb to reclaimed status and his fascination with the wealthy were ongoing. Given an opening, he was glad to preach before new, more respectable audiences.

His opening appeared in the form of his friend and sponsor Lady Huntington. Throughout 1747, he saw her regularly and worked with her to establish a number of methodist chapels. On August 22, 1748, he was appointed her chaplain and agreed to preach at her estate. In a letter he wrote to her that month, he revealed his great desire to reach the wealthy, employing the familiar Pauline identity: "Paul preached privately to those that were of reputation. This must be the way I presume of dealing with the nobility, who yet know not the Lord. O that I may be enabled, when called to preach to any of them, so to preach as to win their Souls to the blessed Jesus!"

With the change of audience, the character of the Oxford servitor returned, though now with an Oxford degree and the additional title "chaplain to the Countess of Huntington." Whitefield deferred to his aristocratic betters with all the old ingratiating skills he had learned at the Inn. When addressed once by Huntington as co-worker and "friend," Whitefield confessed that "when your Ladyship stiled me 'your friend,' I was amazed at your condecension. I am ashamed to think your Ladyship will admit me under your roof, much more am I amazed that the Lord Jesus will make use of such a creature as I am." To modern eyes, such exaggerated deference and groveling seems almost pitiable. Yet it was one with Whitefield's highly ambivalent love/hate relationship with privilege and class.

In short order Whitefield became a hit with the aristocracy. Always the conversationalist, he soon regaled this highbrow company with dramatic stories spanning several continents and cultures. Few full-time adventurers had seen as much of the world as Whitefield had seen, and he had a story-teller's gift for describing it. Combine this with his knack of ingratiation and he was almost guaranteed to please, if not to persuade.

With Huntington's patronage, Whitefield added another "field" to his ministry outside of the established church, this time in the posh drawing rooms and parlors of the English aristocracy. With barely concealed enthusiasm, he wrote a friend that he was preaching twice weekly "among great com-pany" at Huntington's London estate. Included among the frequent guests and visitors were such luminaries of polite society as Lord Chesterfield, Lord Bolingbroke, the Earl of Burlington, Lord Melcombe, the Earl of Aberdeen, and William Pitt the First Earl of Chatham.

Although he did not convert many noblemen to the methodist discipline, he did garner rave reviews from the highest quarters. In a letter to Lady Selina, Lord Bolingbroke marveled at the performance: "He has the most commanding eloquence I ever heard in any person; his abilities are very considerable; his zeal unquenchable; and his piety and excel-lence genuine — unquestionable." In similar terms Lord Chesterfield remarked that "Mr. Whitefield's eloquence is un-rivalled — his zeal inexhaustable; and not to admire both would argue a total absence of taste."

If Whitefield converted few noblemen, the same could not be said of the noblewomen who flocked to hear his message and then took up the cause. Included among the noblewomen Whitefield counted as "lasting converts" were Lady Fanny Shirley, Lady Anne Frankland, Lady Gertrude Botham, the Countess DeLitz, Lady Rockingham, Lady Hyndford, Lady Chesterfield, and Lady Betty Germain. Many of these women gave liberally to the causes of the Tabernacle and the chapels, and others worked in other ways to continue the good work. The Countess DeLitz followed Huntington's example and opened her home to Whitefield's preaching. In a letter to Lady

Huntington he remarked, "on Saturday I had the honour of being almost all the day long with Lady F, Lady H, Lady C, and the Countess of D. Lady F. and the Countess received the blessed sacrament before the others came, and I think they both grow."

Whitefield's relationship with Huntington and company stood in stark contrast to his relationship with his family. The close ties that the Wesleys had with their mother Susannah, or Jonathan Edwards with his wife Sarah, had no equivalent in Whitefield's life. Like other male and female methodist itinerants, he sought sustenance and meaning from within the methodist fellowship. Throughout this period there was little correspondence to suggest close connections to his wife or mother. Only a handful of letters to his mother survive, and their tone is cool. Instead of sounding like a grateful son, Whitefield tended to take on the tone of pastor, concerned more for his mother's spiritual estate than her more immediate temporal and emotional needs. This was, after all, the destiny she had given him, and it was what he gave back to her.

Upon returning from his American tour in 1752, he learned that his mother had died. The news did little to interrupt his ministry or plans for the funding and construction of a new tabernacle at Moorfields. The woman who had done so much to shape his destiny had not elicited warm affections later in life, nor much comment in death. Few — including many of Whitefield's later biographers — even took notice of the event. Perhaps on a level Whitefield could never have recognized, alongside public praise came private resentment for a mother who had so definitively carved his destiny without consultation. In any case, her death did nothing to interrupt his regular preaching in the Tabernacle, around London, and among the London nobility.

Following a winter at the Tabernacle, a restless Whitefield prepared again in the spring of 1753 for travel. He wrote once more to Lady Selina from Scotland confirming that "people flock more than ever, and earnestly entreat me not to leave

215

them soon." From Edinburgh, he took the now well-worn road to Glasgow, again addressing crowds "larger than ever." He also retained the interest and support of the Scottish aristocracy. Then in the summer he went to Bristol and Wales, preaching twenty times in two weeks and over a course of three hundred miles — this at a time when England had almost no reliable roads, in the modern sense of firm, dry highways secure from flooding and thieves.

With all his newfound respectability and interest in the English aristocracy, Whitefield never lost interest in the American colonies. They dominated his conversations outside the pulpit and engaged his deepest loyalties. Alongside regular correspondence and offerings for the orphan house, Whitefield looked to assist other American causes. When his friend Governor Joseph Belcher moved from the Massachusetts to New Jersey, he sought Whitefield's help in promoting the Log College (which eventually settled in Princeton, New Jersey). Whitefield was happy to oblige, seeing in that college the best pattern for a revival-centered "school of the prophets." While in Scotland, Whitefield urged William McCulloch and Gillies to support the New Jersey college, noting its strategic value for the revival: "the spreading of the gospel in Maryland and Virginia, in great measure depends on it." Through his efforts, substantial contributions were raised at a critical time in the history of what would later become Princeton University.

American guests were always welcomed in Whitefield's London home, and he continued to promote their interests on the Old World side of the Atlantic. In January 1754, on the eve of his fifth visit to America, he entertained the Presbyterian revivalist Gilbert Tennent and his young associate Samuel Davies as they visited the isles on a fund-raising mission for the College of New Jersey. In the course of the visit, Davies heard Whitefield preach for the first time. In technical terms, he observed, "the Discourse was incoherent." There was little of the text-doctrine-application schema taught in the schools. But the effects were unparalleled and, on reflection, wrote

Davies, the dramatic manner "seemed to me better calculated to do good to mankind than all the accurate, languid Discourses I have heard." The lessons Davies learned were unforgettable and would find expression in the young minister's own evangelical preaching in the American South.

By March 1754, Whitefield was again en route to America. A brief stopover in Lisbon allowed him the opportunity to visit many Catholic churches and observe their services. Nothing in what he saw persuaded him that Catholicism was anything other than papist "superstition," but the dramatist in him could not help but recognize the power of the ritual. On one occasion he described a reenactment of the crucifixion replete with a stage, cross, and wooden statue of Jesus surrounded by weeping disciples. At length the "corpse" was taken down and placed in an open sepulcher amidst the grieving disciples: "John and Magdalen attended the obsequies; but the image of the Virgin Mary was placed upon the front of the stage, in order to be kissed, adored, and worshipped by the people. Thus ended the Good Friday's tragic-comical, superstitious, idolatrous farce."

Another exhibit made his blood run cold, as he indicated in a letter to a friend:

> As I stood near the altar, over against the great door, I must confess my very inmost soul was struck with a secret horror, when, upon looking up, I saw over the front of the great window of the Church, the heads of many hundred *Jews,* painted on canvas, who had been condemned by what they call the *Holy Inquisition,* and carried out from the church to be burnt — Strange way this, of compelling people to come in! Such was not thy method, O meek and compassionate Lamb of God! Thou camest not to destroy men's lives, but to save them — But bigotry is as cruel as the grave. — It knows no remorse.

Age had done nothing to dampen Whitefield's harsh censures of Catholicism on religious and political grounds. And

217

as war with France was again looming on the horizon, he was prompted to remind his correspondents that "never did civil and religious liberty appear to me in such a light as now. . . . O happy England! O happy Methodists!"

Once in America, Whitefield worked in his usual tireless fashion to shore up past connections and forge new alliances. Georgia having been reestablished as a royal colony in 1752, slavery was now allowed, and there was no longer a need for the South Carolina plantation. All resources were transferred to Bethesda, including a force of slaves for whom, Whitefield rejoiced, "nothing seems to be wanted but a good overseer, to instruct the negroes in sowing and planting." He also instructed them in Christianity. Together with evangelical planters such as Jonathan Bryan, James Habersham, and William Knox, Whitefield became notable for his efforts to Christianize the slaves. Beginning with the work of these men, slaves were given the resources for constructing their own slave religion in evangelical terms that eventually led to the creation of an autonomous black church.

Throughout the summer, Whitefield traveled widely through the middle colonies and New England with undiminished zeal and unsurpassed public adulation. At Princeton, the college repaid his constant support with the award of an honorary M.A. degree. At the Old North meetinghouse in Boston the audience was so large that he had to enter the church through a window, in a move reminiscent of his first triumphant tour of New England. Elsewhere the results were the same, leading a rejuvenated Whitefield to write John Gillies that "my reception has been far superior to that of fourteen years ago."

In ways that Whitefield never fully understood, he had become an American hero whose life and words reflected the yawning ambitions and libertarian rhetoric of the young colonies. If he no longer generated controversy, it was not so much because his message had changed as because the American people had. The spiritual and social lessons they had learned in the outdoor revivals were irreversible. Rich and poor alike now conceded the legitimacy of open-air, popularly sanctioned mass assemblies. Even more, they acknowledged that the people had a right to judge what was best for their religious and civil lives. When a writer to the *Boston Gazette* complained that Whitefield had no right to speak in the marketplace or public buildings, a respondent stated that such places belonged to "the people" and could be used in any manner the people saw fit: "they are Englishmen and have a Right to meet in them when they judge they have occasion for it, either for Civil or Religious purposes."

Whitefield knew little of the "Commonwealthman Ideology" that celebrated the rights of Englishmen, but he understood the rhetoric perfectly. It was as much his creation as anyone's. In time this libertarian rhetoric would grow to a revolutionary pitch. But from its first expression it was identified with Whitefield. As Americans moved ever forward in their great "experiment in liberty" the name Whitefield would continue to lead them and be identified with their quest.

12   An Uncommon Friendship

Of all Whitefield's friendships, two stand out: those with Howell Harris and Benjamin Franklin. Harris introduced Whitefield to the fields, taught him how to be brave in the pulpit, and later found him a wife. Franklin introduced Whitefield to the American press and later served as his Pennsylvania agent for orphan-house funds. Harris was an austere methodist of such moral stature that he gave the woman who loved him to Whitefield rather than be tempted by her affection. Franklin was a resigned humanist whose dalliances with women he fully revealed in his memoirs. It is ironic, then, that Whitefield's friendship with Harris was eventually strained over Harris's indiscretions with a woman, while his friendship with Franklin grew stronger with every passing year. In the end, Franklin became Whitefield's best American friend and, reciprocally, Whitefield was Franklin's only evangelical friend.

Unlike many public figures, Whitefield avoided to a remarkable degree the temptations peculiar to his calling — greed, denomination-founding, and womanizing. His fortitude was simply underscored by the news that Harris had taken up with a female admirer. At the time of the scandal, Harris was married to a young convert named Anne Williams. While preaching in North Wales in 1748, Harris met another methodist convert, Sidney Griffith, the wife of a ne'er-do-well Welsh squire. Griffith soon became strongly attracted to the aggressive "Hammer and Axe" Harris. Before long she was sharing with him divine "revelations," which she believed would enhance his ministry. Harris, himself recovering from a bad head wound inflicted by a mob, accepted her inspiration, and the two became collaborators. Soon Griffith deserted her husband and, with Anne Harris's consent, moved into the Harris home. The relationship between preacher and convert grew warmer. With "Madam Griffith's" encouragement, Harris moved in ever more charismatic directions, believing that her inspiration would "rise me with the great" saints of the church.

So dependent did Harris become on Griffith that the two began traveling together. This Whitefield could not tolerate. Such behavior called the entire methodist enterprise into question. Already critics hinted that the ultimate outcome of charismatic, passion-based ministries was, as with the stage, sexual indiscretion. Now Harris was providing fuel for such accusations. Whitefield had no choice but to distance himself from his friend, however painful it might be. In August 1751, Whitefield refused to open the Tabernacle pulpit to Harris unless he repented. But only in 1752, when Griffith died, did a repentant Harris return to the methodist fold. It was too late. The once-dear friendship with Whitefield had sustained a numbing blow from which it never revived.

Franklin was a different story. His sexual indiscretions were well known, but they were of no real consequence to the methodist cause and had no potential to compromise Whitefield's ministry. Indeed, Franklin's youthful charm and easy access to female company may even have won a secret admiration in the shyer, more repressed Whitefield. Surely here, as in many other places, each man must have seen in the other an appealing road not taken. In addition, Franklin would have seen in Whitefield a cleric whose Christianity and sense of charity were bigger than his denomination. And Whitefield would have viewed Franklin as a virtuous public man whose dedication to public works and charity had few Christian equals. Such was their mutual affection that Franklin forever encouraged Whitefield to look after the state of his badly deteriorating health, while Whitefield continually encouraged Franklin to look after the state of his badly deteriorating soul. Through their solicitations both earthly and heavenly, they displayed the deep concern they had for each other.

Throughout the period of Whitefield's disillusionment with Harris, his friendship with Franklin continued to grow. Already by the summer of 1752, over a decade of steady communication and mutual concern had accumulated between them. When not in America, the two had kept up a steady correspondence, partly over publishing business, but more often simply to share events in one another's lives. When in 1752 Franklin's pathbreaking experiments with electricity came to Whitefield's attention, they prompted a warm letter apprising Franklin that in England "you grow more and more famous in the learned." By the time Franklin retired from the printing business, this unlikely friendship had grown even stronger. In fact, Whitefield celebrated Franklin wherever he traveled, while Franklin memorialized Whitefield in his *Autobiography*.

On the face of it, there could have been no more unusual a combination for friendship than the creed-despising Franklin and the deist-despising Whitefield. Each was on public record as opposing much of the philosophy the other stood for. Yet on further reflection, there appear deeper similarities and affinities that make their friendship intelligible.

To begin with, both had an uncommonly direct and perceptive understanding of the transitional age in which they lived. A seventeenth-century Whitefield or Franklin would have been inconceivable. With no postal service (Franklin's

222

invention), no newspapers, urban market centers, regular transatlantic travel, or religious toleration, the kind of entrepreneurial creativity evidenced by Franklin and Whitefield could not have existed. The old monarchical, aristocratic, and coercive social order was changing in ever more individualistic and voluntaristic ways. From their respective sides of the ocean, and in their respective careers, Whitefield and Franklin had developed a transatlantic sense of, and an instinct for, the new markets that were reshaping their world — and both had discovered how to exploit these new forces.

In particular, both exhibited a precocious appreciation for the art of promotion and the consequent power of popularity. Whether through personal charisma in the case of Whitefield or through the power of the press in the case of Franklin, both knew how to exploit the temper of their times. They capitalized on the departure from traditional associations that was moving their worlds toward new networks premised on voluntary association and self-interest. In voluntary methodist "societies" and in political "juntos," engines of enormous power were created capable of challenging   and defeating — entrenched authority in church and state.

Franklin's effective use of the newspaper in Pennsylvania politics was a model for Whitefield in his pioneering work with religious magazines and letters to the press. Besides being Whitefield's most reliable American printer, Franklin taught Whitefield the power of the popular news sheets. All the learned pamphlets in the world could be arrayed against Whitefield, but if he dominated the popular press, he could overcome all obstacles.

In like manner, Whitefield taught Franklin invaluable lessons in the art of self-promotion. Whitefield's *Journals* were, as we have seen, notable both for their shameless egocentricity and for the creation of a persona deliberately crafted for public dissemination and image. Franklin, in his own way, imitated this in his memoirs, leaving historians a deliberately constructed persona that forever hides the man behind the pose.

223

The memoirs of both tell the story of self-made men who through sheer determination tapped the new forces reshaping their society. In the process, both offer didactic warnings against "cheap grace" that seeks to circumvent unceasing labor in the cause. For Whitefield, the moment of truth had come as the Oxford servitor faced his inability to win divine favor or social status. For Franklin the moment had come when Gov. Thomas Penn proved an unreliable benefactor, forcing a young Ben to go to work to pay off his debt. Through carefully selected personal examples and personality sketches, each of the memoirs creates a popular persona in a highly dramatic manner accompanied by engaging dialogue. Both the forlorn Oxford servitor and Poor Richard adopt colorful styles and autobiographical lessons designed to teach people — particularly young people — the way to happiness, whether temporal (Franklin) or eternal (Whitefield).

In their married lives as well, the two evidenced remarkable, though in this case regrettable, similarities. Both displayed decreasing rather than increasing care for their wives. As Whitefield was frequently absent from home in preaching, so Franklin was separated for years from Deborah, with little show of regret. Franklin's letters to Deborah were perfunctory and mostly matters of bookkeeping and enjoinders to thrift. And both husbands seemed almost embarrassed to be seen with their wives. However different their reasons, and however different their responses to women generally, both suffered an emptiness in their private lives that they filled with unceasing public service. More important than shared market instincts or obsessions with public service, however, were the warm feelings that Franklin and Whitefield shared for one another. Indeed, these feelings found expression in no other context — feelings of loyalty, concern, and well-meaning that did not depend on ideological connection or obligation but grew out of sheer affection. The inner selves both hid so well from the public were the caring selves they unveiled to one another in moments of intuitive recognition. With each other, Whitefield the actor-preacher and Franklin the literary persona became real people living out the moral codes they proclaimed.

Ironically, the unshakable loyalties that Franklin and Whitefield shared stood in sharp contrast to the betrayals both experienced in their professional associations. For all his methodist proclamations, Whitefield came to feel betrayed by the defections of many of his closest methodist affiliates, including John Wesley, James Hutton, John Cennick, John Syms, Elizabeth Delamotte, and Howell Harris. Left with uncertain religious allies and a superficial marriage, Whitefield may well have valued his friendship with Franklin as highly — if not more highly — than he did his shared faith with methodist co-laborers. In like manner, many of Franklin's closest political and business associations and alliances soured as his reputation rose and fell on both sides of the Atlantic. On more than one occasion, Whitefield lent his pen to restore Franklin's credibility.

Contained in the friendship of Whitefield and Franklin is a testimony to the power of a changing, increasingly mobile and impersonal world to mold relationships. These men lived in a public world to a far greater extent than most of their contemporaries, and both were uniquely placed to base friendship on feeling rather than traditional bonds of family, neighborhood, or shared ideologies. Neither the church nor the local community constituted the center of Whitefield's or Franklin's peripatetic worlds. Both men, in fact, were most at ease in transit, and they invariably recorded their greatest pleasures far from home. In a sense, both *had* to establish friendships outside of traditional boundaries: traditional friendships were out of the question. So they injected great emotional energy instead into their transitory friendships. Although personal contacts between Whitefield and Franklin were few and far between, their emotional bond remained strong, finding sustenance in their correspondence as well as their ongoing efforts to do favors for each other.

For both Franklin and Whitefield, the antithesis of per-

225

sonal trust and voluntary commitment was institutional fiat. Neither could serve two masters. In their experience-driven worlds, hierarchical institutions could not be trusted. At the same time, new personal associations forged in voluntary settings had become natural. Franklin's bitterness toward entrenched political interests is well known. Equally evident was his hostility to all religious denominations. Instead of promoting gospel works of charity, he believed, denominations existed for their own sake and actually worked at cross purposes to the universal gospel they proclaimed. Hierarchical and aristocratic denominations (particularly Anglicans and Presbyterians), Franklin complained, "serv'd principally to divide us and make us unfriendly to one another." His use of the term *unfriendly* is significant. He considered friendships forged in coercive institutions to be suspicious and illegitimate; often as not they rested on artificial foundations bereft of personal experience and so tended "to lessen the good Opinion another might have of his own Religion."

Franklin's personal response to denominational factionalism was to cease attending church altogether, reserving Sundays as a day of private prayer and study. Franklin hardly ever went to church, and when he did, he invariably left with a feeling that the true gospel had been left outside. A visit to Philadelphia's Presbyterian church convinced him that the minister, Jedediah Andrews, knew nothing of truly disinterested moral works: "his Discourses were chiefly either polemic Arguments, or Explications of the peculiar Doctrines of our Sect, and were all to me very dry, uninteresting and unedifying, since not a single moral Principle was inculcated or enforc'd, their Aim seeming to be rather to make us Presbyterians than good Citizens."

Whitefield agreed, except that he would have substituted "good Christians" for "good Citizens." But instead of avoiding religious affiliation, he sought to transcend it. Like Franklin, Whitefield saw in religious denominations an ossification and perversion of the spontaneous religion recorded in the gospel accounts he re-enacted. Churchmen of all denominations were more concerned with perpetuating their institutional trusts than with furthering the evangelical and charitable imperatives of the gospel. In his own way, Whitefield too balked at the petty institutional rivalries of denominations. In so doing, he became, with Franklin, a voice speaking out against traditional institutions and looking toward more spontaneous, popular bases of association that would free individuals from the shackles of privilege and hierarchical interest.

Besides sharing an antipathy toward traditional institutions, both men placed a premium on voluntary charity rather than institutional tithes. Almost alone among eighteenth-century churchmen, Whitefield consistently fused his gospel message with unceasing nondenominational plans of charity and good works. The orphan house and Pennsylvania school for blacks were merely the most conspicuous extrainstitutional religious agencies he promoted. He frequently took up offerings for local charities throughout Britain and in Germany for schools and orphan houses and for public relief, and he dug deeply into his own pocket when he did. At the same time, he refused to contribute moneys to his own Anglican church.

As Franklin saw Whitefield in a peculiarly humanitarian light, so Whitefield encountered a more religious Franklin than most saw. In fact, Franklin's religious cavils were directed less at religion per se than at religious *institutions*. Underneath his objections was a passionate religious seeker. In conversations and correspondence with Whitefield, he confessed a deep-seated religious consciousness that affirmed his belief in a personal God and an eternal afterlife of rewards and punishments. Though unwilling to speculate on the divinity of Christ, Franklin confessed in his *Autobiography*,

> I never was without some religious Principles; I never doubted, for instance, the Existence of the Deity, that he made the World, and govern'd it by his Providence; that the most acceptable Service of God was the doing Good to Man; that our Souls are immortal; and that all Crime

227

will be punished and Virtue rewarded either here or hereafter; these I esteem'd the Essentials of every Religion, and being to be found in all the Religions we had in our Country I respected them all, tho' with different degrees of Respect as I found them more or less mix'd with other Articles which without any Tendency to inspire, promote or confirm Morality, serv'd principally to divide us and make us unfriendly to one another.

The inner consistencies and unities shared by Franklin and Whitefield are also revealed in their correspondence. In letters and conversation, religion was often discussed. Franklin allowed himself to be drawn out on the subject of personal religiosity with Whitefield as with no one else, finding in Whitefield a listener he could trust — if not agree with. Ever the evangelist, Whitefield followed up his praise for Franklin's electrical experiments with a customary entreaty: "As you have made a pretty considerable progress in the mysteries of electricity, I would now humbly recommend to your diligent unprejudiced pursuit and study the mystery of the new birth." Such sentiments were vintage Whitefield, yet his tone was one of sympathy and the mutual understanding of friends. He always presented his advice to Franklin in the context of concern rather than controversy. Aware that his own views were perfectly understood by Franklin, he could close with a good-natured "what do you expect?" from a revivalist: "you will excuse this freedom. I must have *aliquid Christi* [something of Christ] in all my letters." This was the integrity that Franklin had come to expect.

And Whitefield knew what to expect from Franklin. When Whitefield told Franklin he had no place to stay on an early visit to Philadelphia, Franklin replied, "You know my House, if you can make shift with its scanty Accomodations you will be most heartily welcome. He replied, that if I made that kind Offer for Christ's sake, I should not miss of a Reward, — And I return'd, *Don't let me be mistaken; it was not for Christ's sake, but for your sake.*"

The religious Franklin that emerged in his correspondence with Whitefield bore little resemblance to the scoffer at religious hypocrisy and institutionalized religion that appeared in his public pose. To Whitefield he revealed a deeply reflective religious consciousness struggling to come to grips with the contradictions between gospel morality and the immorality of Christians. Franklin's ethical emblem, no less than Whitefield's, was Christ, but a Christ known chiefly through his ethical concerns and actions rather than his divinity and saving atonement. In one letter to Whitefield, Franklin noted that, unlike many churchmen, Christ "thought much less of those outward appearances and professions. . . . He professed that he came not to call the righteous — but sinners to repentance, which implied his modest opinion that there were some in his time who thought themselves so good, that they need not hear even him for improvement." So too, in Franklin's experience, there were too many who talked the New Birth but lived the old lies: "I wish it was more productive of good works — works of kindness, charity, mercy and public spirit, not holy day keeping, sermon reading — or making long prayers — full of flatteries and compliments."

In another letter, Franklin sought to further clarify his religious faith. At base, it was profoundly ethical and self-deprecating: "You will see by my notion of good works, that I am far from expecting to Merit Heaven by them," Franklin explained. By "heaven, we understand a state of happiness infinite in degree, and eternal in duration." Of this blissful state, Franklin confessed, "I can do nothing to deserve such rewards."

In fact, Franklin thought much about heaven, and in another letter confessed that "that Being who gave me existence, and thro' almost threescore Years has been Continually showering his Favours upon me, whose very Chastisements have been Blessings to me, can I doubt that he loves me? And if he loves me, can I doubt that he will go on to take care of me not only here but hereafter?" Franklin's destination, like Whitefield's, was heaven. And in both cases, they understood the agency to be an unmerited divine invitation that was profoundly unimpressed with the various cheap graces of this world. To Franklin and Whitefield — outwardly proud, assertive achievers — humility may well have been their greatest strength. Franklin expressed it passionately in a letter to Whitefield when he confessed, "we are all of a family. For my own Part, when I am employed in serving others, I do not look upon myself as conferring favors but paying debts. . . . I can only shew my gratitude for those mercies from God by readiness to help his other children and my brethren."

In Whitefield, Franklin saw someone who was different from other churchmen. Beneath Whitefield's bombast and showmanship, Franklin saw a truly virtuous character who did not hesitate to throw in his lot with slaves, women, Indians, and orphans — those eighteenth-century lepers ignored by most clerics.

Yet there was also something Franklin found disturbing in Whitefield's humility, for at the heart of Whitefield's actions was the experience of the New Birth — an experience Franklin never felt. This experiential void became the source of religious crisis. If Franklin was deeply religious, it was ultimately a somber religion, lacking the comforts of Whitefield's evangelical piety. Franklin hoped, but could never believe, in an actively involved, caring deity. The Incarnation was, for him, a matter of speculation that he chose to reject. With no Incarnation, there was no embodied assurance of a caring, involved God. In a later letter to Whitefield, written in the midst of brewing colonial tensions, he confessed,

> I *see* with you that our affairs are not well managed by our rulers here below. I wish I could *believe* with you, that they are well attended to by those above. I rather suspect, from certain circumstances, that though the general government of the universe is well administered, our particular little affairs are perhaps below notice, and left to take the chance of human prudence or imprudence, as either may happen to be uppermost. It is, however, an uncomfortable thought, and I leave it.

230

To this, Whitefield scrawled across the bottom: *"Uncomfortable indeed! and, blessed be God, unscriptural."*

Here we see the greatest difference separating the religious worlds of Franklin and Whitefield. For Franklin, the experience of personal friendship could not be translated into an experience of personal faith. The result was profound pessimism. Ironically, Franklin's personal religion was more serious and filled with a sense of ultimate depravity than Whitefield's Calvinistic — but ultimately optimistic — methodism. Franklin, the outwardly jovial humorist, and Whitefield, the outwardly stern Calvinist, were at heart opposites. In all his activities, Whitefield was forever buoyed by the hope of a caring God, while the unceasingly active Franklin felt forever tortured by the fear that no one took note of his petty "little affairs." Whitefield built a revival confident that the drama in which he played at center stage was a divine one. Franklin built a nation plagued by the fear that no one ultimately cared.

Whenever Whitefield traveled to Philadelphia he was a guest in the Franklin home, and he won the affection of the whole family. He routinely inquired into the affairs of Franklin's children. And Franklin evidenced a reciprocal concern with Whitefield's shaky health and troubled finances. As orphan-house debts mounted, Franklin even contrived schemes to raise money by public subscription and donated £75 from his own pocket.

But the most remarkable gesture of friendship and trust between Franklin and Whitefield appeared in a letter written by Franklin in July 1756. At that time Whitefield was in England while in America the colonists were absorbing one devastating defeat after another at the hands of the French. The future of the Anglo-American hinterland seemed in question. In this troubled atmosphere, Franklin wrote Whitefield with a remarkable proposition. He began by musing about their lives and about the possibility of finishing them with something big. In terms certain to arouse Whitefield's interest, he observed that "life like a dramatic piece, should not be conducted with reg-

231

ularity, but, methinks, it should finish handsomely. Being now in the last act, I begin to cast about for something fit to end with." Each had accomplished great things in his life. Perhaps, the time had arrived to do something together that would bring the best of both of their worlds together in a united effort. Why not, Franklin continued, "settle a colony in Ohio?"

Franklin undoubtedly recognized that such a request to Whitefield came out of the blue, so he immediately followed with some practical considerations. The colony would serve both as a frontier buffer between France and the seaboard and as a model of virtue and piety. The implication here was that Franklin would take care of the virtue, and Whitefield would handle the piety. Ever the entrepreneur, Franklin envisioned a planned settlement like the colonies of old that would be both prosperous for the colonists and beneficial to the Indians: "Might it not greatly facilitate the introduction of pure religion among the heathen, if we could, by such a colony, shew them a better sample of Christians than they commonly see in our Indian traders?" With the two of them working together, the experiment in virtue and piety could not fail. Surely God would bless their endeavor "if we undertook it with a sincere regard to His honour, the service of our gracious King, and (which is the same thing), the public good."

Unfortunately, no record survives of Whitefield's response. The proposition would undoubtedly have been appealing as it spoke to precisely the sort of project Whitefield would seek to implement and suggested precisely the right friend. Yet the timing was bad. Whitefield's health was shaky at that time, and he could not travel widely. While Franklin was wrong about his own imminent "finish," he was not far off the mark with Whitefield. Nevertheless, the proposition stands as an unequaled testimony to the trust and friendship Franklin exhibited toward his itinerant friend.

With Franklin in England from 1757 to 1762, the two continued to enjoy their friendship and, as we shall see in a later chapter, to help each other greatly. Even as Franklin offered support for the orphan house and Whitefield's dream of converting Bethesda into a southern college, so Whitefield supported Franklin's efforts to establish the Philadelphia Academy (later the University of Pennsylvania) and urged that the school use the "New Building" originally constructed for his revivals. Whitefield also proved to be Franklin's steady political ally in the face of critics in both England and America.

Franklin termed their friendship not a spiritual affinity but a "mere Civil Friendship." Yet the "mere" should not be taken to imply superficiality or a passing acquaintance. In fact, for these two with lives so utterly public and so privately bankrupt, their friendship proved uniquely reliable. In important ways their friendship was stronger *because* there was no spiritual affinity. In effect, each humanized the other and, in powerful ways, confirmed the other in the choices they made. Without the common foundation of methodist society or junto, each was freed to see in the other a true friend who transcended party interests, a friend who could be trusted in a profoundly untrustworthy world.

Neither converted the other, though Whitefield never ceased trying. After reading the cleverly composed epitaph in which Franklin likened his life to an old volume that, with death, would hopefully be restored "in a new and more perfect Edition, corrected and amended by the Author," Whitefield replied: "I have seen your *Epitaph*. Believe on Jesus, and get a feeling possession of God in you, and you cannot possibly be disappointed of your expected second edition, finely corrected, and infinitely amended."

Though unconverted, Franklin was not unappreciative. Whitefield, alone among clergymen, had earned the right to preach to him. Small wonder, then, that in a letter to his brother John written toward the end of Whitefield's life, Franklin inquired into the health of his old friend and closed with the poignant confession: "He is a good man and I love him."

233

13 Dr. Squintum

At the same time Whitefield was introducing his spectacular brand of revivalism to Anglo-American audiences, the English theater was undergoing a transformation of its own. The age of Whitefield was no less the age of David Garrick, and audiences thrilled to the actor Garrick's novel presentation of a more "natural" drama. Interestingly, descriptions of Garrick's popular performances are virtually interchangeable with descriptions of Whitefield's preaching. A contemporary description of Garrick's debut before London audiences in the summer of 1741 by Garrick's friend and biographer Arthur Murphy reads much like accounts of young Whitefield in the fields:

> The power of his imagination was such, that he transformed himself into the very man; the passions rose in rapid succession, and, before he uttered a word, were legible in every feature of that various face. His look, his voice, his attitude, changed with every sentiment. . . . He made a most astonishing impression on the audience. . . . In all this, the audience saw an exact imitation of nature.

234

In advance of established churches and other arts, both the world of the revivals and the world of the stage recognized the signs of the times and responded creatively. Both appealed to the new popular, democratic, and marketing forces that were shaping the age in ways that repudiated conventional and aristocratic rhetorical formulas. In their capacity both to entertain and to mold powerful cultural myths, the theater and revivals were without rival. Sports could entertain and literature could enlighten, but neither could do both with the power and appeal of theater and mass revivals. In both, ordinary people discovered characters like themselves at the center of discourse. Whether caught up in a contemporary stage romance or re-created in a Whitefield rendition of Zaccheus, ordinary people saw themselves become the subject of record. They took from this a newfound sense of importance and in turn gave their eager support — and money. What they began has continued to the present electronic age, and it has become clear that religion and drama represent the two most popular and powerful myth-makers in modern American society.

Inevitably the innovators of stage and revival found themselves locked in mortal combat with one another as they attacked the mores of their culture from opposite sides — the actors flouting their "immorality," and the evangelicals renouncing the world. Yet, in profound if unacknowledged ways, the two were unwitting allies in a united campaign against a passing traditional order. Both were countercultures that stood at the margins of traditional institutions and responded with alienation and opposition. Both called into question social and sexual customs as well as attitudes toward dress and hair style. Female methodist exhorters and female actors (both innovations on their respective "stages") could be found smoking pipes in public and speaking in loud, aggressive voices that defied traditional customs and challenged established gender roles. Finally, and most significantly, both appealed with unrivaled power to the private self in a world increasingly deprived of traditional moral and spiritual public centers.

Despite their different worlds, eighteenth-century actors and revivalists became increasingly aware of one another. When the youthful Garrick introduced his natural rendition of Shakespeare's Richard III, an angry rival actor, James Quin, dismissed him with the quip that "this is the wonder of a day; Garrick is a new religion; the people follow him as another Whitefield, but they will soon return to church again." In fact, Garrick's audiences, like Whitefield's, were there to stay. But the parallels to Whitefield were not lost on Garrick. In response to Quin's public quip, Garrick composed an epigram playing positively on the interconnections of theater, church, and Whitefield:

> Pope Quin, who damns all Churches but his own,
> Complains that Heresy infests the town;
> That Whitefield Garrick has misled the age,
> And taints the sound religion of the Stage.
> He says, that Schism has turn'd the Nation's brain,
> But eyes will open, and to Church again,
> Thou GRAND INFALLIBLE! forbear to roar;
> Thy Bulls and Errors are rever'd no more
> When Doctrines meet with general approbation,
> It is not HERESY, but REFORMATION.

For his part, Whitefield recognized the theater as the church's greatest rival. Wherever he preached, he did his best to close down the playhouses. On his first visit to Philadelphia, he caused a great stir by converting the dancing school master and changing the school into an institution for blacks. In Charleston, one of the American centers where theater got a start, he railed against the art and took pride in decreased theater attendance during his stay there. On his seventh visit to Scotland in 1753, he spoke near a Glasgow theater and angrily denounced playgoing. Later, when the playhouse was dismantled, authorities blamed Whitefield for inciting the mob that brought it down. The irony was certainly not lost on Whitefield. The notion that he, of all people, would incite a mob was "entirely false." Nevertheless, he did concede that "I thought it my duty to shew the evil of having a play-house erected in a trading city — almost, too, before the very door of the university."

In London, Whitefield's blasts against the major playhouses at Covent Garden and Drury Lane were well known and frequent. Yet actors and playwrights frequently attended his performances and invariably saw in him one of their own. Garrick, like Franklin, could immediately distinguish the polished performances from the new creations. By the tenth or fifteenth performance, Whitefield's delivery was so tuned that Garrick marveled at his art and was led to exclaim, "I would give a hundred guineas if I could say 'Oh!' like Mr. Whitefield." Playwright, actor, and comedian Samuel Foote also attended Whitefield's sermons and was impressed by the art, if not the subject matter. According to the ex-Methodist and ardent theatergoer James Lockington, "Mr. Foote was struck by stepping in by chance, and once hearing Whitefield; the mixture of whose absurdity, whim, consequence, and extravagance, pleased his fancy and entertained him highly."

Others from the theater were more than simply pleased or "entertained." Whitefield, alone among eighteenth-century preachers, converted actors. In New York, one of his converts, a "strolling player," left the theater to work at the orphan house. In London, the renowned comic actor Edward Shuter became a frequent visitor to the Tabernacle and a great supporter of Whitefield's ministry. Whitefield, in turn, gave Shuter the dubious honor of being addressed directly in one of his sermons, recounted here by Cornelius Winter:

> The famous comedian, Shuter, who had a great partiality for Mr. Whitefield, showed him friendship, and often attended his ministry. At one period of his popularity he was acting in a drama under the character of Ramble. During the run of the performance he attended service on sabbath at Tottenham-court chapel, and was seated in the pew exactly opposite to the pulpit, and while Mr.

Whitefield was giving full sally to his soul, and in his energetic address, was inviting sinners to the Saviour, he fixed himself full against Shuter, with his eye upon him, adding, to what he had previously said, "And thou, poor Ramble, who hast long rambled from him, come you also. O end your rambling by coming to Jesus."

Shuter was understandably unnerved by the direct public reference, but he remained an admirer. Whitefield, in turn, paid Shuter the ultimate tribute by allowing his own listeners one trip to the Garrick stage: to see Shuter in a benefit performance.

As long as Whitefield and the theater kept a respectful distance, all was well. But when either strayed too close to the other's turf — and customers — trouble followed. If players performed too close to churches or schools, Whitefield screamed. And if Whitefield spoke on the greens on market days, he encountered sustained opposition from the actors.

A crisis was reached in 1756 and 1757. In casting about for new preaching locations, Whitefield sought to gain a preaching stronghold at Long Acre, a fashionable street adjacent to the theater district. The Long Acre chapel had been built earlier, and the Wesleys had preached there without disturbance. But Whitefield was another story. He threatened theater business directly with his pulpit attacks and entertaining style. Those of the theater world viewed his preaching there as an encroachment on their market. Whitefield so effectively wedded drama to pulpit that they feared the secular theater would founder. People's need for dramatic expression would be satisfied in the revivals, while their own performances would be suppressed as a perversion of gospel drama.

Throughout 1756 Whitefield preached at Long Acre and railed against the stage. And the more he preached, the more he coveted the location as a permanent preaching place modeled on the Tabernacle: it was the perfect location from which to bait the actors in their lair. Throughout his twice-weekly sermons, he invariably singled out actors and theatergoing for condemnation and sought to reduce the theaters' audiences.

Not every actor took Whitefield's censure as lightly as Edward Shuter, though many came to a grudging admiration of him as a worthy competitor. James Lockington, present at many of Whitefield's services, rated his pulpit drama "beyond compare." This, he added, was not surprising, for Whitefield "had been really and truly an actor on the stage in the early part of his life."

Lockington's educated ear for dialect, mimicry, and improvisation enabled him to capture Whitefield's pulpit style and speech in a way that eluded most journalistic and ministerial descriptions. Most noticeable to Lockington was Whitefield's distinctive enunciation: "*Lurd* instead of Lord, *Gud* instead of God, as *O Lurd Gud.*" In one sermon at Long Acre, Lockington recorded Whitefield's extemporaneous remarks, diction and all. Knowing that many of his hearers had just come from a play, Whitefield used the occasion to condemn the theater:

> "You go to plays! and what do you see there! Why, if you will not tell me, I will tell you what you see there! — When you see the players on the stage, you see the devil's children grinning at you; and when you go to the playhouse, I suppose you go in ruffles — I wonder whether St. Paul wore ruffles? No; there were no ruffles in those days. I am told," he continued archly, "that people say I bawl, and I will bawl — I will not be a velvet-mouthed preacher, I will not speak the word of *Gud* in a sleepy manner, like your church preachers — I'll tell you a story. The Archbishop of Canterbury in the year 1675, was acquainted with Mr. Butterton the player. One day the arch bishop . . . said to Butterton . . . "pray inform me Mr. Butterton, what is the reason you actors on the stage can affect your congregations with speaking of things imaginary, as if they were real, while we in church speak of things real, which our congregations only receive as if they were imaginary?" "Why my Lord says Butterton, the reason is very plain. We actors on the stage, speak of things imaginary, as if they were real, and you in the

239

pulpit speak of things real, as if they were imaginary."
"Therefore," added Whitefield, "I will bawl, I will not be
a velvet-mouthed preacher."

Sermons like this, both entertaining and biting, did not
sit well with the actors' guild. In response, they did their best
to disrupt Whitefield's Long Acre preaching. The loud clang-
ings of bells, drums, clappers, and cleavers all interrupted the
itinerant's sermons. When this seemed insufficient, the actors
pelted Whitefield and his supporters with stones. While no
serious injuries ensued, there was great irritation.

Whitefield sought redress for the disturbances. In a letter
to Bishop Pearce, he complained that inside the chapel "some
of the windows were stopped up, to prevent, in some degree,
the congregation being disturbed by the unhallowed noise; but
large stones were thrown in at another window, and one young
person was sadly wounded." Beyond this, he darkly hinted
that the rioters had "been hired by subscription," perhaps by
actors, perhaps by bishops.

When the bishop ignored Whitefield's letter, he wrote
another, insisting that the disturbance was "more than noise.
It is *premeditated rioting.*" The noise was so loud that "many
women have been almost frightened to death."

In fact, the physical damage done seems to have been
minimal. The real weapon was the noise. Whitefield wanted a
toehold in the theater district, and the actors were equally
determined that he should not have it. This was one battle
Whitefield would not win. The Wesleys — who never
threatened the theater as Whitefield did — would stay nearby,
but Whitefield would not. Unable to overcome the incessant
noise, he finally gave up the Long Acre project and shifted his
efforts to the construction of a new building at Tottenham
Court. The building was completed in late 1756, allowing
Whitefield to divide his London time between it and the Tabernacle. Thereafter, Long Acre remained out-of-bounds.

When read as cultural history, Whitefield's contest with the

Long Acre players represents a fascinating window into social change and the new forces appearing in the English marketplace. As we have seen, Whitefield and the theater were both voices of the future for many of the same reasons. Yet the futures they represented would not begin to be reconciled until the twentieth century. Throughout much of modern Protestant history, the theater and motion pictures have been viewed as the "devil's workshop." Only with the advent of television has secular drama been approved — and consumed — in evangelical circles.

Whitefield apparently never perceived — certainly never articulated — the parallel ways in which he and the theater were creating new markets for their particular services. But the parallels were not lost on his opponents. After one particularly hostile anti-theater sermon, a writer for the *Monthly Review* defended the art of the theater by exposing Whitefield's own theatricality and self-marketing. The stone throwing and noise were no less regrettable than Whitefield's rash identification of all contemporary theater with Satan:

> We hope the pious orator, Mr. Whitefield, made some reserve in favour of those who frequent the theatres. . . . But, after all, it were no wonder, that a Whitefield, or a Wesley should be jealous of so powerful a rival as Garrick; or even a Woodward, a Shuter, or a Yates. However, it must be allowed uncharitable in any performers, or managers, thus to consign each other's audiences to the devil. We hope our good friends of Drury Lane and Covent Garden have never been chargeable with such unfair and unChristian dealings. Emulation is certainly commendable, while accompanied with honesty and decency; and if we can improve and extend our traffic by furnishing a better commodity than another can, why, it is all fair; but neither decency nor honesty will allow us to break the windows, or to abuse or frighten away the customers, of *our rivals in trade.*

The writer's insights are important. At base, Whitefield and the actors made similar complaints. Each accused the other

241

of driving away their "customers" and, in the process, of inter-
rupting the "trade" between the performer and his "audience."
In the emerging new order, Whitefield and the theater fought
for a market share according to new rules governed less by
mercantile controls and elite institutions — be they church,
state, or aristocracy — than by market forces and the sheer
power of public opinion. As countercultures, both the revivals
and the stage threatened the life of well-regulated traditional
churches and communities. Both served notice on the established order of church and society that its days were numbered.
And both conducted their assaults through the avenues of the
passions and the imagination — the two central domains of the
modern private self.

In their own ways, both Whitefield and Garrick were
"charismatic" personalities whose power derived from their
ability to plumb the depths of human passion and literally
re-present the human condition in all its various poses. Both
Whitefield and Garrick were accused of being "licentious." In
a literal sense, they *were:* both took license with the old forms
and rules of society to create new forms capable of speaking to
a new society.

As Whitefield sought to use his stage, the pulpit, to destroy the theater, so the theater took after Whitefield in its own
way. Garrick, Foote, and Woodward all saw in Whitefield a
rival worthy of contest. They challenged him not with stones
and bells but on the stage itself, using the most powerful weap-
ons at their disposal: mimicry, comedy, satire, and ridicule.
They crossed the line separating art and reality to attack religion as they had earlier attacked courtly politics, legalistic
morals, and polite manners. And they produced a living satire
using Whitefield as they had used other real people in the
imaginary setting of the stage — with devastating consequences. By holding their opponent up to ridicule, they effectively cut him down to laughable, life-sized proportions.

The first staged attacks on Whitefield actually dated from
1746, when Drury Lane produced Charles Macklin's play *A*

Will and No Will. The play was followed by a scurrilous "after-piece" that introduced a Methodist itinerant preacher caught in an adulterous situation. In the play an older widow, Shark, confessed to her Uncle Skin that she was pregnant. When asked to identify her "bedfellow" she replied,

> You must know uncle, I am greatly addicted to be afraid of spirits, ghosts, witches, and fairies, and so to prevent terrifying dreams and apparitions I took a religious gentleman, a very good man, to be with me — an itinerant Methodist, one Doctor Preach Field.

SKIN: "Doctor Preach Field, I have heard of him."
SHARK: "O he's a very good man uncle I assure you."

With that, the comedy was on, and the field preacher exposed for his base, sensual ends.

As theater and Whitefield shared many of the same dramatic secrets, so they directed at one another the same charge of sexual immorality. Both worked to establish their cases in the eighteenth-century contest of virtue and vice. Actors ridiculed both the integrity of revivalists, suggesting abuse of their charisma for immoral purposes, and their theology, suggesting a form of cheap grace that entitled the sinner to continue in immorality, certain of being saved by faith alone.

The actors' campaign against Whitefield peaked in 1760, when Samuel Foote wrote and starred in a satiric comedy entitled *The Minor* at Garrick's Drury Lane Theater. The play opened with two characters, named Crank and Foote, musing over possible new characters to satirize. Crank suggested a Scotchman or an Irishman, but this was old hat. Foote then made the daring suggestion that they ridicule an "itinerant field orator." Crank was not sure; fooling around with a churchman could be dangerous. But Foote assured him this was wrong-headed. Itinerants were not untouchable. In fact, Foote claimed, they operated in the very same world as the theater:

FOOTE: Now I look upon it in a different manner. I consider these gentlemen in the light of public performers like myself; and whether we exhibit at Tottenham-Court, or the Hay-Market our purpose is the same, and the place is immaterial.

Foote went on to note that satiric comedy was the only weapon players could use in responding to the itinerant's condemnations. They had no force of arms or institutional allies to fight the methodist challenge: "ridicule is the only antidote against this pernicious poison. Methodism is a madness that arguments can never cure; and should a little wholesome severity be applied, persecution would be the immediate cry. Where then can we have recourse but to the comic muse?" Actors were no more rioters than itinerants. And, like itinerants, they could call upon no traditional institution or agency for protection. They had no traditional controls to invoke because, like the methodists, they were extrainstitutional. Like the preachers, they would have to attack their enemies and defend their persons solely on the basis of their power to persuade and move an audience.

With that the decision was made. Whitefield was to have one last character to play — or rather to be played for him. The character was "Dr. Squintum." In a classic case of reality imitating art, Whitefield would forever after be burlesqued in prints, cartoons, and satires as the Foote character "Squintum." The cross-eyed stare that enhanced his speaking presence was singled out for attention and satire on the stage.

In the play, Squintum was cast alongside a procurer named Mrs. Cole, who frequented Squintum's sermons and rejoiced when he "stept in with his saving grace, got me regenerate, and another creature." Despite her conversion, Mrs. Cole continued to ply her illicit trade, prompting another character to observe "with what ease she reconciles her new birth to her old calling! No wonder these preachers have plenty of proselytes, whilst they have the address so comfortably to blend the hitherto jarring interests of the two worlds."

As the play progresses, a theologically naive Mrs. Cole encourages a young girl to a life of methodism and prostitution with the words: "Don't you remember what Mr. Squintum said? A woman's not worth saving, that won't be guilty of a swinging sin; for they have matter to repent upon."

Foote would have been the first to acknowledge that Whitefield never encouraged immorality, let alone prostitution, in his preaching. Yet Foote made an underlying point. By proclaiming a message of free grace to the exclusion of all works, and by promising perfect strangers that a New Birth could erase any old sins, Whitefield could all too easily encourage a transformation of free grace into cheap grace. And undoubtedly that was a licentious message that some of Whitefield's common hearers took from his sermons.

Foote perverted Whitefield's theology to make a point, but his satire of itinerant preaching was no more a perversion of reality than Whitefield's damnation of all theater as "the devil's masterpiece." Each saw weaknesses in the other that he was incapable of seeing in himself.

Foote's play generated a scandal which, like all scandals, simply increased public interest. After a successful run at Drury Lane, the play repeated its success at Covent Garden. Soon it was playing in all the provinces, with later editions turning up as far away as Charleston and New York City.

Foote had hit upon a successful theme. *The Minor* was soon followed by other productions that added methodist religion to their list of victims for ridicule. In 1761, Garrick followed up with *The Register Office,* a comedy in the new mode of two acts, in which "Mr. Watchlight" and "Mrs. Snarewell" played to Squintum and Mrs. Cole. That same year Foote produced another assault unambiguously titled *The Methodist.* This play, however, exceeded even the theater's broad toleration, and Garrick suppressed it.

Methodists were predictably scandalized by the theater attacks. Lady Huntington implored Garrick to halt production. He refused but promised to soften some of the more biting commentary. Later Whitefield biographers shared in the outrage. Luke Tyerman mentioned the plays only to dismiss them as the work of that "profane and filthy-minded comedian" Samuel Foote.

Criticism of the theater's satire was not limited to methodists and their supporters. Respectable reviewers also found it reprehensible. Indeed, if anyone was more distasteful to them than a strolling itinerant, it was a licentious actor or playwright. In August 1760 the *Monthly Review* condemned Foote and Garrick for "debasing the stage" by introducing "real and living characters into his pieces." A follow-up letter protested "such Scandalous liberties with Names" as an "insufferable" contempt. Once again, the upstart stage had struck too close to home by blurring the line between art and reality. If ministers could be reviled by name, so also could magistrates and aristocrats, and with that, all social order would be brought into contempt.

Foote and Garrick defended the plays on the grounds of art. Like Whitefield twenty years earlier, they were challenging the right of hierarchy to prescribe morality or delineate the boundaries of art. In their own ways, actors and field preachers were both demanding the freedom to define their art before the bar of public opinion. In the new courtroom, success, not classical categories of art, would be their criterion and barometer. Between them, revivalists and theater owners made "head counts" a science in the emerging social order governed by market forces and voluntary support rather than direction from above.

As a celebrity, Whitefield soon became fair game not only for newspapers and playwrights but also for the popular new markets in prints and caricatures. Once introduced to the public spectacle, he took his place with other celebrities and became the frequent butt of their jokes to a much greater extent than the Wesleys or Moravians. Indeed, a whole genre of Whitefield prints appeared portraying the itinerant in an unfavorable light. Most notable was a spate of portraits and cartoons suggesting that Whitefield was having an affair with an American Indian princess.

In 1761 William Hogarth brought his biting satire to bear on Whitefield again with a print entitled "Credulity, Superstition and Fanaticism," in which he depicted an audience of insane people driven to bedlam by a cross-eyed preacher. Others followed suit. In middle age, Whitefield had become transformed from the comely young celebrity to the squint-eyed ranter. When not mocking the enthusiasm of Whitefield's ignorant listeners, the printers portrayed the itinerant's presumed immorality. In one print, Whitefield appeared in the pulpit holding a bag of money and crying out: "You are all Damn'd that go to hear Foote. Verily I say unto you he is a Child of Hell." In the same print, however, Whitefield is pictured surrounded by female listeners and admirers. One old lady remarks, "O what a Pious Creature he is." Next to her, a young woman mischievously exclaims, "I wish his Spirit was in my Flesh." Through much of his life, Whitefield had been on the offensive with his barbs and biting sarcasm. Now, older and weakened, he found himself the object of parody.

In May 1763 a print emerged explicitly linking Whitefield to Foote's play. Entitled "Dr. Squintum's Exaltation or the Reformation," it shows Whitefield in the marketplace surrounded by lewd and disorderly listeners. Beneath the print appears some doggerel including the following lines:

> While Methodist Villains infest the whole Nation,
> And suffer'd to robb on the Plea Reformation;
> Permit me Good Friends the whole Breed to describe,
> Whose Hearts (tho they're Steel'd) are not steel'd aginst
>   the Bribe
> Take a walk to Bell Yard and you'll see in a Trice
> These Informers — I mean — these Reformers of Vice;
> With their soul-saving cant and their pious Grimaces,
> I wish that Old Nick had his Fork in their A-ss-s.

Throughout the scurrilous campaign on stage and in print, Whitefield said very little. His refusal to reply to the new round of public attacks was motivated less by saintly withdrawal than by illness and an inability to rise to the occasion. As the crescendo peaked in the early 1760s, Whitefield was partially disabled, preaching on a drastically reduced schedule, and cutting down his correspondence and public appearances. Unable to do serious battle with theater, he was nonetheless aware of the play and may even have taken perverse pleasure in seeing himself on stage. To one friend he confided in a letter: "I am now mimicked and burlesqued upon the public stage. All hail such contempt!"

Throughout all this satire, the lesson was clear. If religion could be marketed, then, like politics, quackery, and prostitution, it could also be mimicked, demeaned, and condemned. On one level — the level seen by Whitefield's early biographers — the insults were a scandal. On another level — the level Whitefield himself recognized — they were back-handed tributes to his status as a celebrity. No other religious personality had scaled such heights. No other understood the media — or, for that matter, the market — as Whitefield did.

In their own ways, Whitefield and Garrick, to say nothing of Franklin, were of a piece. They gave as good as they got, and they asked no quarter save that the market be open and they be given a fair chance to tap it. The age belonged to all of them. Garrick and Franklin lived out most of their century presiding over a new stage and a new nation. Time would not be so kind to Whitefield. But there was still one more hurrah.

14 American Icon

By December of 1760, as the theater battles peaked, Whitefield was unable to rise to the occasion. Indeed, such was the state of his health that he was barely able to rise at all. Through much of the following two years he was a virtual invalid, confined to bed and forbidden to preach. The traditional cures no longer worked as they had in his earlier bouts with illness and exhaustion. A visit to the mineral waters at Bath left him as weak "as before." In October 1761, on the advice of Edinburgh's finest physicians, he entered a regimen of mild exercise, mustard seed, and silence — the latter being "the painful thing," and in fact impossible. While still in Edinburgh he confided to John Wesley that he could not resist a little exhortation: "I spoke a little . . . in a private room." And then added the almost desperate wish, "may you, my Dear Friend, never be stopped till you breathe your last."

Unable to preach, a recovering Whitefield determined to travel. If travel was always Whitefield's best remedy, America was always his favorite destination. War with France and his own waning health had precluded an American visit for eight long years, but in that time Whitefield had remained fully informed concerning religious and political developments in the New World. He had read American newspapers regularly and frequently expressed his frustration at the extended separation. In a cajolatory letter to Lady Pepperell during the war with France, he confessed, "How did I wish to be transported to America! How did I long to stir up all against the common enemy. . . . Dear New England, — dear Boston lies upon my heart!"

With the Peace of Paris signed in 1763, Whitefield planned an immediate return to America, but again his body let him down. Excited planning brought on asthmatic difficulties, and the trip had to be postponed to summer. He did not arrive in Virginia until August, at which point he immediately left for the cooler climes of Pennsylvania and his beloved Presbyterian audiences.

In Pennsylvania he resumed preaching at the reduced rate of three times a week. His reception was predictably large and enthusiastic, but old friends noted that the past eight years had not been kind. Whitefield's body showed the ravages of time. In place of the buoyant, youthful-looking Whitefield, audiences encountered a much older and more corpulent Whitefield — the figure who in fact is featured in most of his portraits. He moved and breathed with difficulty, and could not sustain the bursts of passion that had formerly marked his ministry.

But still the crowds flocked. They came partly from respect, partly from curiosity, and partly just to hear an American legend. Absence did little to dim the American memory of their great evangelical friend or lessen their appreciation. Wherever Whitefield traveled, word-of-mouth reports spread the news of his arrival. Listeners who were too young personally to remember the earlier Whitefield heard stories from those who had been there. Sales of Whitefield's journals increased as Americans reminded themselves of the fearless institution baiter who could draw thousands at the mention of his name.

Ministers recalled the effects of Whitefield oratory on their parishioners. The German pietist Henry Melchior Muhlenberg had been present at many of Whitefield's sermons over the years and marveled at his continued ability to move audiences. He recalled how "the honorable Mr. Whitefield had the gift [of oratory] in his younger years, and by it whole crowds were sometimes carried away as though they had been betwitched." By way of illustration, Muhlenberg recalled one occasion on which Whitefield arrived late to his preaching destination. Another preacher had begun a sermon on a "powerful text," but to no effect. Then Whitefield arrived. On seeing him, the ineffective preacher immediately gave up the discourse and, with hardly a minute's thought, Whitefield picked up on the same text. The effects were electric:

> Mr. Whitefield had scarcely spoken for a minute on the same text when the whole *auditorium* could be seen to be deeply moved, to be in tears, and to be wringing hands, and the sighing, weeping, and shouting of the people could be heard. Is it not possible that name and fame, preconceptions and fancies play a part in the synergism? Weeping, laughing, yawning, sneezing, etc. are contagious, and they seem to have something in common with electricity.

On another occasion, Muhlenberg recalled how a German woman had come on foot to hear Whitefield preach in Philadelphia. She did not speak English, but such was the power of Whitefield's "gestures, expressions, look, and voice" that "on her return she asserted that never in all her life had she had such a quickening, awakening, and edifying experience."

Besides identifying himself with the earlier American revivals, Whitefield invariably identified himself — and his hearers — with the cause of America. Memories of victory over France were still fresh, and Whitefield did not hesitate to identify the same divine providence in war that he had earlier associated with revival. His unending bursts of passion for the

New Birth he now coupled with increasing celebrations of his "dear America." Thirteen separate colonies were well along the road to a collective identity, and no single figure was more representative of that unity than Whitefield.

In short, since the Louisbourg campaign of 1745, Whitefield had become an American icon — the first intercolonial hero. In America, the religious lessons of the revivals automatically contained political applications. If Americans could unite successfully in religion, then they could unite in politics and war — a transition that Whitefield exemplified as recruiter for the Louisbourg expedition.

In an era about to experience a new generation of political revolutionaries and statesmen whose names would dominate "American" history, it is easy to forget that America's first intercolonial hero was a preacher, not a politician. From a twentieth-century vantage point, it is also easy to forget how extraordinarily difficult it was to forge a common identity for thirteen colonies that were, in effect, separate nations. Unparalleled pluralism and intercolonial rivalries virtually precluded any single magistrate from "speaking for" the larger, as yet uncreated whole. Here Whitefield was particularly well placed for success. He claimed no particular American region as his own nor promoted any denomination over another. All Americans could claim Whitefield *without* sacrificing their particularity.

Not only had Whitefield brought American Calvinists together, but he had done so in a brash, combative style with a hostility toward external authority that fit well with American self-confidence following war with France. Americans knew and read of Whitefield's frequent sermons on their behalf during the war with France and of his many charitable efforts on behalf of Boston and the American colleges. Although separated, he remained present through his unending campaign for colonial causes. No one dared condemn the self-made hero.

Only Whitefield, the Anglican Calvinist with an American soul, had bridged the cultural, religious, and linguistic chasms separating colonial identities and shown how true unity could be achieved. By the 1760s he had come to symbolize that unity in ways that transcended religion altogether. The new corporate consciousness he personified was at once religious, cultural, and, in a short time, ideological and military. The lessons first learned in the mass revivals — the virtue of popular mobilization, the rhetoric of a "common cause," submission to the "public will" — all contained double meanings that Whitefield would not discourage in the years to come, even as the "tyrant" label shifted from France to England.

Throughout 1764 and 1765, there was no angry American theater belittling Whitefield on the stage. Neither were there any working-class mobs disrupting his ministry in the "fields." Wherever he traveled, old battles were forgotten and old antagonisms washed away in a sea of good feelings. When preaching in Philadelphia and New York, he invariably encountered a "prodigious crowded auditory," including many who were seeing the famed evangelist for the first time. They knew nothing of the "Great Awakening" that first launched Whitefield's American career, but they knew Whitefield the American symbol, and they flocked in numbers that exceeded the records of 1740. In Boston, such was the enthusiasm that audiences ignored the travel prohibitions brought on by a smallpox epidemic and took their chances just to see Whitefield.

The colleges were no less grateful than the citizenry. Princeton had always been Whitefield's favorite American college because of its connections to the Log College. By the unanimous request of president, tutors, and students, Whitefield attended Princeton's commencement and delivered a "very striking and animated exhortation" to the graduates. Harvard College had long since forgiven Whitefield his youthful indiscretions but had not forgotten how he had worked in England to secure books for their library after a devastating fire. They welcomed him to the campus as a "friend" both to the college and America. Yale College followed suit and urged him to preach to the students. An ailing Whitefield complied and went beyond the allotted time when President Clap pleaded to "give them one more quarter of an hour's exhortation."

Most significantly, the ever-expanding colonial press fell unanimously in line behind Whitefield. His revivals had helped create the sort of news that fueled the establishment of newspapers in every large city in the colonies. In 1764, as the concerns of the press shifted, they did not forget the Grand Itinerant. Ever since Louisbourg, the newspapers had been directing public attention from revivals to politics and war. But Whitefield proved an exception. Wherever he spoke, printed itineraries prepared the way, together with lavish praise for his ongoing triumphs. Even opposition editors fell in line. The *Boston Evening Press*, once his greatest American antagonist, joined the wave of praise with extended descriptions of Whitefield's sermons and an editorial lament: "what a pity that such a god-like man's constitution is almost worn out by Apostolic Labours!" Papers throughout the colonies reported Whitefield's visit to a New York jail where, "being informed that no provision was made for the support of the debtors, he generously gave, out of his purse, enough to purchase ten cords of wood for the use of the poorest prisoners." They also carried the story of his public citation in Boston for efforts to secure relief in London for Bostonians left homeless by the Great Fire of 1760.

In June of 1764 Whitefield delivered his Boston farewell sermon in the friendly confines of the Old South meetinghouse. The gathering proved somber as many realized they might be hearing Whitefield for the last time. The following report appeared in the *Boston Gazette* and was picked up by newspapers throughout the colonies:

> The notice he gave of his departure was sudden; and it was the more affecting to his friends, as there is but little reason to expect he will ever have an opportunity of making another visit here. His lectures have been at-

tended by persons of Figure and Rank, as well as others;
and in the opinion of those of his Hearers who are allowed
to be the best Judges, they have been adapted to promote
the common cause of Christianity.

Contained in these accounts were many of the accolades
that could be found in earlier accounts of Whitefield in America
and Scotland. But there was also something new. A new language, more political than religious, had begun to shape descriptions of American revivals. Revivals had always given
political lessons, but a dawning political self-consciousness was
now giving back its vocabulary to religion. Increasingly, descriptions of Whitefield's style and message were fused with
the rhetoric of America's rising political consciousness of itself
as a free people. A distinctively American phraseology appeared in journalistic accounts of the revivals, peppered with
such phrases as "common cause" and describing popular
audiences as "the best judges" of who and what they would
support. Such rhetoric was not conspicuous among Scottish
Presbyterians or English methodists but came increasingly to
express the American temper in religion and politics.

This language would soon grow far louder in political
contexts than in the earlier religious debates of the 1740s. In
all of this, Whitefield was identified by his Bostonian hearers
as a champion and fellow spirit. No one demurred when the
Boston Evening Post summarized his tour with the recognition
that "he has met with great acceptance among all Denominations of judicious Christians, and we trust Religious Impressions which will never be erased, are formed upon the minds
of many."

From Boston Whitefield traveled slowly south, spending
the month of October in Philadelphia. By late fall he was in
Virginia and the Carolinas, where he observed yet another
"great awakening," this time in the South. He did not know
that this was to be the last American "revival" he would witness. In response to the impassioned exhortations of Baptist

itinerants, Presbyterian New Lights such as Samuel Davies, and evangelical Anglicans such as Deveraux Jarratt, huge numbers of Virginians were entering the churches. Whitefield rejoiced to play a part in awakenings in which such a "vast alteration" could be recognized among the people. Although weakened by the travel, he preached at Northern Neck, likening the enthusiasm there to the halcyon days of revival in Philadelphia, Boston, and Cambuslang.

On December 3, 1764, eighteen months after his arrival in America, Whitefield at last arrived "home" at Bethesda. Bethesda had never been Whitefield's residence for more than a few months at a time, yet it had secured a lifelong loyalty and substantial financial commitment from him. Soon after his arrival, Whitefield printed a formal accounting of orphan-house finances. The widely reported results were staggering. With no help from the Georgia legislature or the Anglican Society for the Propagation of the Gospel, Whitefield had managed to raise amounts of money without equal in American philanthropy to that time. Though never wealthy himself, Whitefield's own contributions totaled over £2,000. Even more impressive were the public offerings accumulated over the preceding twenty-five years. In all, "the sum of £12,855 has been laid out for the same house since the 7th of January 1739 to this day" — a figure exceeding the entire budget of the Georgia legislature in 1764. Along with this report came the auditor's record "that it doth not appear that any charge has ever been made by the said Rev. Mr Whitefield, either for travelling charges or any other expenses whatever; and that no salary has been made for any person whatever."

Reports of Whitefield's munificence at the Georgia orphan house worked the same transformations in southern elite attitudes that had been evoked in the North. Perhaps no single figure had done more to establish the colony than Whitefield. In a letter from Georgia reprinted in the *Boston Evening Post*, a writer noted that "many sensible people say that if it had not been for this house, the Province would have been deserted;

for the new settlers (poor people) had recourse here, after their work was done, to good lodgings and Provisions on free cost." Whitefield himself was pleased to note that "peace and plenty reign at Bethesda. His Excellency dined with me yesterday, and expressed his satisfaction in the warmest terms."

Whitefield took advantage of his new acceptance by pursuing an idea that had begun to germinate in England during his ministry to the nobility. Why not transform the orphan house into a college? Like Franklin he wanted to end with something big — a grand gesture. In fact, neither man was immune to the allure of creating a personal monument. And for both, the preferred location was America. In Whitefield's case, the monument of choice would be a new, evangelical American college. Whitefield would not be the last revivalist to translate an anti-intellectual style into an academic college of his own, but he was the first. Having repudiated all invitations to found denominations, he settled instead on transforming Bethesda into an evangelical college for the South. This would be his crowning legacy to posterity.

It had been apparent to Whitefield for some time that the South needed a "school of prophets" modeled on institutions in their neighboring colonies to the North. The recent advances of southern evangelicals confirmed the need for an institutional training ground that could prepare responsible citizens and gospel preachers. Princeton served as Whitefield's model. After speaking at the commencement ceremonies there, Whitefield spent an additional week studying the college's charter, curriculum, and organization. Much of what he saw there he incorporated in his own preliminary plans for "Bethesda College."

Clearly a college required far more support than the not insubstantial needs of the orphan house. The Princeton study convinced him that additional resources would have to be secured from church and state, and this meant courting old antagonists. Given the secular as well as religious purposes of the college, Whitefield turned initially to the Georgia legislature.

In a memorial to Gov. James Wright, he outlined the successful history of the orphan house and went on to request a grant of two thousand acres to establish a college "for the education of persons of superior rank . . . to serve their king, their Country, or their God either in Church or State." Taking Princeton as his model, Whitefield was careful to state his case in general academic terms that downplayed his evangelical designs. Without a college of its own, he argued, Georgia would lose its most talented youth to northern schools. In addition, Georgia would be unable to attract talent from other parts, particularly the "British west islands." To this calculated appeal to regional self-interest Whitefield added the personal promise of an additional £2,000 gift to build additional lodgings and support ten "poor students as servitors to the rest."

Whitefield assured the legislature that, once established, the day-to-day needs of the college would be covered by the same slave labor that had saved the orphan house. By his calculation, thirty slaves were more than enough to make Bethesda College self-supporting. Ever the Oxford servitor, he went on to urge "that the Negroe children belonging to the College shall be instructed in their intervals of labor by one of the poorest students [and] an additional provision for educating and maintaining a number of Indian children, which I imagine may easily be procured from the Creeks, Choctaws, Cherokees, and others." In return for lands and a charter, Whitefield promised both Georgia and the Privy Council that he would "make a free gift of all lands, negroes, goods, and chattels" to the college in his will.

Whitefield's petition was enthusiastically received by both houses of the Georgia Assembly. Again personal friendships were important. James Habersham, Whitefield's old ally and co-founder of the orphan house, had become a leading planter and president of the Upper House. With Habersham's encouragement, the Assembly awarded Bethesda the lands Whitefield requested, together with a commendatory preface endorsing the whole enterprise. In their widely printed endorsement, the legislators praised the proposed college as one more instance of "the many and singular obligations Georgia has continually laid under to that Rev. Gentleman." It seemed that Georgia would soon have its college.

With lands, buildings, and slaves in place, Whitefield next turned to another old foe, the Anglican Church. With a charter from the Church, he could gain additional support through the offices of the Society for the Propagation of the Gospel in Foreign Parts. In a petition that again minimized his evangelical and dissenting designs, he appealed to the Archbishop of Canterbury for a charter. This time, however, the appeal was denied. Unlike the Georgia legislature, the archbishop did not forget old grudges. Feelings still ran high against Whitefield's past censures, and the threatening growth of Methodism in England continued to be identified with his name. When presented with a bill for the college, the Archbishop signified his approval only on condition that "extempore" prayers not be allowed. That, of course, would eliminate the "broad bottom" of Whitefield's substantial support in the dissenting, evangelical communities, and thus effectively scuttled immediate hopes for an Anglican charter.

Undeterred, Whitefield returned to England in June 1765, determined to see his last ambition through. For help he turned to his old friend Benjamin Franklin, then in England as colonial agent. Earlier the two had "interviewed" often about "Georgia College" and its charter. Despite Franklin's frequent and impassioned arguments on behalf of the college, however, the Church remained adamant in refusing to grant any charter for an institution that was not explicitly Anglican and anti-Methodist. Whitefield's American college, it was clear, would have to go it alone.

On returning to England, Whitefield had hoped to concentrate his waning energies on preaching and on the creation of his college. But events were mounting that would soon divert those energies to another American cause, one in which his friend Franklin played a central role.

In March of 1765, Parliament passed a Stamp Act tax in an effort to recoup debts incurred during the Seven Years War. As the chief beneficiary of these debts, Parliament had assumed that the colonists would be willing — if not eager — to shoulder some of the costs. Parliament was sadly mistaken. Instead of complying with the tax, Americans balked, citing their lack of representation in Parliament — an offense, they contended, against England's own constitution and the principle of popular representation in government. Throughout the summer of 1765 Whitefield's most consistent booster, the *Boston Gazette*, was filled with letters and essays protesting the Stamp Act as unconstitutional.

Even as Whitefield's hopes for a monument were fading, Franklin's were just beginning to grow with this storm. And Whitefield would be enlisted for badly needed support. In the summer of 1765, as colonists observed the zealous prosecutions of the vice admiralty courts and waited for the stamp tax to go into effect, voices of protest grew louder. The storm center was Boston, where many ministers, together with radical "Sons of Liberty" and minor officials such as Samuel and John Adams, joined to protest the act as an infringement on British "liberties." This was a language Whitefield understood well. But now its context was politics, not religion, and its focus was Parliament, not France or Catholicism. On August 14 the colonial protest spilled into violence as the Sons of Liberty attacked the home of the stamp collector Andrew Oliver. Twelve days later, violence flared again with attacks on the homes of William Story, deputy register of the vice admiralty court, and Benjamin Hallowell, comptroller of customs. From there the mob turned on the home of Deputy Governor Thomas Hutchinson, leaving nothing standing but the "the bare walls and floors."

Similar outbursts occurred in other colonies from New England to Georgia. While no respectable civil or ecclesiastical leaders approved of the violence of August 26, neither did they issue blanket condemnations of the mobs. The experience of the revivals had taught elites the futility of seeking to silence the populace once it had been aroused. New England's Congregational clergy, including many of Whitefield's closest allies, played a central role in protesting British "tyranny." In Boston, Samuel Cooper, together with Whitefield's old antagonist Charles Chauncy, had a hand in penning the libertarian letters pouring from the *Boston Gazette*. Throughout the autumn of 1765, Lyme's pro-revival pastor, Stephen Johnson, published a series of libertarian essays in the *New London Gazette* reminding American readers that "if you tamely part with [your liberties], you are accessory to your own death, and entail slavery on your posterity."

With growing alarm, Whitefield realized he might have to make a choice between his native England and his beloved America. His life's ministry had been premised on the broadest possible union of Anglo-American evangelicals. Now politics was threatening to undo everything and make a shambles of his international revival. Others, like John Wesley, were faced with similar dilemmas. But Wesley would remain loyal to England, and Whitefield could not. His institutional attachments and personal identification with the colonies were stronger than his loyalty to the crown.

Although far removed from the scene of the riots, Whitefield followed the news closely and relied on his American correspondents for information. A worried James Habersham wrote him in January 1766 describing "much confusion" ensuing from the Stamp Act. Personally, Habersham continued, he disapproved of the act, but not royal authority. The mob frightened him more than unconstitutional taxes: "Dreadful it is to find one's Person and Property at the Disposal of a giddy multitude." This, Habersham realized, was not the view of many American "patriots," nor was it Whitefield's perspective. Knowing his friend's loyalties and proclivity for sharing letters, he closed with a worried request that reflected the tensions of the time: "I must insist on your not making a use of this scrawl."

A second letter from Habersham, dated February 7, 1766, reported little improvement in "the terrible confusion we have been in here on account of the Stamp Act." His own sympathies to the crown had grown stronger in the aftermath of mounting colonial protests: "I detest and abhor, from every human and divine the intemperate Zeal, to say no worse shewn on this occasion throughout this Continent."

Although no friend to the "mob," Whitefield could not share Habersham's loyalties. Many patriot leaders were responsible members of Presbyterian and Congregational churches, and had always been more faithful allies than Anglicans, who tended to remain loyal to the crown. Whitefield's recent disappointment in the college charter only heightened his identification with the Calvinist dissenters and a movement that was increasingly theirs. Their grievances, moreover, echoed many of the religious issues that revivalists had raised earlier. At base, both involved questions of the extent of popular sovereignty.

In February of 1766 an embattled Franklin was called to answer before an angry House of Commons. Whitefield attended the sessions as Franklin's friend and consort. Throughout the hearings, the interrogations were sharp and hostile. If British courts would not countenance anti-Methodist mobs, even less would they tolerate American mobs opposed to their own authority. Somehow Franklin had to explain that there was a difference in American protests — namely, that they were not an expression of an American defiance of British law but rather loyalty to it. To Whitefield's pride and satisfaction, Franklin more than held his own in the debates. The critical issue was the subject of taxes. With mounting drama, Franklin held firm before his questioners:

> Q. If the Stamp Act should be repealed, would it induce the assemblies of America to acknowledge the right of parliament to tax them, and would they erase their resolutions?
> A. No, never.
> Q. Is there no means of obliging them to erase those resolutions?

A. None, that I know of; they will never do it, unless compelled by force of arms.

Q. Is there a power on earth that can force them to erase them?

A. No power, how great soever, can force men to change their opinions.

Throughout the hearings Whitefield praised and defended his American friend: "Dr. Franklin has gained immortal honour by his behaviour at the bar of the House. His answer was always found equal to the questioner. He stood unappalled, gave pleasure to his friends, and did honour to his country." Whitefield's reference to Franklin's "country" is indicative of the independent American identity that he had grown to respect.

In response to Franklin's testimony and out of a desire to quiet controversies in the colonies, an angry Parliament repealed the Stamp Act. At the same time, however, they retained the Revenue Act as a symbolic show of authority. Franklin's testimony had convinced them (erroneously) that Americans objected chiefly to "internal" rather than "external," or trade taxes. In both cases, however, sovereignty lay with the Parliament. To confirm this, Parliament issued a Declaratory Act that claimed sovereignty over colonial affairs "in all cases whatsoever." Discerning minds saw in that Declaratory Act a portent of trouble. Clearly the immediate tensions had passed, but the underlying issues remained.

While Franklin's defense pleased Whitefield and did much to effect the repeal of the Stamp Act, it did not please all Americans. Many felt compromised by Franklin's distinction between internal and external taxes, believing that all such taxes from Parliament were unconstitutional. Soon Franklin came under fire from both sides. His sister had gotten angry letters in America, and Franklin encouraged her with some words from Whitefield:

So my dear sister, when you meet with any more such

letters . . . don't let them give you the least Uneasiness;
but call to mind what your Friend good Mr. Whitefield
once said to me on such an Occasion; "I read the Libels
writ against you, says he, when I was in a remote
province, where I could not be inform'd of the Truth of
the Facts; but they rather gave me this good Opinion of
you, *that you continued to be USEFUL to the Publick:* For
when I am on the Road, and see Boys in a Field at a
Distance, pelting a tree, though I am too far off to know
what Tree it is, I conclude it has FRUIT on it."

Having already defended Franklin before his English critics, Whitefield was more than prepared to support him before
Americans. At this time, Whitefield was a far more popular
figure in the American eye than Franklin. A word on Franklin's
behalf from the eyewitness Whitefield could move mountains
of popular distrust and opposition. In a calculated attempt to
stem American hostility to Franklin, the Philadelphia patriot
Joseph Galloway asked Whitefield for a character reference and
testimony, believing that his words would "clear up [Frank-
lin's] reputation to all the American world. For who dare deny
Mr. Whitefield's authority — will the Church? Will the Presbyterians?"

Whitefield happily complied with the request and went
one step further by enlisting the support of his letter-writing
network to spread the word of Franklin's patriotism. Calvinist
readers throughout the colonies learned how Franklin "spoke
very heartily and judiciously in his country's behalf." Soon the
newspapers picked up on Whitefield's praise. By April of 1766,
William Franklin wrote his father,

You cannot conceive the Satisfaction which the Accounts
of your Examination at the Bar of the House of Commons
have afforded your friends. Dr. Fothergill and Mr.
Whitefield have mentioned your Behaviour on the Occasions in High Terms. I am told the latter says America
owes the Repeal of the Stamp Act to the assiduous Endeavors of . . . Dr. Franklin.

On more than one occasion, Franklin had stood by Whitefield in the face of public accusation and libel. Now Whitefield returned the favor.

When not busy with political affairs, Whitefield preached at the Tabernacle and continued working for his college. Further opportunity for him to comment indirectly on American affairs occurred when six methodists were expelled from Oxford for their extemporaneous prayers and background in the "manual trades." Having already been defeated on the issue of a charter for the college, and publicly sympathetic with the colonies, an outraged Whitefield took the offensive and published a pamphlet in the methodists' defense.

The defense was clearly written for audiences on both sides of the Atlantic. Whitefield skillfully interwove the local issue of dismissed students with broader American fears of an imposed New World Anglican bishop. While Parliament hoped to solidify its jurisdiction over the colonies, wrote Whitefield, the Anglican church hoped to centralize its authority in the New World with an American bishop. This, Whitefield warned, would lead to tyranny. If bishops could expel methodist students in England for nothing more than a dissenter's piety, their overseas missions could clearly not be trusted. An American bishop would be as intolerant as his English counterpart. In fact, Whitefield complained, the overseas mission of the Anglican Church was not a "Society for propagating the Gospel" but a "Society for propagating Episcopacy in foreign parts." He went on to ask, "how must it increase the prejudices of our colonists . . . against the establishment of Episcopacy."

Whitefield's letter provoked a wave of bitter opposition from the Church in England. Lying behind the opposition was a sense that Whitefield spoke not only for methodists but also for the "rebellions" of the American colonists. One especially outraged writer recommended that British authorities "make an example of Tabernacle preachers, by enacting a law to *cut out their tongues.*"

265

At the same time the letter aroused controversy in England, it confirmed old friendships in America. The defense was reprinted in Boston and widely serialized in the press. Americans, no less than the English, saw the double message in the defense. Again, the Anglican-ordained evangelist attacked his own church, this time on grounds as clearly political as religious. Whitefield knew little of colonial law or political theory, but he understood the politics of popular mobilization as well as anyone, and he recognized that if he was to play a role in that drama, it would be around the familiar ecclesiastical issue of an American bishopric rather than the constitutional issues of taxation and representation. "Tyranny" existed throughout English society and must be combated in the English church no less than the English Parliament. Whatever outrages American Anglicans may have felt over this assault were muted. Whitefield held the American imagination, and any criticism of him would be an act of self-destruction. In fact, it was far easier for American loyalists or neutrals to criticize Franklin than to criticize Whitefield.

Although Whitefield could not ignore politics, it would never become all-consuming for him. From first to last, Whitefield remained a preacher and continued his tours of England and Scotland. Following his June 1768 tour of Edinburgh, he rejoiced that "our Orphan House Park assemblies [were] as large and attentive as ever." In Scotland as in America, reports of his preaching increasingly assumed an air of nostalgia. Whitefield himself was visibly moved to see how "twenty-seven-year-old friends and spiritual children remember the days of old. They are seeking after their first love, and there seems to be a stirring among the dry bones." Whitefield had grown up in turmoil and confrontation; now he grew old in waves of nostalgia that hid the pressing issues of the age. While on tour, political issues paled before the ongoing revival. No one could tell Whitefield, as long as he preached, that the revivals had passed.

On returning from Edinburgh, Whitefield learned that

Elizabeth was gravely ill. On August 9, his long-suffering and silent companion of twenty-seven years died. The loss shook Whitefield but did not deter his life's course. No time was lost to grief. Two days after her burial he wrote a friend, "Let us work whilst it is day." Two weeks later he opened Lady Huntington's college at Trevecca with a sermon and charge to the Methodist students. And from there he prepared to leave for America again.

Whitefield's nonstop preaching after Elizabeth's death had a predictable effect. Overexertion led to a ruptured blood vessel and a period of forced convalescence from September through the new year. In January of 1767 he took Cornelius Winter into his home as aide and secretary. Left without a wife and in ailing health, Whitefield longed to return "home" to America. On March 17 he wrote the orphan-house managers to expect him shortly: "I am every day, every hour, almost every moment, thinking of, and preparing for America. A pilgrim life to me is the sweetest on this side of eternity." Whitefield knew himself better than anyone, and he knew that he needed public targets and public audiences to sustain his life. America was the scene of great actions that fueled his will to live. He would see it for one last stand.

On the eve of his departure, Whitefield received word from Franklin that Parliament had dispatched troops to Boston and warned of the possible outcome. It was, Franklin confided, a "dangerous step. . . . I cannot but fear the consequences of bringing them together."

Undeterred, Whitefield pressed ahead. On August 30 he preached farewell sermons to the loyal congregations at the Moorfields Tabernacle and Tottenham Court Road Chapel. This was where it had all begun. Observers noted that much of the old verve was gone. Whitefield rambled more than before and evoked the nostalgia of a friend taking leave of friends, perhaps for the last time. An admirer in the audience, Joseph Gourney, recorded both sermons in shorthand. To his loyal followers, Whitefield explained that "this is the thirteenth time

267

of my crossing the mighty waters, it is a little difficult at this time of life . . . but I delight in the cause, and God fills me with a peace that is unutterable." The times, Whitefield cautioned, were ominous: "clouds are growing thick" and great "storms" appeared on the horizon. Whitefield's prayer was that "the great and gracious God may avert every impending storm." As for himself, he was visiting America to heal, not to found a movement: "witness against me, if I ever set up a party for myself."

The concluding remarks, taken verbatim by Gourney, capture the pathos of the moment:

> I dare not meet you now, I can't bear your coming to me to part from me, it cuts me to the heart and quite over-comes me, but by and by all parting will be over, and all tears shall be wiped away from our eyes.

A seventeen-year-old future itinerant was in the crowd that day and recorded his thoughts: "I remember a thought which passed my mind, I think, as I was going to hear his last sermon, 'which would I rather be, Garrick or Whitefield?' I thought each, in point of oratory, admirable in his way. I doubt not conscience told me which was best."

15: Final Scene

In September 1769, an ailing Whitefield sailed for his seventh and last visit to America. He had always spoken as if any visit would be his last, but this time the weakness was palpable. Aware of his precarious health, he brought two apprentice companions with him, Cornelius Winter and Richard Smith. Winter had been living with him in London since Elizabeth's death and would remain in Georgia to begin a mission to the slaves. Smith would accompany Whitefield on his northern speaking tour.

Whatever fears Whitefield had for his health did not show. To Winter's eye, he seemed to enjoy the voyage, "familiarizing himself to his naval situation [and] acquainting himself with the crew and passengers." As in the old days, he filled his hours observing the sea and composing sermons and letters for the press. But this time another subject also caught his interest. Tensions between England and her colonies turned his attention to constitutional histories of England and the subject of liberty.

In the past, Whitefield had shown little interest in political history or in the ideological questions that separated England from Scotland or her colonies. External enemies and wars he had cast solely within the context of "popery," anti-Christ, and loyalty to the English crown. All that was changing in the heated aftermath of the Seven Years War and the Stamp Act, as American colonists challenged Parliament's sovereignty and, with that challenge, raised ideological questions of popular rights and constitutional balance to the forefront of Anglo-American consciousness. British troops were on their way to Boston at the time Whitefield sailed, and Franklin was besieged in the House of Commons. For Whitefield, as for those on all sides, questions of English rule — and English constitutional history — became compelling. Whitefield's considerations brought him down on the side of the colonial patriots.

Late in life, Whitefield now added "real Whig" republican to his enduring identity as a revivalist. His crash course in the history of liberty, though recent and unavoidably superficial, could not have been alien to him. He had spent much of his career seeking to achieve religious rights for methodists using arguments similar to those employed by colonial patriots. And his own embattled relationship to the Church of England closely paralleled the colonies' increasingly strained relationship with Parliament. If Whitefield did not wish to abolish institutions or dispel deference, neither did most of his clerical friends among the patriot leaders. Instead, they sought extra-institutional means to transcend a traditional order, and they demanded that laws and courts grant them the freedom of speech and assembly that such transcendence required. In plain terms, they demanded a recognition of their "rights" as English citizens and English Christians.

Whitefield's well-known American sympathies simply enhanced his already legendary popularity in the colonies. It was clear that the attraction between Whitefield and his American audiences was more than simply religious or charismatic. In fact, both were brash and experimental voices outside the mainstream that saw in one another the shape of a new religious and political future. If they could not yet articulate that future in theoretical terms, they could and had experienced it in the form of translocal revivals and Stamp Act "congresses." They would leave it to others to catch theory up to practice. Both Whitefield and his beloved Americans were tilting against the past in perfect confidence that the future would sing their praises and perpetuate their legacy.

On November 30 Whitefield's party landed in Charleston and he began preaching immediately. For several days he preached in that city, delighted to discover that his body held up to the demands of weekly sermons. As always, he took it as a sign that he should take on more work — in this case, a return to daily preaching really the only life he knew. The added efforts would kill him before long, but not before he completed the work at Bethesda and one last tour.

From Charleston, Whitefield was conveyed to Bethesda in the familiar mode of slave-paddled canoe. It had been four years since he had last visited Bethesda, and many then had thought they would never see him again. So the reunion was all the more joyous, both at the orphan house and throughout the Georgia colony. Whitefield stayed there through the winter, preaching weekly and working to establish his college.

The college had become nearly an obsession. The London Tabernacle had always been important to him, but only instrumentally as a place to preach. The college, on the other hand, captivated his soul for reasons he could only dimly see. The pietist in Whitefield forsook any claims to a spiritual prominence that would displace Christ, and the anti-institutional strain in him prevented any identification with one denomination, but the proud performer in him wanted to live beyond the last curtain. Obviously there could be no Christian stage. Nor was the Tabernacle well suited to express the transatlantic, transdenominational shape of Whitefield's genius. It was in Bethesda College that Whitefield identified his longed-for monument. In all regards, it was a fitting symbol. It took in

271

orphans and deserving "servitors" for college training, it trained ministers for service in revivals, it inculcated the methodist lifestyle of devotional simplicity, and, most important, it dwelt in the newest colony of the brave new world Whitefield had come to love. Nothing in the old country had captivated his soul as the new had, and so now in his final years it was the New World college that received his fondest institutional attention.

Having failed to secure a charter from the archbishop, Whitefield concentrated his energies on the Georgia legislature and his own considerable fund-raising capabilities. A surprise legacy from Scotland left Whitefield some discretionary income for the first time in his life, and with this he immediately paid off the remaining orphan house debt and announced that the leftover money would be used to begin construction of additional buildings for the college.

Whitefield preferred that the college not bear his name, but in every other respect, from funding to rules and curriculum, he made sure it would bear the mark of his personal attention and direction. He drew up a series of rules for the college and basic curricular requirements. In it he included daily prayers — both liturgical and extemporaneous — and memorization of the *Thirty Nine Articles*. To satisfy nonconformists he also recommended readings from such English Puritan worthies as Matthew Henry, Doddridge, Poole, and John Edwards. His own shipboard libertarian reading showed its impact in his requirement that "the history of Georgia, and the constitution of England, [be read] before being taught the history of Greece and Rome." Much of his direction he borrowed from Princeton and conceived out of his own private sense that Bethesda College would be chiefly an engine of evangelization.

Ever mindful of the slaves, Whitefield made careful provision for their welfare. As in the orphan house, slave labor was to sustain the college. In return, the college would provide for "the young negro boys to be baptized and taught to read;

the young girls to be taught to work with the needle." By eighteenth-century American standards, such provisions put Whitefield and such fellow evangelical planters as Hugh Bryan and James Habersham at the forefront of enlightened slave ownership. The goal of supplying slaves with literacy skills was novel and dangerous, but it was consistent with Whitefield's lifelong insistence that the slaves had souls — and minds — of their own. He was not afraid to give them everything other students would have — everything but their freedom.

With rules and curriculum set, Whitefield still lacked buildings, students, and tutors. But these, he felt, would come in time. In the interim, he could certainly set the stage. And so, as a preview of coming attractions calculated to impress the Georgia Assembly, he announced a celebration dinner at Bethesda. The governor, council, and assorted dignitaries were invited to welcome their new college.

The honorable party arrived from their ten-mile journey in a train of twenty carriages. Every dignitary in the colony arrived to pay respects to Whitefield and his planned college. In return they were treated to a sumptuous feast perfectly orchestrated in collegial fashion by Whitefield. The newly founded *Georgia Gazette* described the event in words that were reprinted throughout the colonies. The evening began with a formal procession led by the orphan boys "in flat caps and black gowns, like the servitors in the university." The group processed into the chapel, where the governor and his council slowly mounted the chapel steps and sat in "great chairs" of prominence.

Once assembled, the dignitaries heard Whitefield preach a portentous sermon from Zechariah 7: "And who hath despised the day of small things?" The sermon was both self-promoting and nostalgic as Whitefield recalled those who had paid their dues in the past to make a stable present and a glorious future for Georgia. Many in his audience could recall the difficult beginnings in the "once despised deserted province of Georgia," where "lands which now sell for three pounds an acre might have been purchased for three shillings." The orphan house mission, together with a handful of merchants, had saved the colony from extinction and laid the basis for an enduring settlement. With continued growth, and now with a college of its own, the colony would assume its rightful place among the crown jewels of the British empire. Whitefield concluded by noting that construction on the college had already begun.

Following the sermon, the party adjourned to feast in the great room. The meal was followed by toasts to the crown. In patriotic New England no such toasts would have been made, but at Bethesda, where much of the assembly remained Loyalist, the gesture was not out of place. In fact, throughout his stay in the South, Whitefield was careful not to express his more extreme patriotic sentiments. As reported in the *Georgia Gazette*, "when the governor drank the king, Mr. Whitefield added, 'And let all the people say Amen,' which was immediately echoed back with a repeated loud Amen from one end of the room to the other."

All, including Whitefield, left the feast certain that the college would become Georgia's crowning religious and civic achievement. None could foresee how Whitefield's imminent death and the looming war with Great Britain would destroy the charismatic transatlantic foundation on which the college rested. But for that brief moment Bethesda College was a reality in the minds and imaginations of all those present.

With spring came the time for final farewells at the orphan house and for the move north. By the time Whitefield arrived at Philadelphia in early May, political tensions had sharpened again. News of the "Boston Massacre" on March 5, 1770, when five rioting Bostonians were shot by British troops, had raised colonial grievances to a fever pitch. The little resistance to England that Whitefield had noticed in the South grew progressively more radical as he moved north. It was not an easy trip; Whitefield's health prevented any activity other than preaching. But his heart went out to the colonial protesters.

Wherever Whitefield traveled, he got a hero's welcome — and attention. Philadelphians knew of his defense of Franklin and welcomed him as a special guest at the commencement of the Philadelphia Academy begun by Franklin. Whitefield's themes were once again nostalgic. As reported in the *Pennsylvania Chronicle*, he preached a short sermon praising the colony and its college and then "in particular expressed high Pleasure in beholding a House, [the Long Building] which he had laid the Foundation of thirty years ago, thus continued and improved for the lasting Advancement of Religion and useful knowledge."

In fields and pulpits throughout Pennsylvania, Whitefield attracted large, diverse audiences. Henry Muhlenberg recorded an occasion at the Zion Church on Sunday, May 27, where Whitefield preached before a combined congregation of English and "German people of every religious persuasion." Muhlenberg picked Whitefield up at his lodgings, and "when we reached the church, it was so crowded and closely packed that we had to crowd through the tower door with him and get him in this way." At first Whitefield complained of a cold and hoarseness, but once begun, "he preached quite audibly" and powerfully. In Muhlenberg's observation, he played perfectly to his audience:

> He made impressive remarks . . . and referred to our Reverend Fathers, the late Mr. Francke and Mr. Ziegenhagen. . . . He properly deserves to be called *Gachswungsrorachs* [saw] in the North American tongue, for, in the hands of his Master, he is a sharp saw to cut through the knotty, gnarled, streaky hearts with their countless prejudices, false opinions, excuses, etc., and to scatter sawdust about. . . . When he concluded his sermon he called upon us to close the service with a German hymn, *"Nun ruhen alle Walder,"* etc. Our parishioners, scattered about upstairs and down, most of them women, sang so charmingly, devoutly, and sublimely that the English people were quite enraptured and are still speaking of it to this day.

As always, women were conspicuous in the crowd. The language of liberty did not extend to them politically, but it did religiously. Women found more central roles in Whitefield's revivals than they would ever be allowed in politics.

By the end of July, Whitefield had traveled a five-hundred-mile circuit throughout the middle colonies. His health had not fully improved, but his spirits were so taken up by the euphoria of preaching that he determined to resume "daily preaching" — a decision that would soon prove fatal. Meanwhile, wherever he preached, he witnessed "revival" and raised additional funds for the orphan house and college. In a letter to his friend at the Tabernacle, Robert Keen, he rejoiced, "O what a new scene of usefulness is opening in various parts of the new world! All fresh work where I have been. The Divine influence has been as at the first." As always, invitations poured in "from many quarters."

From the middle colonies Whitefield traveled north, hoping to avoid the seasonal heat so that he could continue his daily preaching. There was no letup in his schedule, and the New England itinerary read much like his earlier tours. To many outside observers, the pace seemed suicidal — or at the least irresponsible. In fact, it was entirely consistent with Whitefield's life and message. He had at all times demonstrated a callous disregard for his private self, both body and spirit. The preaching moment engulfed all, and it would continue to do so, for in fact there was nothing else he lived for.

In New England, the public reception was predictably enthusiastic. Not only was Whitefield a self-confessed spiritual heir of New England's Puritan progenitors but he was also a symbol of liberty at a time when Boston was besieged. The newly founded *Massachusetts Spy*, published by Isaiah Thomas and given over largely to political commentary, carried the happy news that on August 15 "the Rev. Mr. George Whitefield arrived here, in good health, from Providence . . . and preached this afternoon to a very crowded audience at the old-North meeting House." Whitefield responded to his embattled New

England friends with genuine sympathy. In a letter to Robert Keen he evidenced a far stronger sympathy with the patriot cause than he had ever exhibited in Georgia: "Poor *New England* is much to be pitied. *Boston* people most of all. How falsely misrepresented! What a mercy that our *Christian charter* cannot be dissolved as easily as Parliament threatens to dissolve popular government in America."

Again Whitefield pushed himself relentlessly. Much of his New England travel was rough, done on horseback with frequent stops. Still, he went on, insisting to friends that "I would rather wear out than rust out." He ignored the danger signs, in particular asthmatic "colds" that brought "great difficulty" in breathing. Instead of resting, he rode on, preaching more rather than less, depending on the moment of preaching to bring out a "good pulpit sweat" that would grant him one more day's reprieve. Daily travel and preaching were now joined with frequent "exhortations," marked by almost the same sort of frenzy that had characterized his first tour in 1740. The pace continued even after he was "taken in the night with a violent lax, attended with retching and shivering."

Clearly, Whitefield sensed the imminence of death and was pushing himself beyond prudence. In effect, he was living each day as if it were his last. And this meant that, regardless of health, he must preach and travel each day, so that if — and when — the last day arrived, it would fulfill the character with which he wanted to close out his career: the ever-zealous revivalist whose last breath was spent preaching Christ.

Throughout those days, Whitefield did not appear depressed or suicidal. Indeed, he evidenced a spiritual fervor and ideological solidarity with the colonists suggesting that he was acutely alive and engaged with all that was going on around him. As long as he could, he would preach gladly and with exuberance, for he knew that when he lost that freedom, he would have nothing to fill the void. The private man and the family man had long since ceased to exist. In the final scene, there was only Whitefield in his pulpit.

Whatever fears Whitefield may have harbored concerning death he never articulated. Descriptions of deathbed scenes were a commonplace in Protestant piety, and Whitefield evidently intended to play the role fully. He had already composed a hymn for his funeral entitled *Ah! Lovely Appearance of Death* and had spoken freely of his eagerness to be taken up in heaven. Now, with the end approaching, he supplied his public with a script worthy of his name. Just as he had always found in the pulpit the courage to confront life, so also would he find in the pulpit the arena where he could challenge death itself with complete composure.

A complete account of Whitefield's last days and his last act appears in newspaper reports and personal memoirs. Inevitably, these accounts read like the final scene in a play. They tell how Whitefield rejected the doctors' advice and returned to daily preaching. They describe all his stops at familiar places and the joy he frequently expressed traveling in his "pilgrim mode." They portray not a depressed Whitefield but a preacher-actor seizing the last moment in the limelight and giving the show of his life.

On Saturday morning, September 29, Whitefield concluded another successful sermon at Portsmouth, Massachusetts, and immediately set out for the next stop at Newburyport. Eyewitnesses described him, nearly collapsed, being helped onto his horse and then plodding on despite the entreaties of concerned friends and admirers. At a mid-day stop in Exeter, Whitefield was enjoined to preach, and he complied. One friend, on observing the "oppressive heavings of his bosom," counseled, "Sir, you are more fit to go to bed than to preach." Whitefield ignored the warning and answered with a prayer: "Lord, if I have not yet finished my course, let me go and speak for Thee once more in the fields, seal thy truth, and come home and die!"

Whitefield's prayer was answered. His last discourse took place mid-afternoon in the fields, atop a hogshead. His text was "Examine yourselves, whether ye be in faith," and his subject

278

was the great Puritan theme of faith versus works. A listener in the fields recounted the event for the press,

> He rose up sluggishly and wearily, as if worn down and exhausted by his stupendous labours. His face seemed bloated, his voice was hoarse, his enunciation heavy. Sentence after sentence was thrown off in rough, disjointed portions, without much regard to point or beauty. [But then] his mind kindled, and his lion-like voice roared to the extremities of his audience. He was speaking of the inefficiency of works to merit salvation, and suddenly cried out in a tone of thunder, "Works! Works! a man get to heaven by works! I would as soon think of climbing to the moon on a rope of sand."

The eyewitness account was widely printed in the press and in subsequent collections of sermons and memoirs. Another account recorded Whitefield's closing words on departing Essex as follows: "I soon shall be in a world where time, age, pain, and sorrow are unknown. My body fails, my spirit expands. How willingly would I live for ever to preach Christ! But I die to be *with* Him."

Following the sermon, according to the stories, an exhausted Whitefield insisted on continuing his journey, once more against the advice of friends. His destination was the home of his old Presbyterian friend Jonathan Parsons, who had defended him so vigorously in the early years. It was also home of the "Old South" Presbyterian Church. Earlier, he had expressed a wish to be buried before Old South's pulpit if he died in America.

Upon arriving at Parsons's house, he was too ill to dine and announced his intention to go to bed. But again a crowd of admirers waited on him, and eventually received a "brief exhortation."

The exhortation would be Whitefield's final public words. According to Richard Smith's account, he retired to his quarters immediately thereafter, complaining of difficulty in breathing. At 5:00 A.M. a worried Smith called for Parsons to come to their quarters immediately. By then, Whitefield was running from window to window in desperate attempts to breathe, worrying all the time he would be unable to preach the next day.

Parsons ran to the room and, recognizing the gravity of the situation, immediately called for a physician. But the cause was lost. According to Smith's account,

> When the doctor came in, and saw him in the chair lean-ing on my breast, he felt his pulse, and said "He is a dead man." Mr. Parsons said, "I do not believe it, you must do something, doctor." He said, "I cannot; he is now near his last breath." And indeed, so it was, for he fetched but one gasp, and stretched out his feet, and breathed no more. This was exactly at six o'clock. We continued rubbing his legs and hands and feet with warm cloths, and bathed him with spirits for some time, but all in vain. I then put him into a warm bed, the doctor standing by, and often raised him upright, continued rubbing him, and putting spirits to his nose for an hour, till all hopes were gone.

When news of Whitefield's death reached Boston, a party of ministers and friends set out immediately for Newburyport to claim the body so that he might be buried in Boston. As his life began in gospel analogies to Bethlehem, so would it end in a bizarre rendition of the opened sepulcher. The clergy were met by Parsons and told in no uncertain terms that Whitefield would be buried in the Presbyterian church, in a "Brick Tomb under the Presbyterian Meeting-House." In a sense, this last unpleasantness was fitting: for one who had made controversy a foundation of his career, a little controversy at the end rep-resented the perfect capstone.

On Tuesday, September 31, a number of ministers gathered at the Rev. Parsons's manse and led an extraordinary procession to the burial site. The pallbearers were ecumenical in makeup and included the Presbyterian Parsons, the Anglican

Edward Bass, and Congregationalists Samuel Haven, Daniel Rogers, Jedediah Jewett, and James Chandler.

The funeral procession extended over a mile in length as it made its way to the meetinghouse. Nothing in Newburyport annals had ever matched such an assembly. Six thousand mourners packed the church, and thousands more lined the street grieving. The bells of the town were tolled, and guns were fired from the harbor.

A mahogany-stained casket costing £8 was built for Whitefield, and he "was buried in gown, cassock, bands and wig." His corpse was placed at the foot of the pulpit. The Rev. Daniel Rogers offered the prayer. It was to Whitefield's ministry in the early years, Rogers confessed, that he owed his own conversion. The memory of this so gripped him that he broke off the prayer in tears, exclaiming "O my Father! my Father!"

Following the prayer, the coffin was placed in a newly prepared tomb beneath the pulpit. Before the tomb was sealed, the Rev. Jedediah Jewett delivered a brief address, mixing pathos with politics. After describing Whitefield's ministry, Jewett went on to exclaim, "what a friend he has been to us, and our interests, religious and civil; to New England, and to all the British colonies in the Continent!" As the body was placed in the tomb, another prayer was offered, and then the "immense crowd departed, weeping through the streets, as in mournful groups they wended their way to their respective homes."

If Whitefield could not have been more dramatic in the hour of his death, neither could his admirers have been more impassioned. His death provoked widespread displays of tears and sorrow without precedent in the American colonies. Not until the death of George Washington would there be a more universal display of sadness and loss.

Such was Whitefield's public reputation that people having no personal acquaintance with him interrupted their journals to enter the historic death. In Brookfield, Massachusetts, the Old Light pastor Nathan Fiske made an extraordinary entry in his manuscript diary: "Last evening we were informed by a melancholy Messenger from Newbury-Port that yesterday morning Whitefield had died." Fiske was not given to tributes in his diary, let alone tributes to New Lights, but this occasion was different. It called for a personal statement. And so, appended to the usual one-line entries was the following assessment:

> In his public Performances throughout Europe and . . . in most parts of British America . . . [Whitefield] has for a long number of years astonished the world as a Prodigy of Eloquence and Devotion. . . . With what divine Pathos did he not plead with the impenitent Sinners to the Practice of Virtue and Piety.

Fiske's entry is revealing not only for the way in which it registers the impact of Whitefield's death but also for the nature of the remembrance. Already a mythologization of sorts was taking place. As in all myths, Whitefield was invoked for qualities that expressed the ethos of the speaker. In Fiske's case, what was remembered was neither Whitefield's piety nor his Calvinism but his "Eloquence," and "Practice of Virtue."

American friends of the revival remembered Whitefield's "Puritan" character. At the Thursday Lecture in Boston on October 11, Whitefield's staunch ally Ebenezer Pemberton delivered the eulogy. He remembered especially how Whitefield preached "those great Doctrines of the Gospel which our venerable Ancestors brought with them from their Native Country." In so doing, he engrafted Whitefield into the American Puritan mythology. American "typologists" were long in the habit of paralleling their experiences and leaders to ancient Israel and the New Testament church. Now Whitefield was joining that American typology. In Philadelphia, the Presbyterian James Sproutt spoke for all when he noted that Whitefield's preaching produced "probably more [conversions] than any one man since the Apostolic age." In fact, he implied, Whitefield was an American Paul.

As memorable as Whitefield's evangelicalism was his

character. In eulogizing Whitefield, Pemberton turned from the itinerant's evangelical successes to his charity and generosity: "with large opportunities of accumulating wealth, he never discovered the least Tincture of Avarice. . . . His benevolent Mind was perpetually forming Plans of extensive Usefulness." Instead of private wealth, the orphan house and college would be "lasting monuments of his Care, that Religion and Learning might be propagated to future Generations."

Perhaps most remarkable in the accounts of Whitefield's death, however, was the sense of personal loss expressed by many who never knew him personally. Everywhere people were devastated by the news. In ways befitting the unique relationship of Whitefield and his admirers, the mourners became as much a part of the news as Whitefield himself. As word of his death spread, the drama heightened with an ever-growing number of mourners. In every colony and urban center, a public service and eulogy honored his passing. And at every stop, the press carried news of the audience as well as the occasion. The audience, after all, had made Whitefield as much as he had made them.

The greatest public mourning took place in Georgia. Cornelius Winter was preaching to the orphan house slaves when word came from James Habersham of Whitefield's death. "As soon as I heard it," Winter recalled, "I retreated to pray, and pour out my soul to God. I can truly say, the cause of God at large lay near my heart, and I had a persuasion that the work over which he had presided would not die with him." In a subsequent letter, Winter went on to describe the scene of mourning in Georgia:

> You have no conception of the effect of Mr. Whitefield's death upon the inhabitants of the province of Georgia. All the black cloth in the stores was bought up; the pulpit and desks of the church, the branches, the organ loft, the pews of the governor and council, were covered with black. The governor and council, in deep mourning, convened at the state-house, and went in procession to

283

church, and were received by the organ playing a funeral dirge. Two funeral sermons were preached, one by Mr. Ellington, which I was desired to compose; the other was preached by Mr. Zubly. All the respect showed to his memory at his death, kept my sensibility alive.

Whitefield's death left Winter "set up doing the best I could for the poor negroes. . . . I had settled it in my own mind in submission to the will of God, that I would, being put into a capacity of usefulness, live and die in Georgia, a devoted servant of servants."

In fact, Winter would not be allowed to remain in Georgia. Despite the efforts of Habersham in Georgia and Franklin in England, the cause came to naught. Though this *could* have been Whitefield's greatest legacy, it was not. But his concern for the slaves and their connection to Whitefield was clear, and so it is not surprising that perhaps the greatest mourning was expressed among the slave community. A seventeen-year-old black Boston servant and self-trained poet named Phyllis Wheatley expressed her sense of loss in a widely printed elegy that registered the emotion of the black community:

Hail happy saint on thy immortal throne!
To thee complaints of grievance are unknown:
We hear no more the music of thy tongue,
Thy wonted auditories cease to throng.
Thy lessons in unequal'd acents flow'd!
While emulation in each bosom glow'd;
Thou didst, in strains of eloquence refin'd
Inflame the soul, and captivate the mind.
Unhappy we, the setting Sun deplore:
Which once was splendid, but it shines no more;
He leaves the earth for Heaven's unmeasur'd height:
And worlds unknown, receive him from our sight;
There WHITEFIELD wings, with rapid course his way,
And sails to Zion, through vast seas of day.

Questions of the correlation between conversions and changed lives in Whitefield's revivals can be debated, but in the case of the slaves, the changes were indisputable. More than any other eighteenth-century figure, Whitefield established Christian faith in the slave community. His support of slavery remains a blot on his memory that has deprived him of heroic status in African-American history. But in 1770, while many Americans continued to doubt that slaves had souls, Whitefield stood as the slaves' greatest champion, and at the time he was mourned as such.

Throughout the colonies, newspapers suspended political commentary to eulogize Whitefield. The press and Whitefield had grown up together in the colonies, one as hero and the other as hero-maker. Never was there a better fit. In Boston, the *Massachusetts Spy* took space away from the Boston Massacre to praise Whitefield in mythic terms as revivalist and patriot. Appropriately, it went on to reprint an elegiac essay composed by "a *Female* reader." In Philadelphia, the *Pennsylvania Chronicle* reported Sproutt's sermon noting "the Presbyterian Church in Arch Street was hung in black, in Testimony of their Regard for the late Rev. Mr. George Whitefield, when five Hymns one of which was composed by Mr. Whitefield himself, for his funeral, were sung." That hymn, noted the *Boston Evening Post,* expressed the man: "He seem'd to have a clear view of the entertainments of another life; and would commonly converse so familiarly of death, as tho' he was a fine friend he was waiting for, and even long'd to receive the summons."

In New York, the *New York Gazette* described the "melancholy occasion" of Whitefield's memorial service, echoing the theme of his "fervency of zeal, perhaps unequalled since the Days of the Apostles." In Providence, the *Providence Gazette* reported services at St. Paul's, where the Rev. William Stringer set forth the "shining qualities of the deceased." And the *Gazette* contributed yet another elegiac poem, this in the form of an acrostic, the first letters of each line spelling GEORGE WHITEFIELD.

Friends in England and Scotland were as saddened as

their American counterparts. Of all the eulogies, the only one Whitefield expressly requested took place in London at his two home pulpits: Moorfields Tabernacle and Tottenham Court Road Chapel. There, on Sunday, November 18, his old friend and sometime rival John Wesley delivered the funeral sermon at morning and afternoon services. The two had been reconciled during Whitefield's last stay in England and had found a common footing in their shared Oxford experience of the New Birth. In death, it suddenly became clear to Wesley *why* these rivals had been rejoined, and the olive branch went to Whitefield. Of all Whitefield's qualities, Wesley recognized, the most striking was that he was a good and loyal friend. His "servant to all" credo did not stop short of friends. "I have frequently thought," Wesley exclaimed, "that this, of all others, was the distinguishing part of his Character. How few have we known of so kind a temper, of such large and flowing affections? Was it not principally by this, that the hearts of others were so strangely drawn and knit to him?"

John Gillies memorialized Whitefield in terms similar to Wesley's. Both knew him well and recognized the man beneath the talent. Whitefield's "strong and musical voice," "lively imagination," and dramatic style were all important, but none accounted for the full measure of the man. Most significant, Gillies concluded, was a capacity for friendship to all that invariably transcended doctrine and turned on charity: "he had a heart deeply exercised in all the social as well as the pious and religious affections."

In England, word reached Benjamin Franklin of his friend's death. His wife wrote, "Yisterday came the a Counte of the Death of our verey kind Friend Mr. WhiteFeld. It hurte me indeaid. You will see all a bought him in the Papers." To his sister Jane Mecom, Franklin wrote, "I condole you on the Death of my dear old Friend Mr. Whitefield which I have just heart of." Later, in a letter to the Georgia Assembly, he paid tribute to his old friend: "I knew him intimately upwards of thirty years. His Integrity, Disinterestedness, and indefatigable

Zeal in prosecuting every good Work, I have never seen equalled, and I shall never see exceeded."

All of these eulogies illustrate the man behind the movement. The public self was the private self, and it was a self "charismatic" in both the ancient and modern senses of the term. If Whitefield was a modern promoter with a shameless ego, he was also a spirit-filled, caring minister who directed his work first at the soul and second at charity, and never one without the other.

For one brief moment, religion again claimed center stage in American public assembly. Whether or not his mourners realized it, Whitefield's passing coincided with the passing of an era. Americans were doubly crushed. They had lost not only a beloved evangelist but an English Anglican who had openly sympathized with their plight and championed their cause. As in Whitefield's life, so in his death, timing was everything. Whatever reservations he may have harbored concerning colonial resistance were never known. He died a Pauline evangelist *and* an American patriot.

A Note on the Sources

For all of the references to George Whitefield and the "Great Awakening" in the historical literature, there has been a surprising lack of scholarly biographies. However, significant Whitefield materials may be found in more general histories of eighteenth-century revivals and in the periodical literature. Joseph Tracy's nineteenth-century work *The Great Awakening: A History of the Revival of Religion in the Time of Edwards and Whitefield* (Boston, 1841) is still unexcelled for its breadth of coverage. Also useful are the following: Edwin S. Gaustad, *The Great Awakening in New England* (New York, 1957); Alan Heimert, *Religion and the American Mind: From the Great Awakening to the Revolution* (Cambridge, 1966); Jon Butler, *Awash in a Sea of Faith: Christianizing the American People* (Cambridge, Mass., 1990); Patricia U. Bonomi, *Under the Cope of Heaven: Religion, Society, and Politics in Colonial America* (New York, 1986); C. C. Goen, *Revivalism and Separatism in New England, 1740-1800* (New Haven, 1962); Michael J. Crawford, *Seasons of Grace: Colonial New England's Revival Tradition in Its British Context*

(New York, 1991); and Nathan O. Hatch, *The Democratization of American Christianity* (New Haven, 1989). Two superb documentary histories of Whitefield and the Great Awakening are *The Great Awakening: Documents on the Revival of Religion*, ed. Richard L. Bushman (New York, 1969); and *The Great Awakening: Documents Illustrating the Crisis and Its Consequences*, ed. Perry Miller and Alan Heimert (Indianapolis, 1967).

Among the substantial number of filiopietistic biographies and appreciations of Whitefield produced by Calvinist and Methodist admirers of Whitefield, three have proved indispensable to this work as repositories of biographical and anecdotal information: Luke Tyerman, *The Life of the Rev. George Whitefield*, 2 vols. (London, 1876); Stuart Henry, *George Whitefield: Wayfaring Witness* (Nashville, 1957); and Arnold A. Dallimore, *George Whitefield: The Life and Times of the Great Evangelist of the Eighteenth-Century Revival*, 2 vols. (Westchester, Ill., 1970, 1979).

Among the more important periodical essays on Whitefield and the Great Awakening are: William H. Kenney, "George Whitefield, Dissenter Priest of the Great Awakening," *William and Mary Quarterly* 26 (1969): 75-93; Jon Butler, "Enthusiasm Described and Decried: The Great Awakening as Historical Fiction," *Journal of American History* 69 (1982): 305-25; Susan O'Brien, "A Transatlantic Community of Saints: The Great Awakening and the First Evangelical Network, 1735-1755," *American Historical Review* 91 (1986): 811-32; Timothy L. Smith, "George Whitefield and the Wesleyan Witness," in *Whitefield and Wesley on the New Birth*, ed. Timothy L. Smith (Grand Rapids, 1986); Eugene E. White, "The Decline of the Great Awakening in New England, 1741-1746," *New England Quarterly* 24 (1961): 35-52; S. Durden, "A Study of the First Evangelical Magazines, 1740-1748," *Journal of Ecclesiastical History* 27 (1976): 255-78; and S. J. Royal, "Religious Periodicals in England during the Restoration and Eighteenth Century," *Journal of Rutgers University* 35 (1971): 27-33. A superb article by Frank Lambert — "George Whitefield and the Great Awakening," *Journal of American History* 77 (1990): 812-37 — appeared after the completion of this biography but reaches many of the same conclusions.

To situate Whitefield in his times, I have relied on a variety of primary sources representing him and his contemporaries. Apart from a handful of autographs preserved in scattered archives, virtually all of Whitefield's manuscript sources have been lost or destroyed. Nevertheless, there is a substantial body of printed materials that serve the biographer well. Still unsurpassed as a single-source respository for Whitefield's sermons, letters, and pamphlets is *The Works of the Reverend George Whitefield*, 6 vols., ed. John Gillies (London, 1771-72).

Other important collections of Whitefield's writings can be grouped in four major categories: journals, letters, newspaper accounts, and printed sermons. The most convenient reprinting of Whitefield's journals is *George Whitefield's Journals* (London, 1960), a compilation of all seven published journals from 1738 through 1741, together with an unpublished journal of 1744-45. Besides the Whitefield correspondence reprinted in the Gillies edition of Whitefield's *Works*, the other major collection of Whitefield's correspondence is reprinted in "Newly Discovered Letters of George Whitefield, 1745-46," ed. John W. Christie, *Journal of the Department of History of the Presbyterian Historical Society* 32 (1954), nos. 2, 3, and 4.

Of the vast body of published Whitefield correspondence, the following appear in this biography: Whitefield, *A Letter to the Lord Bishop of London* (London, 1739); Whitefield, *Letter from the Rev. George Whitefield to the Rev. John Wesley* (London, 1740); Whitefield, *Letter from George Whitefield to John Wesley on Universal Redemption* (Boston, 1814); Whitefield, *A Letter to Harvard College* (Boston, 1745); Whitefield, *A Letter to the Rev. Dr. Durell* (London, 1768); Whitefield, *An Expostulatory Letter Addressed to Count Zinzendorff* (London, 1753); John Green, *The Principles and Practices of the Methodists . . . in a Letter to the Rev. George Whitefield* (Cambridge, 1761); Whitefield, *A Letter to the Religious Societies* (London, 1740); Charles Chauncy, *A Letter to George*

Whitefield (Boston, 1745); Whitefield, *Three Letters from the Rev. Mr. George Whitefield* (Philadelphia, 1740); Alexander Garden, *Six Letters to the Rev. George Whitefield* (Boston, 1740); Whitefield, *A Continuation of the Account of the Orphan-House in Georgia* (London, 1743); Whitefield, *A Letter from the Rev. Mr. George Whitefield to the Religious Societies of England* (Edinburgh, 1742); Whitefield, "Letter to Benjamin Coleman," dated 4 July 1740 and pasted inside the cover of a copy of Benjamin Dorr's *History of Christ Church in Philadelphia* (Philadelphia, 1881) in Huntington Library; "Jonathan Edwards's Letter of Invitation to George Whitefield," ed. Henry Abelove, *William and Mary Quarterly* 29 (1972): 487-89; Thomas Church, *A Serious and Expostulatory Letter to the Rev. Mr. George Whitefield* (London, 1744); and Benjamin Franklin, "Dr. Franklin to George Whitefield," dated 15 June 1753, in mss. collections of Huntington Library.

A surprisingly neglected Whitefield source has been the eighteenth-century press. Among the religious newspapers and histories consulted for this biography, the most useful were Thomas Prince Jr.'s *Christian History* (Boston), *Weekly Miscellany* (London), *The Weekly History* (London), *Scots Magazine*, *Glasgow Weekly History*, and the *Christian Monthly History* (Edinburgh);

In the secular press, significant Whitefield materials were located in the following newspapers: *Pennsylvania Gazette, American Weekly Mercury, Pennsylvania Journal, Boston News-Letter, Boston Post-Boy, Boston Evening Post, Boston Gazette, New England Weekly Journal, South-Carolina Gazette, Georgia Gazette,* and the *Providence Gazette.*

Despite Whitefield's reputation as an extemporaneous preacher, collections of his printed sermons abound. In addition to the sermons preserved in Whitefield's *Works,* I have drawn from the following eighteenth- and nineteenth-century collections: *Memoirs of Rev. George Whitefield,* ed. John Gillies (London, 1772); Whitefield, *Sermons on Various Important Subjects by the Rev. George Whitefield, A.M.* (Boston, 1741); Whitefield, *A Short Address to Persons of All Denominations Occasioned by the Alarm of an Intended Invasion* (Boston, 1756); Whitefield,

Nine Sermons (London, 1750); Whitefield, *Fifteen Sermons* (New York, 1794); Whitefield, *Sermons on Various Important Subjects* (London, 1739); Whitefield, *Britain's Mercies and Britain's Duties* (Philadelphia, 1746); and *Eighteen Sermons Taken in Shorthand,* ed. Joseph Gurney (New York, 1809).

Among the seventeenth- and eighteenth-century sources quoted in this biography, the most important are the following: William Seward, *Journal of a Voyage from Savannah to Philadelphia* (London, 1740); William Prynne, *Histrio-Mastix: The Players Scourge* (London, 1633); John Bulwer, *Pathomyotamia; or, A Dissection of the Signifative Muscles of the Affections of the Minde* (London, 1649); John Bulwer, *Chirologia, Chironomia; or, The Art of Manuall Rhetorique . . . Touching the Artificiall Managing of the Hand in Speaking* (London, 1644); John Hill, *The Actor; or, Guide to the Stage* (New York, 1823); Samuel Foote, *The Minor: A Comedy* (New York, 1813); James Lockington, *Memoirs of James Lockington* (Newburgh, 1796); *The Journals of Henry Melchior Muhlenberg,* 3 vols., trans. Theodore G. Tappert and John W. Doberstein (Philadelphia, 1942-58); *The Journal of Charles Wesley,* 2 vols., ed. Thomas Jackson (London, 1849); "The Spiritual Travails of Nathan Cole," ed. Michael J. Crawford, *William and Mary Quarterly* 33 (1976): 89-126; James Habersham, "The Letters of Hon. James Habaersham 1756-1775," in *Collections of the Georgia Historical Society,* vol. 6 (Savannah, 1904); *The Journal of William Stephens, 1741-1745,* ed. E. Merton Coulter (Athens, Ga., 1958); Nathan Fiske, "Diary," Manuscripts Collection, American Antiquarian Society; *Memoirs of the Late Reverend Cornelius Winter,* ed. William Jay (Bath, 1808); Ann Hester Rogers, *An Account of the Experience of Hester Ann Rogers* (New York, 1828); John Wesley, *Thoughts on Marriage and a Single Life* (Bristol, 1743); Alexander Garden, *Regeneration and the Testimony of the Spirit* (Charleston, 1740); Benjamin Colman, *A Letter to the Rev. Mr. Williams* (Boston, 1744); and *Diary of Rev. Daniel Wadsworth, 1734-1747,* ed. G. L. Walker (Hartford, 1894).

The Cambuslang conversion narratives cited in this biography are located in the manuscript archives of New College

Library, University of Edinburgh. Contemporary accounts of Whitefield in Scotland include the following: *The Life and Diary of the Rev. Ralph Erskine of Dunfermline*, ed. Donald Fraser (Edinburgh, 1834); John Maclaurin, *Sermons and Essays* (Edinburgh, 1772); Henry M. Wellwood, *Account of the Life and Writings of John Erskine* (Edinburgh, 1818); James Robe, *A Faithful Narrative of the Extraordinary Work of the Spirit of God at Kilsyth* (Glasgow, 1742); Alexander Webster, *Divine Influence: The True Spring of the Extraordinary Work at Cambuslang* (Edinburgh, 1742); *An Apology for the Presbyterians of Scotland Who Are Hearers of the Rev. Mr. George Whitefield* (Edinburgh, 1742); John Erskine, *The Signs of the Times Considered; or, The High Probability, That the Present Appearances in New-England, and the West of Scotland, Are a Prelude of the Glorious Things Promised to the Church in the Latter Ages* (Edinburgh, 1742); and John Erskine, *A Fair and Impartial Account of the Debate in the Synod of Glasgow and Air Sixth Oct 1748 anent Employing Mr. Whitefield* (Edinburgh, 1748).

The "paper war" of 1745 fought by Whitefield's supporters and detractors in New England generated an unrivaled body of polemical literture. I have consulted the following: Thomas Foxcroft, *An Apology in Behalf of the Rev. Mr. Whitefield* (Boston, 1745); William Hobby, *An Inquiry into the Itinerancy of George Whitefield* (Boston, 1745); William Shurtleff, *A Letter to Those of His Brethren* (Boston, 1745); Aaron Cleveland, *A Letter to the Rev. Mr. Foxcroft* (Boston, 1745); Daniel Wadsworth, *Testimony of the North Association in Hartford* (Boston, 1745); Theophilus Pickering, *Letter to Mr. Whitefield* (Boston, 1745); *The Declaration of the Association of New Haven* (Boston, 1745); John Cleaveland, *A Twig of Birch for Billy's Breach* (Boston, 1745); Nathaniel Eells, *A Letter to the Second Church in Scituate* (Boston, 1745); JF, *A Letter to the Rev. Mr. Hobby* (Boston, 1745); Samuel Niles, *Tristiae Ecclesiarum* (Boston, 1745); *A Letter from the Rev. Mr. Thomas Clap Rector of Yale College* (Boston, 1745); Nathanael Henchman, *Reasons Offered . . . for Declining to Admit Mr. Whitefield* (Boston, 1745).

Among the many funeral sermons delivered on the occasion of Whitefield's death, I have quoted from the following: John Wesley, *A Sermon on the Death of the Rev. Mr. George Whitefield* (London, 1770); Ebenezer Pemberton, *Heaven the Residence of the Saints* (London, 1771); Jonathan Parsons, *To Live Is Christ, to Die Is Gain* (Portsmouth, 1770); James Sproutt, *Funeral Discourse on the Death of the Rev. George Whitefield, A.M.* (Philadelphia, 1771); Henry Venn, *A Token of Respect to the Memory of the Rev. George Whitefield, A.M.* (London, 1770); and Phyllis Wheatley, *An Elegiac Poem on the Death of George Whitefield* (Boston, 1771).

The body of secondary literature on eighteenth-century religion and society is immense, and I can list only the most essential sources for this biography. For recent works dealing with the impact of an incipient "commercial revolution" on eighteenth-century society, I have been especially enlightened by the recent work of T. H. Breen, especially: " 'Baubles of Britain': The American and Consumer Revolutions of the Eighteenth Century," *Past and Present* 119 (1988); and "An Empire of Goods: The Anglicization of Colonial America, 1690-1776," *Journal of British Studies* 25 (1986). Also suggestive are "Toward a History of the Standard of Living in British North America," *William and Mary Quarterly* 45 (1988): 116-70; Christine L. Heyrman, *Commerce and Culture: The Maritime Communities of Colonial Massachusetts, 1690-1750* (New York, 1984); *The Birth of a Consumer Society: The Commercialization of Eighteenth-Century England*, ed. Neil McKendrick, John Brewer, and J. H. Plumb (Bloomington, 1982); Roy Porter, "The Language of Quackery in England, 1660-1800," in *The Social History of Language*, ed. Peter Burke and Roy Porter (Cambridge, 1987), 73-103; and R. Paulson, *Popular and Polite Art in the Age of Hogarth and Fielding* (Notre Dame, 1979).

One recent study of theater and a consumer society that has been especially enlightening is Jean-Christophe Agnew, *Worlds Apart: The Market and the Theater in Anglo-American Thought, 1550-1750* (Cambridge, Mass., 1986). Other major works on theater, religion, and society used for this study include the following: Edmund S. Morgan, "Puritan Hostility to the Theatre," *Proceedings of the American Philosophical Society* 110 (1966): 329-47; Jonas Barish, *The Anti-Theatrical Prejudice* (Berkeley, 1981); M. C. Bradbrook, *The Rise of the Common Player* (Cambridge, 1962); Francis Fergusson, *The Idea of a Theatre* (Princeton, 1944); Elizabeth Burns, *Theatricality: A Study in the Theatre and in Social Life* (New York, 1972); Leslie Hotson, *The Commonwealth and Restoration Stage* (Cambridge, Mass., 1928); and Harry W. Pedicord, *The Theatrical Public in the Time of Garrick* (New York, 1954).

On Whitefield and Methodism, see Douglas Macleane, *A History of Pembroke College Oxford* (Oxford, 1897); *Two Calvinist Methodist Chapels, 1743-1811*, ed. Edwin Welch (London, 1975); J. D. Walsh, "Methodism and the Mob in the Eighteenth Century," in *Popular Belief and Practice*, ed. G. J. Cumming and D. Baker (London, 1972), pp. 213-37; and Mary Tucker, *Itinerant Preaching in the Early Days of Methodism* (Boston, 1872).

On Whitefield in England and the British Isles, I have relied on the following: George H. Wicks, *Whitefield's Legacy to Bristol and the Cotswolds* (Bristol, 1914); Hugh J. Hughes, *Life of Howell Harris the Welsh Reformer* (London, 1892); Edward Morgan, *The Life and Times of Howell Harris, Esq.* (Holywell, 1852); Andrew Drummond and James Bulloch, *The Scottish Church, 1688-1843: The Age of Moderates* (Edinburgh, 1973); Marilyn J. Westerkamp, *Triumph of the Laity: Scots-Irish Piety and the Great Awakening, 1625-1760* (New York, 1988); Andrew Hook, *Scotland and America, 1750- 1835* (Glasgow, 1975); and Arthur Fawcett, *The Cambuslang Revival: The Scottish Evangelical Revival of the Eighteenth Century* (London, 1971).

A substantial but already dated bibliographic guide to women and Methodism in the age of Whitefield is Kenneth E. Rowe's *Methodist Women: A Guide to the Literature* (North Carolina, 1980). A particularly enlightening analysis of women and English Methodism is Deborah Valenze's *Prophetic Sons and Daughters: Female Preaching and Popular Religion in Industrial England* (Princeton, 1985). I have also consulted the following:

295

Frank Baker, "John Wesley and Sarah Crosby," *Wesley Historical Society Proceedings* 27 (1940): 76-82; Aaron Seymour, *The Life and Times of Selina, Countess of Huntingdon* (London, 1840); and Earl K. Brown, *Women of Mr. Wesley's Methodism* (New York, 1983).

On Whitefield's relationship with Benjamin Franklin, the primary Franklin sources include *Benjamin Franklin's Autobiography*, ed. J. A. Leo Lemay and P. M. Zall (New York, 1986); and *The Papers of Benjamin Franklin* (New Haven, 1959——). Two suggestive studies of Whitefield and Benjamin Franklin are John Williams, "The Strange Case of Dr. Franklin and Mr. Whitefield," *Pennsylvania Magazine of History and Biography* 102 (1978): 399-421; and David T. Morgan, "A Most Unlikely Friendship: Benjamin Franklin and George Whitefield," *The Historian* 47 (1985): 208-18.

On Whitefield and slavery, see the following: Harvey H. Jackson, "Hugh Bryan and the Evangelical Movement in Colonial South Carolina," *William and Mary Quarterly* 43 (1986): 594-614; Betty Wood, *Slavery in Colonial Georgia* (Athens, 1984); William B. Stevens, *A History of Georgia* (New York, 1847); Gary B. Nash, *Forging Freedom: The Formation of Philadelphia's Black Community, 1720-1840* (Cambridge, Mass., 1988); Stephen Stein, "George Whitefield on Slavery: Some New Evidence," *Church History* 42 (1973): 243-56; and Alan Gallay, "Jonathan Bryan's Plantation Empire: Land, Politics, and the Formation of a Ruling Class in Colonial Georgia," *William and Mary Quarterly* 45 (1988): 253-79.

Index

CPSIA information can be obtained
at www.ICGtesting.com
Printed in the USA
JSHW042227260822
29806JS00001B/31